PUTINISM

Also by Walter Laqueur

After the Fall

The Last Days of Europe

Generation Exodus

The Terrible Secret

Soviet Union, 2000

Black Hundred

The Dream That Failed

The Long Road to Freedom

PUTINISM

RUSSIA AND ITS FUTURE WITH THE WEST

WALTER LAQUEUR

Thomas Dunne Books St. Martin's Press New York

THOMAS DUNNE BOOKS.
An imprint of St. Martin's Press.

www.thomasdunnebooks.com
www.stmartins.com

Designed by Meryl Sussman Levavi

The Library of Congress Cataloging-in-Publication Data is available upon request.

ISBN 978-1-250-06475-2 (hardcover)
ISBN 978-1-4668-7106-9 (e-book)

First Edition: July 2015

10 9 8 7 6 5 4 3

In memory of two of my gurus:

George Lichtheim (1912–1973)

Hans (Tom) Meidner (1914–2001)

CONTENTS

ACKNOWLEDGMENTS

I HAVE TO GO BACK IN TIME, MENTIONING THOSE WHO HELPED ME to understand Russia and its people. My interest dates back to my childhood, but about this later on. My training in this field was incomplete and unorthodox. When I arrived, a seventeen-year-old student in Jerusalem, which at the time was in Palestine not long before the outbreak of World War II, I went to see the one and only professor of history, a nice man and a native of my hometown, expressing the wish to study Russian history. He asked me whether I had read the four volumes of Vasily Klyuchevsky's history. My answer was in the affirmative (which was only half-true), whereupon he said that being an expert on early medieval English history, he could not be of help. I joined a kibbutz, where two years later I happened to break my leg while shaving, which I was told was a very rare occurrence in medical history. I was incapacitated for almost two months. When this happened to young women in our collective settlement, they were given socks to mend, but for young men there was no such work.

A neighbor, the mother of a fellow member, Mrs. Pickman, a native of Nikolaev on the Black Sea shore, had been a teacher and was happy to find a pupil. I read Russian with her for many hours a day. After a month, I could read *Pravda,* which I believe at the time had to confine its vocabulary to about eight or nine hundred words so that millions could read it. After two months, I could read Alexander Pushkin's *Kapitanskaya Dochka.* In the months that followed, I found yet another group of teachers. Being a mounted policeman at the time, I spent long nights around a campfire in the fields or on a mountain. My comrades, most of them at least twenty years older, most of them natives of Siberia, quite a few of them the offspring of Christian sectarian families who had converted to Judaism, taught me Russian songs mostly of the *katorga i sylka* (prison and exile) variety, many of which I remember to this day. These men came from little places in Siberia with unlikely names such as Balagansk ("Balagan" in Russian means a state of utter confusion and disorder). They also enriched my vocabulary with many words and phrases not normally found in dictionaries.

In the years that followed, I worked as a writer and journalist, but one of my main interests was still in the Russian field. In 1956 in London, I became the founding editor of *Soviet Survey,* later *Survey,* a quarterly (later a bimonthly) covering political and cultural trends in the Soviet Union. I came to know most of the people working in this field in the United States and the United Kingdom, but also on the European continent. It would take a long time and much space to mention all of them (they were my teachers at this time), but I should single out Jane Degras, who helped me enormously with my early work. She had been with the Marx-Engels-Lenin Institute in Moscow but moved on to Chatham House in London.

I spent some time at the Harvard Russian Center in the 1950s but had no formal education. I stayed with *Survey* for a decade and then moved on to another position that led me in very different directions—European and Middle Eastern affairs. This I did not regret because I felt about Russia what Kipling had written about England: *What do you know of Russia who only Russia know?*

All these years I suffered from an obvious handicap. I had read about Russia, I had talked to Russians, but I had never been to the country. This was soon to change. The parents of Naomi, my late wife, lived in a resort in the Northern Caucasus. Her father had been a professor of medicine at Frankfurt, specializing in the history and philosophy of medicine. He had to leave Germany rather quickly in 1936, and the only country that wanted to have him was the Soviet Union. He was a wholly apolitical being and therefore very surprised, and even shocked, when he arrived in Moscow and no one pretended ever having heard of the *Narkomzdrav* (Ministry of Health), his deputy, and the others who had invited him. In the end, a receptionist took pity on the bewildered foreigner and told him, first, to get as far away from Moscow as he could (these were the days of the purges and the Moscow trials) and, second, not to learn the local language. He followed this advice and found himself and his family in one of the resorts in the Northern Caucasus. We went to visit them first in the 1950s, and then for a while we visited them almost every year. At that time, it was not easy to get a visa to Russia, especially not for visits outside Moscow. I did not quite trust our good luck, fearing that one day someone would ask us to pay for this privilege. But the day never came; they may have never heard of *Survey* or of me. It taught me a lesson about Russia and bureaucracies in general: never to underestimate the role of accident and never to assume that the left hand would be aware of what the right was doing.

I have written in some detail about this chapter in my life in my autobiography (*Thursday's Child Has Far to Go*) and do not wish to repeat myself. I came to like the Caucasus (at the time, Switzerland without the tourists), and these frequent visits and prolonged stays gave me insights most visitors and tourists did not have; we seem to have been for years among the first foreign visitors in that area. Friedrich Richardovitch, my brother-in-law, was an excellent guide.

However, the anticlimax came one day when driving in the mountains. This was in the early Leonid Brezhnev era, and it occurred to me that while in years past Russia had been very interesting, since apparently about anything could happen, it had now entered a period of stability, or rather immobility (Russians called it *zastoi*). As far as I was concerned, it had become boring, and I had learned what I could in the circumstances, and so the time had come to pursue other interests.

This, then, was what I did for the next twenty years, until suddenly, under Mikhail Gorbachev, history began to move very fast, a new period of change dawned, and events in Russia became exciting. This coincided with an urge for professional change. I had been teaching in the United States but had no wish to do this full-time; I had left the London Institute I had been heading in competent hands. We moved to Washington, D.C., and I owed much to Ambassador David Abshire, head of the Center for Strategic and International Studies in that town, who let me do more or less what I wanted. A great deal had to do with Russia and the people in government, the academic world, and elsewhere, following events there.

But where to look for the early origins of my interest in Russia? This is another strange story. When I was a boy, my parents told me that one of my ancestors had been the physician of the Russian empress. They did not specify which empress. I dismissed this as sheer fantasy even at that early age. But years later, my interest was suddenly reawakened. I began my research, and the following emerged: The story was not quite right, but neither was it entirely wrong, and as is so often the case in such family legends, there was a grain of truth. Around 1800, my family lived in a little place in Silesia. My great-great-grandfather was a rabbi and in his spare time wrote undistinguished poems in Hebrew. His brother Moritz (born 1787) wanted to study medicine, but this was impossible because the family was very poor. One day a missionary appeared and made Moritz an offer he felt he could not refuse. He would be given the means to study if he would convert to Protestantism. This he did, and a number of years later he graduated in medicine (and rhetorics; medicine was apparently not a full-time subject) from the University of Dorpat (now Tartu) in what is now Estonia. The job he got was less than exciting. He was made head of the quarantine station at Taganrog, at the Black Sea. Moritz became Boris, and since Russian has no umlaut, the name was now Lakier. This would have been a dead-end job, but the unexpected happened: The czar (Alexander I) visited southern Russia, came to Taganrog, and died there in 1825. The government of the day feared (rightly, it would appear) that there would be allegations of foul play and therefore tried to get as many physicians as possible to sign the death certificate. Having come from abroad, Boris was in particular demand, and his name appears on the death certificate. This meant that he became a nobleman, belonging, alas, to the landless nobility. The family moved to Moscow, and among his three sons one, Aleksander Borisovich (1825–1870), was of particular interest to me. He was a well-known writer in his day, author of one of the first serious full-scale Russian books on the United States (it was published in English by the University of Chicago Press more than a hundred years after it had appeared in Russian). Before, he had been secretary of the government committee dealing with the liberation of the Russian peasants from the prevailing form of serfdom. He was also the author of the first Russian work on heraldry (republished in Moscow a few years ago) and provided a rather ugly coat of arms of the Lakier family, which can be found on the Internet. He married the daughter of P. A. Pletnev, friend of Pushkin's and rector of St. Petersburg State University. The lady died in childbirth. After a number of years he married again, this time a lady of the Komnenos Varvakis clan in Taganrog. Anton Chekhov, a native of Taganrog, wrote that there lived only three or four honest people in his hometown; I am sure my uncle three times removed was among them. The Komnenos family had been the royal house of Byzantium. So I found myself (albeit by considerable distance) related to all kind of historical figures, some distinguished and interesting, others of doubtful reputation.

However, there was a little problem: Boris, the doctor and master of rhetoric, had found it necessary following his arrival in Russia to acquire a "legend," as it is known in the world of intelligence services. According to this version, he was not born a Jew in Silesia, who having been married there had left a daughter behind; his background was purely French aristocratic. They hailed from Toulouse, and he had arrived in Russia with Napoleon's army. I can understand the need for a cock-and-bull story of this kind in Russia at that time, but he should have concocted something more plausible, for it was not widely believed. He died in Moscow and is buried in the cemetery for foreign religions. I have met some of his descendants.

These, then, were the Russian connections of my family.

There could have been no better research assistant than Christopher

Wall. I am grateful to David Boggis and Michael Allen as well as Joshua Klein and Irena Lasota for help with editing this book and also to Misha Epstein and Michael Hagemeister for helping me to understand certain specific points. It goes without saying that the opinions expressed are my own. The literature on contemporary Russia in Russian and English has grown immensely in recent years, and some of the essential sources are listed in the bibliography at the end of this book. The number of relevant Web sites is increasing even more rapidly and has become almost unmanageable. Johnson's Russia List and Paul Goble's Window on Eurasia, published daily, are of particular help as far as access is concerned. Russian Web sites, too many to mention, have also been of great assistance.

PUTINISM

INTRODUCTION

THIS IS AN ATTEMPT TO ASSESS THE PROSPECTS FOR RUSSIA'S FUTURE and above all the emerging "Russian idea" (ideology or doctrine) replacing communism. Such an endeavor involves various scenarios, some more likely than others. Unfortunately, quite often the less likely have happened—or some that appeared so outlandish, no one dared mention them (or did so under the wrong assumptions).

Of the last half dozen leaders chosen to govern the Soviet Union and Russia, all but the last came as no great surprise. All were members of the Politburo, the leading governing body: It stood to reason that a member of this body would be the next leader of the country. The choice of Vladimir Putin was far more accidental, but the policies he pursued were not. Observers of the Russian scene have argued that Putin's rise to power was resistible—influenced perhaps by one of Bertold Brecht's less impressive plays written during the Nazi era about the resistible rise to power of Arturo Ui, the king of the cauliflower trade. But the evidence for such claims is not exactly overwhelming. True, in principle about anything could have happened following the disastrous and chaotic Yeltsin years. But given all that was known about Russian history and traditions and current Soviet affairs, the emergence of a nationalist autocracy was far more likely than any other development even in the 1990s. (Walter Laqueur, *The Long Road to Freedom*, New York, 1989). Some economists have written that the oil and gas bonanza can account only for half of the Russian national income in the Putin era. True again, but the oil and gas income was decisive, it accounts to a large extent for the rise in the economy in general, for the various social and political schemes initiated by the Putin government from which the population benefitted, and last not least for Putin's foreign and military policy in 2014/5. At the present time, the choice of the next leader or leadership will likely prove difficult because there is no Politburo anymore.

It seems obvious to predict that Putin's successor will conduct the same or similar policies, domestically and abroad. It is unlikely that he will be more moderate. But there are no certainties. Much depends on the situation prevailing at the time within as well as outside Russia. Much may depend on the strength or weakness of the successor, the presence (or absence) of a rival (or rivals). Perhaps there will be a struggle for power among several candidates.

To pursue a discussion along these lines, it is necessary to go over familiar ground, to recapitulate (or try to interpret) the events that have taken place since the fall of the Soviet Union—the rise of Mikhail Gorbachev and the other parents of glasnost and perestroika, the age of Boris Yeltsin and of Putin.

More than twenty years ago, in a study of the extreme Right in Russia (*Black Hundred*), I tried, as I put it at the time, "to differentiate between the legitimate concerns of Russian patriotism and the pathological fantasies of the extreme Right." I also said that given Russia's precarious situation, "the Right holds firm to its belief that time works for us and it is their ambition to restore Russia's position as a global power." Moreover, "The Far Right will play a crucial role in the coming years." I mentioned Pushkin a few times but Putin did not appear in this book. In fact, he did not appear in any book known to me. On the other hand, I dealt with Alexander Dugin in some detail—his was not yet a household name at the time. But there is true sincere patriotism and *krasnoi* (beer hall) patriotism, rejected and ridiculed as empty and meaningless by leading Russian nineteenth-century thinkers such as Belinsky.

What did I mean by the phrase "the legitimate concerns of Russia"? Precisely this: the attempt to regain at least some of what had been lost. I am not particularly proud of this feat of prophecy. But I find it difficult even now to understand the optimism among many with regard to the prospects of democracy and freedom in Russia. Most likely it was wishful thinking, the satisfaction that the Cold War was finally over and we could devote our time, energy, and resources to the truly important tasks facing us at home. Given Russia's history, what ground was there for such optimism?

It seemed obvious that Russia would try to regain its status as a world power once the conditions to do so existed. After all, Germany had been defeated in World War I and had to suffer the consequences—yet within fifteen years, it was back as a leading power. Such comebacks have happened repeatedly in history and most likely would happen again.

It seemed equally obvious that the general trend of the Russian search for a new doctrine and mission would be toward the authoritarian Right, though I should admit that I did not anticipate it would go quite so far and happen so fast. To clarify this point: Russia at the present time is a dictatorship with much popular support, but I do not believe that the invocation of fascism is very helpful. Nor do I think it likely that it will reach this stage in the near future. Comparisons with the "clerical" Fascist regimes in Europe during the 1930s, with Francisco Franco's Spain, or with some of the dictatorships in the developing countries after World War II seem closer to the mark.

But Russia has gone far in this direction. How much further will it go?

I found it strange, even ludicrous, that the Left outside Russia has hardly been aware of the ideological and political changes in Russia and continues to think of Russia as left-wing in some ways. Perhaps it has to do with the fact that the distance between populism of the Left and populism of the Right has become difficult to detect. What difference is there between present-day Russian communism and the

Vladimir Zhirinovsky party? Since both vote with the government on all the important issues, there is no true political opposition in Russia. Sometimes it appears that even the intelligentsia in Russia has disappeared. The extreme Right in Europe has been much quicker to understand the changes in Russia and adjust its propaganda and policy accordingly.

I am dealing in the present book with the new doctrine gradually emerging in Russia. Most countries, even most great powers, are able to exist without a doctrine and a mission or manifest destiny, but not Russia. Its doctrine or ideology has several components: religion (the doctrine of the Orthodox Church, Russia's holy mission, the third Rome, and the New Jerusalem), patriotism/nationalism (with occasional leanings toward chauvinism), geopolitics Russian style, Eurasianism, the besieged-fortress feeling, and zapadophobia (fear of the West, coined by the philosopher-ideologue Nikolay Danilevsky as *zapadnichestvo*, for "Westernism"). Students of early Russian literature know that the belief in Russia's uniqueness goes back virtually to its beginnings; the writers (often merchants) who had been abroad returned with the conviction that "Rus" was unique, without parallel. This goes, for instance, for Afanasy Nikitin from Tver, who had been to India many years before Vasco da Gama; for Nestor Iskander, who wrote about the fall of Constantinople; and for Maxim Maximus, a monk from Mount Athos who had been invited to Russia and settled there. Further, this conviction was usually paired with another belief—the suspicion of Russophobia, the certainty that all foreigners were against Russia. (Such fears were not specifically Russian; in the very first articles in which an American manifest destiny is mentioned in the 1830s, we also find references to the assertion that virtually all foreigners were hostile toward the United States.) Why this should have been the case is unclear, for the attitude of the outside world toward Russia under Ivan III and Ivan Grozny (the Terrible) was one not of hostility but of profound lack of interest.

The roots of Russian messianism, the belief in a special mission from God, go deep. They existed in other nations, of course, especially in the nineteenth century; but in most cases the belief was a passing phase, whereas in Russia it persisted even beyond the Slavophiles, the most ardent believers in this kind of mission. It should not therefore have come as a surprise that political messianism had a secular rebirth during the Soviet period and that it resurfaced in our time as part of the search for a new Russian idea.

To a certain extent, this search for a new ideology amounts to a return to the status quo ante before the revolution of 1917, albeit with certain important changes, given that 2014–15 is not like 1914. Such a dramatic reversion is bound to resurrect many painful subjects. For instance, that Leon Trotsky was evil goes without saying; he was a Jew and an internationalist, and what he did harmed Russia. Vladimir Lenin, while perhaps slightly better, was also a negative force. The victory of the Reds in the civil war was a disaster; Alexander Kolchak, Pyotr Wrangel, and Anton Denikin should be rehabilitated—a process that has in fact already taken place.

Joseph Stalin, on the other hand, should not be denigrated. It was a difficult period; he took actions that cannot be justified, but he also made Russia greater and stronger and was therefore a positive force. But how to defend Stalin against the attacks of the "liberals," considering that he was so close to Lenin?

These historical issues are probably best ignored or at least should be accorded less significance. In twenty or fifty years, they will no longer figure prominently.

Religion, or rather the Orthodox Church, is of great importance to any ideological reorientation. Well before 1917, the prestige of the church was low. The intelligentsia may have maintained an interest in religion, but not in the church. Individual churchmen were admired and even loved, but the stupidity, the venality, and the low moral standards of much of the clergy generated a considerable measure of contempt. Under Communist rule, the church suffered. Churches were closed, churchgoers were harassed, and priests were imprisoned, exiled, and even killed.

The church did survive but had to pay a heavy price; it was almost totally penetrated by the secret police and virtually absorbed and integrated into the GPU/NKVD/KGB. All senior appointments in the church hierarchy had to be approved by these organs, sometimes even by the Politburo. Many churchmen, even those at the highest echelons, became informers.

Seen in retrospect, these "compromises" enabled the church to survive, whereas those who had persecuted it did not. But was the survival of the organized church the supreme aim? They certainly did not act like the martyrs of earlier periods in church history.

The church had sinned. But after the fall of communism, it confessed its sins and strove to regard the chapter as closed. Churches were reopened, its activities renewed, and the new rulers regarded the church as an essential, even central, part of the new order. With this, new questions arose. How close should the relationship be between church and state? What gospel was preached by the newborn church? It was often claimed that its spiritual values were universal, but in fact it was a state church. Before the revolution, it had been probably closer to the state than that in any other country. A religious person had to be a patriot, and how a patriot should behave was decided by the government. But this closeness has not been a blessing, and there had been warnings against it even inside the church. For this reason, the Moscow patriarchate has recently shown a little caution: Even while trying to evade conflicts with the state, it has demonstrated that it does not implicitly support every policy mandated by the government.

There were other troubling questions. A great majority of Russians regarded the church as a positive and vital factor in the life of the country. But an equally large majority (almost 80 percent) did not practice religion or even attend church, except on one or two of the most important holidays. Nor did they observe the commandments of religion, the orders, and the prohibitions.

The rituals of the Orthodox Church were clear, but what was it supposed to preach? Was it Christian love, charity, and compassion? Was it the love of God or the hatred of Satan—meaning Jews, Catholics, Masons, liberals, the pope, and all the enemies of Russia?

These questions had to be confronted in the wake of the Orthodox revival, along with other elements of the new Russian ideology, such as neo-Eurasianism, antiglobalism, and *geopolitika*—not to mention the new science of conspirology. Of course, an individual could be a staunch Russian patriot even if he or she did not believe that almost the whole universe was engaged in conspiring against Russia. But in practice, there was almost always a close relationship among these various sets of beliefs.

Some reservations are called for at this stage. First, Eurasianism and *geopolitika* Russian style are obviously of recent date. There were such beliefs in the nineteenth century, but not much more than in other countries, nor were they more deeply held. Under Stalin, these fears received a fresh impetus. As for conspirology, I had assumed that the Russian belief in pervasive conspiracies was of recent date, but I had to revise my views when I encountered the following written by Vladimir Solovyov, the great Russian philosopher, in 1892 (*Sobranie Sochineni*, vol. 5):

> Let us imagine a person healthy in body and strong, talented and not unkind—for such is quite justly the general view of the Russian people. We know that this person or people are now in a very sorry state. If we want to help him, we have first to understand what is wrong with him. Thus we learn that he is not really mad, his mind is merely afflicted to a considerable extent by false ideas approaching folie de grandeur and a hostility toward everyone and everything. Indifferent to his real advantage, indifferent to damage likely to be caused, he imagines dangers that do not exist and builds upon this the most absurd propositions. It seems to him that all his neighbors offend him, that they insufficiently bow to his grandness, and in every way want to harm him. He accuses everyone in his family of damaging and deserting him, of crossing over to the enemy camp. He imagines that his neighbors want to undermine his house and even to launch an armed attack. Therefore he will spend enormous sums on the purchase of guns, revolvers, and iron locks. If he has any time left, he will turn against his family.
>
> We shall not, of course, give him money, even if we are eager to help him, but will try to persuade him that his ideas are wrong and unjustified. If he still will not be convinced and if he perseveres in his mania, neither money nor drugs will help.

One hundred and twenty years later, I cannot think of a better description of the current state of affairs.

To repeat: These afflictions are not specific to Russia. Perhaps the majority of all these beliefs are foreign imports. Some appeared first among the extreme Right of the Russian emigration, while most originated in publications of the post–World War II European "New Right"; the French *nouvelle droite*; and the neo-Fascists, ranging from Alain de Benoist to the Belgian Jean-François Thiriart, the Italian Julio Evola, and other occultists, combining anti-Americanism with anti-Sovietism, admiration for Stalin, Mao, Ceauşescu, and the Fatah.

These influences are clear in the writing of Alexander Dugin, one of the chief philosophers of the new age, but can also be detected in the work of Igor Panarin and others. After a while, it became clear that these obscure, foreign ideas had to be strengthened by homegrown products, and it was at this stage that Nikolay Danilevsky and a few other Russian thinkers with a strong dislike of the West were brought in. Ivan Ilyin (1883–1954), the reactionary émigré ideologist, has been another important influence frequently invoked in recent years by Putin and those close to him.

Nikolay Danilevsky (1822–1885) has been rediscovered. An interesting figure, in his younger years he belonged to the Petrashevsky Circle, a radical literary discussion group studying French socialism, and was promptly arrested. He studied biology, disagreed with Darwin, but also hated Europe, about which he had strong feelings but did not know very much. His book *Russia and Europe* (1869) became the bible of the "hate Europe" school. He sincerely believed that (as his biographer put it) the Russians were the children of light and the Europeans the children of darkness. Europeans were violent and bellicose, whereas the Russians were peace loving. The Europeans wanted war, and war was an evil. In many respects, Danilevsky was an ideal precursor of the anti-Western school in contemporary Russia.

Neo-Eurasianism, an important tenet of the new Russian doctrine, rests on the assumption that the origins of the Russian state are found in Asia rather than in Europe; that the encounter with Mongols, Tatars, and Asian tribes largely shaped Russia; and that, rejected by the West, Russia should look for its future in Asia. A marriage, it could be said, of Anna Karenina and Genghis Khan. The neo-Eurasian school is not identical with the Eurasian thinking of the late nineteenth century and the historical-philosophical school of the 1920s, which was more cautious and intelligent. The neo-Eurasians received an uplift from the writings of Lev Gumilev on ethnogenesis and passionarity, which became fashionable after the breakdown of the Soviet Union. They also gained more popularity with the rise of China and the East Asian / Pacific region in general. The basic tenets of the Russian Far Right have the advantage that their meaning is seldom very clear; they can mean one thing but also another. Passionarity may mean the readiness of a nation or a group of people to make sacrifices for their beliefs.

Given Europe's declining importance, a reasonable case may be made for Russia's heightened interest in East Asian markets and its greater attention to Asia in general. But in view of its origins, past history, cultural influences, and demographics, there is little to support the idea that Russia is essentially an Asian power. The great majority of Russians do not live in Asia, and many of those who live in Siberia wish to leave. Furthermore, Asians are not showing much enthusiasm at the prospect of Russian migration. Thus, neo-Eurasianism may be characterized as an ideology of beliefs and taste, not facts. Unkind critics may regard it as misplaced wishful thinking or even as nonsense on stilts. The fact that Russia had its difficulties with Europe does not make it Asian. However, attempts to expose neo-Eurasianism as a fantasy have been fruitless, precisely because such beliefs do not lend themselves to rational argument.

A paradoxical development took place that was noted by Western and Asian diplomats and scholars alike. While on the ideological level there was a great deal of talk about the importance of Eurasianism and Russia as an emerging Asian power, and much was promised in the way of economic and general development in Russia beyond the Urals, very little happened on the ground. This was the result partly of the usual lethargy but mainly of events in Ukraine and Crimea (and the accompanying anti-Western campaign) that deflected Russian interest from Asia even more.

Few terms have been more frequently used and abused in political discourse in our time than "geopolitics." Originally, it referred to the relationship between politics and geography, an obvious and perfectly legitimate subject. But it has been used in different countries and by people of different political opinion to mean many different things. Sometimes, this may have happened because "geopolitical" sounds more impressive than "political," but quite often it was intended to imply the special God- or nature-given rights and historical missions of a certain country derived from its geographic location. Thus, "geopolitical" can be used to prove that the historical mission of Ruritania is to be Africa's leading power: because it is located in the very heart of the continent or because it has access to three different oceans and four major rivers or because the Ruritania-Utopiana axis makes such a dominating position its destiny—and its policy inevitable. However, the geographic facts mentioned can also be used to prove the very opposite.

"Geopolitical" is particularly useful when the issue at stake is to prove why a certain country has the divine mission to be a great power, a superpower, or an empire. Although the theory is now thought to be outdated, in Russia geopolitics is considered to be a valid justification for action.

The geopolitical message was brought to Russia by Alexander Dugin in the late 1990s. Dugin's thinking (sometimes named the fourth political theory or the third doctrine) aimed at Russian domination of Eurasia, this being a new (third) continent. But since Russia was not powerful enough by itself for military, economic, and demographic reasons, it needed more than one axis to achieve this aim: Moscow-Tokyo and Moscow-Tehran were considered, but both proved to be excessively problematic. Moscow-Berlin, however, found many sympathizers in Russia. This is of considerable interest because Germany had been the traditional enemy and the United Kingdom and France the allies. However, by the time Putin had become president, Germany's record in World War II was forgotten and forgiven.

The intellectual starting point of Dugin was the realm of the irrational, esoteric metaphysical, and mystical. These influences in Russian intellectual history were not exactly new. But Dugin acutely realized that whereas Gurdjieff and Madame Blavatskaya (Helena Petrovna), to name but two in this tradition, were likely to appeal to writers and composers (such as Mahler, Skryabin, and Sibelius) rather than to military men and politicians, whereas *geopolitika* Russian style would do precisely that.

Dugin's message was listened to with great interest by Russian military thinkers and the general staff and Ministry of Defense, although with a curious mixture of great interest and understandable caution, born of the recognition that some of his ideas were not practical. The conduct of foreign policy (as Putin saw it) had to be energetic and aggressive but was best left to men of the world rather than writers of political science fiction showing symptoms of hysteria in stressful situations.

Some of these concepts are bound to strike the reader as curious and strange, yet I have referred so far only to mainstream ideas and doctrines. Even the Dugin of 2014 is usually a little more moderate than twenty years ago.

Once one moves from mainstream to radical views—and much of contemporary Russian political literature belongs to this category—understanding and comment become difficult. Should views be taken literally that are both eccentric and unbelievable? Do their authors exercise what psychologists call confabulation? In other words, have their authors persuaded themselves that they tell us the truth, or do they simply wish to shock or entertain their readers?

The legitimate concerns of Russian patriotism include the aspirations of ethnic Russians in neighboring states who feel discriminated against and would like to be citizens of Russia. Given the fact that no country is wholly homogeneous, how may one do justice to all such aspirations? What of nonethnic Russians, for instance, in the Caucasus? Would regional arrangements bring a solution or merely collide with statism? The insistence on a strong central power (*derzhavnost*) is also a vital part of the new Russian doctrine. To understand Russian policy in this respect, it is probably more helpful to consider Pushkin's attitude rather than Putin's. In 1830, the Poles rebelled against Russian rule; the uprising was suppressed and eight thousand Poles lost their lives in the Battle of Ostrolenka alone. There was much support for the Polish cause in Europe and America, which annoyed Pushkin and many other Russians.

Russian public opinion supported the government reaction almost without exception. In one of his poems, "To the Slanderers of Russia," Pushkin expressed his anger about the Western critics of Russia even more than about the traitorous Poles. Why did they threaten Russia with anathema (sanctions)? What business of theirs was it? Was it not a family struggle of the Slavs among themselves? Had they not been at war for a long time? The Poles had burned Moscow, and the Russians had destroyed Praga, a part of Warsaw. If the enemies of Russia want military intervention, Pushkin said, why do they not send their sons; there is enough space for them in the graves in the fields of our country. Strong emotions, strong words.

Pushkin's feelings were shared even by the most bitter critics of official Russia and its society. Some of them were even afraid that the czar in his magnanimity would not be harsh enough in treating the Poles. But was not Pushkin the poet glorifying freedom rather than tyranny, and had he not suffered for his beliefs? How to explain this contradiction? An attempt to do so was made by Georgy Fedotov, a great theologian and church historian and the most clear-sighted thinker of his generation. Fedotov saw in Pushkin someone whose political views had been shaped in the eighteenth century: Freedom, yes—but not for everyone. Pushkin had been disappointed by his people. His heroes were Peter the Great and the empress Catherine, even though he must have been aware of the great corruption at court. He was not a democrat, but who was in the eighteenth century? As he grew older, Pushkin became more conservative.

There is some resemblance with the present situation in Russia, except that the political outlook of Russia's current rulers and their attitude toward democracy were formed not in the eighteenth century, but while the Soviet Union still existed. The relevant question, therefore, is whether and to what extent the attitude of the next generation will be different.

There has been a massive shift in the ideology of the Russian regime in the years since the downfall of the Soviet Union. Marxism-Leninism has been replaced by Russian nationalism and the glorification of a strong state. This process has been accelerated by the seizure of Crimea, the state of civil war in the eastern Ukraine, and the attack of MH17, the Malaysia Airlines airplane explosion that killed hundreds of passengers. At present, the process of transition from communism to some form of state capitalism under the supervision of the organs of state security is by no means complete, and it is impossible to know where this reorientation, the search for a new Russian idea, will lead.

During the last decades of Soviet power, the importance of Communist ideology was frequently overrated abroad. Only after the downfall of the regime did it become clear that Marxism-Leninism was no longer taken seriously; lip service was still paid to it, but it became the subject of ridicule among those at the very top. Is there a danger that a similar misapprehension may prevail now that political views once found only at the periphery of the political system have moved to its center? It is frequently argued that Russia has become deeply conservative, patriotic, and religious. But sociological investigations so far call for caution, because the fact that the mainline ideology has changed so much does not indicate much about the depth with which these new convictions are held. According to sociological investigations such as those conducted by Vladimir Petukhov of the Russian Academy of Sciences, there is no doubt about the patriotic upsurge that has taken place and the widespread satisfaction that some of the territory lost (such as Crimea) has been regained. However, once the question is raised concerning the sacrifices that will have to be made to restore more of the old glory, the results are less than striking. A great majority would like to see their country a major power, a superpower if possible, but are reluctant to make great efforts, especially financial efforts, to achieve this. Eurasianism might be a topic of intense interest among the intelligentsia, but much less so for the rest of society. The great majority are not motivated by ideology; their psychology and ambitions are primarily those of members of a consumer society.

Contemporary Russia is a traditionalist society, and the majority of its people are averse to change. But conservative values do not overwhelmingly shape their outlook and behavior. There are apparently no more true conservatives than liberals in contemporary Russia. The Orthodox Church plays a far larger role now than in the past, but it is not clear whether it will be able to maintain this position for long: Only a small minority attends church services (at the main holidays the percentage is somewhat higher) or has accepted the other religious duties. According to investigations, religion ranges as an actor of paramount importance for 8 percent of the population. Patriotism, with 14 percent, figures somewhat higher.

These facts concerning the motivation of the majority of Russian society will not necessarily be the only ones to shape Russian policy in the years to come, but they will undoubtedly limit its scope. Hence the need for caution at a time when the ideological declarations of Russian political leaders attract greater interest than usual because they differ so much from those made in the past.

Those ruling Russia today, the *siloviki*, have been described as the new nobility, selfless patriots motivated by pure idealism. It is indeed a noble vision, but how true is it? In the 1980s, a strange situation had arisen: The KGB spent much of its time harassing and persecuting the dissidents, but they believed as little in communism and the Soviet system as their victims. They did what they did because they had been given orders from above. What is known about their real convictions? Deep down many of them were probably cynics, willing apparently to serve any system as long as it preserved their privileged positions. What of the current situation? How important is ideology, and what is the specific weight of power and money? It would be wrong to dismiss the importance of patriotism and the other components of the new ideology altogether as a mere smoke screen; some of the new elite may deeply believe in it, some only a little, and some not at all.

The role of the Russian intelligentsia is a sad story in this general context. During the last century, this most attractive and creative section of Russian society, which contributed much to our culture, has been subject to myriad bloodlettings. As a result of emigration and "liquidation," not much of it has remained; standards and levels have declined. The Russian democrats have been blamed for failing in their reformist attempts following the breakdown of the Soviet Union. This is correct, but could anyone have succeeded given the nondemocratic mind-set of Russian society in general, the desire for a strong hand to guide the country?

A new middle class might be emerging, but so far there are few signs heralding the appearance of a new intelligentsia. Of its remnants, some have made peace with the new regime and support it, but others have thought it wise to withdraw from politics and public life in general. In its cultural history, Russia went through a golden and a silver age, but now there are few prospects even for a bronze age. One feels reminded of Pushkin's reaction having finished listening to Nikolai Gogol reading to him *Dead Souls*: "God, what a sad country, our Russia."

1 | THE END OF THE SOVIET ERA

ACCORDING TO A SAYING ATTRIBUTED TO VOLTAIRE, HISTORY IS ONLY the patter of silken slippers descending the stairs to the thunder of hob-nailed boots climbing upward from below. The question why nations fail and decline has been frequently discussed in recent years, the question why they recover—sometimes for a short period only, sometimes for longer periods—less often. It took Germany a mere fifteen years after the defeat in World War I to regain its military and political power. It took Russia two decades for its comeback after the disintegration of the Soviet Union.

But does it make sense to compare twenty-first-century Russia with other great powers and empires? The emergence of the Soviet Union was sui generis, based on an ideology, the desire to build a society wholly different from all others in history, and it was to be the beginning of a new era, a just and progressive society. It was to be a new beginning in the annals of humankind. As "The Internationale," which was to be the anthem of the country up to World War II, put it:

Du passé faisons table rase

And further on:

Le monde va changer de base

The revolution and the regime to which it gave birth attracted much opposition and hostility in the early days. But after the end of the civil war, there was an enormous amount of enthusiasm, especially among the younger generation. This was the heroic age, and as Anatoly D'Aktil put it:

We are always right in our daring
There are no obstacles for us on land or on sea
We fear no ice, no cloud
We achieve in a year the work of a century
Happiness we take as of right
We carry the banner of our country
Through the whole world and all ages.

Of that heroic age there remained "the march of the enthusiasts," the name of a subway and a metro station on the Kalinin line on the Moscow metro. The author of the poem is now remembered mainly as the translator into Russian of *Alice's Adventures in Wonderland*. He also wrote the "Budyonny March," celebrating the famous commander of the civil war.

But at the time, enthusiasm was in the air. It was the age of *Kak Zakalyalas Stal* (*How the Steel Was Forged*), by Nikolai Ostrovsky, describing the superhuman efforts of young workers to build and work new factories. Ostrovsky was a desperately ill young man (he died at thirty-five in 1936), and his novel sold or was distributed in millions of copies and became the socialist realist bestseller par excellence. It was made into a movie three times and became a television series as late as the 1970s, even though by that time young people no longer felt much empathy for the Pavel Korchagins, the heroes of a past age. Another idol was Magnitogorsk, one of the new centers of the iron and steel industry in the Urals and the regions beyond. Many of the best young people, many of the idealists, volunteered to move to these places. They became the mecca of that period. It was the age of "Shiroka Strana Moya Rodnaya," a song that became something like the second national anthem and the signature tune of Moscow radio. It announced that the Soviet Union was not only a country of many mountains and rivers but also the country *gdye tak volno dyshit chelovyek*—where a man could breathe more freely than anywhere else.

Magnitogorsk played a role of importance in World War II. Today, it is reported to be one of the most polluted places on earth; only 27 percent of the children born there are healthy. Magnitogorsk became a "closed city" to foreigners, opened again only in the age of glasnost. It now has four hundred thousand inhabitants, but many would like to escape from it.

Although 1935 was a good year, it was followed by the Moscow trials and the age of the great fear and tribulations of the war and eventually the great victory. At the end of the war, there was much hope that from now on everything would be better. Enthusiasm had largely vanished, but there still was a great deal of hope.

The earlier internationalism had disappeared. "The Internationale" was replaced by a new national anthem, a patriotic song praising great Russia and its foremost role. The war years saw the emergence of a "Russian party," of which we shall have much more to say. However, the feeling was that the worst was over. Joseph Stalin died, and there were no mass arrests and executions. Supplies of elementary goods slowly improved. A Russian was the first human being to fly into space. Living conditions improved to a certain degree. The Soviet Union had its nuclear arsenal soon after the Americans.

But progress in the Soviet Union was slow, much slower than in the West. True, the devastation in the occupied Soviet territories had been more extensive than the damage that had been caused by the war in the West. This above all was adduced as the reason for the slow Russian recovery. It was a convincing argument for a decade, perhaps even two, but it no longer seemed persuasive after that. By the 1970s, serious doubts arose about the efficacy of the system—something obviously was wrong with it, but what?

The Soviet Union had become a superpower with very strong military forces, and this caused much pride. But maintaining a strong military force was very expensive, and as the economy progressed only slowly and eventually stagnated, it became more and more difficult to keep pace with America and the West. Many Western experts overrated the extent of the Soviet performance, whereas the average Soviet citizen was more aware of the true state of affairs. But they too could not travel abroad at the time and were not fully aware of the true state of affairs. Only the upper reaches of society knew about the true situation, partly because they had been abroad and were able to compare or because they had access to restricted information. From the 1960s onward, there had been manifestations of dissent, but their outreach was limited. The KGB had society very much under control.

But when it came to a test such as in Afghanistan, the showing was not very impressive. In the non-Russian republics, a nationalist mood prevailed. The general malaise of that period was described openly in the novels of right-wing writers, the nationalist *pochvenniki*. By the late Brezhnev period (1981–82), complaints about the situation were made at the highest level—the food shortages were a matter of crucial political and economic importance. There was open criticism, but it was not followed by actions and reforms.

Perhaps most important was the failure to improve the quality of life. Air and water were polluted; the soil was poisoned; the Russian forest, traditionally the pride of the country, was partly disappearing in European Russia. There were some staunch fighters for improving the environment, but their activities clashed with those of the local and central authorities who had to fulfill the plan, and the environment fighters usually failed to have any impact. Alcoholism, always a plague in Russian history, became worse. On payday in the villages and cities, no work was done because everyone was too drunk to make their way to their places of work; the scenes were indescribable. The crime rate was rising, petty and not-so-petty theft was increasing all the time. Much of this was out in the open—described, for instance, in the novels of Valentin Rasputin, perhaps the most gifted of the nationalist writers, a Siberian by origin who spent most of his life in this part of Russia.

It was clear by that time to any unprejudiced observer that the regime had lost its dynamism, that the age of enthusiasm was long over. While interest in Marxism could still be found in American universities, it became difficult to find any of this in the Soviet Union. Some Western observers found certain redeeming factors in the Soviet system: It was, after all, a welfare state of sorts: People were paid pensions and had no fear of unemployment. This was true, but it was welfare on a very low level. Russia was and remained a poor country, and as the years passed, four decades after the end of World War II, blaming the war for most of the misfortunes became impossible.

At the same time, the old idea of catching up with and even overtaking America and becoming the most powerful force on earth persisted. The Cold War meant high and ever-growing military spending. But America was so much richer, and it should have been clear to the Soviet leadership that they could not win this arms race, which might instead ruin their economy. But it was not recognized, and this too contributed to the breakdown.

If there was little opposition inside the country against military spending, this is a reflection that it would have been considered unpatriotic, if not a matter of treason. Furthermore, the facts concerning military spending were known only to a very few. But there was vocal criticism of the allocation of funds to friendly countries abroad. Weapons worth millions of dollars had been delivered to Egypt and other Middle Eastern countries, but not a dollar had ever been paid back. Money and resources that were badly needed at home had been diverted to Cuba and various Asian and African countries. This resentment manifested itself in a growing xenophobia when officials and tourists visited the Soviet Union from African and Asian countries. Relations with China had improved somewhat since the days of open hostility, and there was an alliance with the European satellites, but twice since the war, the Soviet Union had to intervene militarily in Eastern Europe, in Hungary (1956) and in Czechoslovakia (1968). Romania had openly defied Moscow, and with the possible exception of East Germany, there was no trust with regard to the others.

It was widely believed at the time that the Soviet Union was overstretched. This was true, and perhaps some of the Soviet leaders were even aware of it. But if so, they did not know how to terminate the Cold War. Some of them may have believed that it was all the fault of the West. After all, even some of the American experts argued that but for Truman, there might not have been the Cold War. Some Soviet leaders may have believed that the conflict with the West was needed for a domestic reason: How else to justify the many restrictions at home, the whole dictatorial system?

One of the reasons for the collapse of the Soviet Union was the weakness and inefficiency of the top leadership. Leonid Brezhnev was seventy-five years of age when he died in 1982, and a new general secretary of the party had to be elected. Yuri Andropov had not been in good health for years, but his style of leadership was in some respects better than that of his predecessor (he almost always consulted his Politburo colleagues before making important decisions). He was not eager to make changes; the period since the 1970s became known as the *zastoi*—stagnation. The system did work, after all, even if it did not work well, and opposition was negligible, with the security services in full control. By the time Brezhnev died, the party leadership consisted of elderly people out of touch with the problems of the common people. A novel published in the early days of glasnost described the plight of a very high official, a minister or party leader, whose car and driver had not turned up to take the VIP home after a meeting. He tried to make his way using public transport but had the greatest difficulties because he had no idea how to do so.

Yuri Andropov, who had been head of the KGB for a number of years, followed Brezhnev. He had the reputation of being an intelligent leader who was disgusted with the state of the country, above all with the ever-growing corruption, and was eager to carry out reforms. During his stay in office, some eighteen ministers and senior party secretaries were dismissed. But there was no liberalization, stricter repression at home, and no change in foreign policy. Andropov was very sick, unable to attend Politburo meetings. When he felt his end was near, he suggested Mikhail Gorbachev, the youngest member of the leading body, to preside over its sessions and eventually take over. But the majority ignored his suggestion and chose Konstantin Chernenko, who was generally considered an inoffensive character on reasonably good terms with his colleagues. If Andropov had been in office for eighteen months, Chernenko stayed for a mere thirteen months, an old man also, unable to attend many of the meetings of the Politburo. He gave the eulogy at the funeral of his predecessor, but was so weak that he could barely finish it. Since the occasion was shown on television, millions of Soviet citizens watched it, and the impression they gained was devastating. It only added to the prevailing depression and pessimism: a country faced with serious problems in many fields but lacking a reasonably effective leadership. It was after the death of Chernenko that Mikhail Gorbachev came to power.

The Soviet Union was certainly in bad shape at the time, worse than assumed by most people in the West. But was the ultimate breakdown inevitable? Perhaps, but not from an economic perspective. True, even wheat had to be imported at the time, something unheard-of in a country that had once been among the leading wheat exporters. But no one was starving, and if there was widespread dissatisfaction, it had not reached the boiling point. The propaganda machine was telling people that the situation in the West was even worse, and the KGB was effectively suppressing any opposition. If there was dissatisfaction, there was even greater apathy, no burning desire to engage in political activity to bring about political change.

To engage in a brief exercise of counterfactual history: The Putin regime owes its survival and success to one factor and one factor only—the export of oil and gas, which accounts for about half of the Russian budget. Up to 2013, when it was overtaken by the United States, Russia was the biggest global producer of oil and gas. If the price of a barrel of crude oil was $14 in 1988 and $11 in 1998, it was $94 in 2013 and is about $52 now.

If on March 11, 1985, someone other than Gorbachev had been made general secretary of the Communist Party—say, another member of the Politburo (for argument's sake, let him be named Ivan Ivanov)—and if ten or fifteen years later Ivanov had been succeeded by, say,

Sergeev—neither one a liberal reformer but both leaders in the Brezhnev tradition, muddling through the 1990s—they would have benefited from the oil and gas windfall that subsequently occurred, without any particular modernizing effort. The Supreme Soviet would still exist, as would the Communist Party with its political monopoly. The party leadership would be praised for the country's increase in wealth and for its wisdom, energy, farsightedness, and astuteness in making the country richer. Some minor political and ideological reforms might have taken place, but no radical changes. True, the character of such an economic system and such a country would hardly conform to the original Communist vision of a developed industrial (or postindustrial) Marxist-Leninist economy and society. It would more resemble a colonial country, with its economy based on the export of raw materials. But it might not be so difficult to overlook all this. The doctrinal inconsistencies would not greatly matter—what would matter would be the existence of a balanced budget and a higher standard of living. The Communist Party of the Soviet Union would still have a political monopoly, there would have been no secession from the Soviet Union, and the regime would still be authoritarian. It is possible—indeed, quite likely—that precisely because of a rise in the standard of living, new tensions would not have developed, and the continued existence of a command economy would not have been questioned.

Such a development in Russia during the last two decades is by no means unthinkable. The election of a leader who genuinely believed that the system could be reformed was an accident.

Perestroika

Soviet politics in the early 1980s seemed to be frozen, at a standstill. Only after the death of Chernenko did it suddenly gather speed. This came as a surprise to people inside the Soviet Union and observers abroad, who had not expected any important changes in Soviet policy. The events that followed, beginning with the election of Gorbachev as general secretary of the party, have been heavily documented; virtually all those involved have written their memoirs. It is therefore not necessary to go over the ground in any detail.

Very little was known abroad at the time about Gorbachev, and virtually nothing about his personal views (if any) on domestic and foreign affairs. But the same was true with regard to the other members of the Politburo, with the possible exception of Andrei Gromyko, who as foreign minister had been frequently abroad. He had never been a man of many words, and it was considered elementary wisdom at the time, even among the top leadership, to keep one's personal views to oneself, especially if these happened to deviate from the prevailing consensus that had been prescribed by the head of the group. Truer opinions were voiced, if at all, in a small circle of the closest friends and even there only with due caution. Even the leadership had to pretend to be in full agreement or at least to keep silent unless the issues at stake were of minor importance.

Mikhail Gorbachev was born in a small village not far from Stavropol in the Northern Caucasus. It should be noted that while earlier generations of Communist leaders had usually been townpeople whose parents had often belonged to the middle class or intelligentsia, those of Gorbachev's generation who played leading roles in the dramatic events of the 1980s and 1990s more often than not came from peasant families. It is also interesting that even though these families lived far from the centers of political power, they did not escape the consequences of the 1930s. Many were victims of "repression," the term that came to be used in the post-Stalin period. Gorbachev's grandfather was arrested, as was Yeltsin's father (his family had five horses and four cows, which made them kulaks, rich peasants, which at the time was the "wrong" class); few families survived these years entirely unharmed.

Gorbachev was born in 1931 and received his primary education locally. He seems to have been an exceptionally bright young man, for the party became interested in him early on, and it was decided to send him to Moscow State University to study law. This was the country's leading university, and to be sent there and accepted was exceptional. His rise in the party hierarchy was swift. At thirty-five, he was first secretary of the

Stavropol town section, and a few years later he became head of the Stavropol district organization. His reputation spread, and in 1971 he was appointed a member of the Central Committee of the Communist Party. This meant frequent visits to Moscow, where the powerful Yuri Andropov became interested in the capable young man. Various offers of employment followed—the KGB was interested in him, but so was the supreme planning institution, and some of his protectors wanted him to be minister of agriculture. But Gorbachev accepted none of these offers and in 1980 became a member of the Politburo, the most important political institution in the country. He seems to have behaved modestly and inconspicuously, as befitting a newcomer, made a few friends and no enemies.

During his years in Stavropol, Gorbachev became well informed about the local situation, but only in Moscow did he gain a true, wider picture of the state of affairs in the Soviet Union. As a result, he became very critical of current policies or rather the absence of action to improve the situation. He gathered around him a number of like-minded people, hoping, perhaps, to have the necessary support for the day when he would be in a position to influence policy.

We know about one of these meetings, which is of particular interest because it concerns a man considered the ideological father of perestroika, Alexander Yakovlev. Eight years older than Gorbachev, he too was a bright country boy who had risen to the party leadership. Severely injured during the war in August 1942, he was mustered out of the army and sent to study—eventually becoming a member of the Russian Academy of Sciences. Like Gorbachev, he went to Moscow to work in the Central Committee of the Communist Party, mainly in the ideological field. He was among those who suggested that sociology should be taught in Russian universities, which was not the case at the time. However, being less cautious than Gorbachev, he ran into trouble. In August 1972, he published an article in the *Literaturnaya Gazeta* in which he sharply denounced the chauvinist and anti-Semitic trend that he encountered in the country. By that time, these tendencies were already deeply rooted and had powerful supporters in the party leadership. These people demanded that he should not be permitted to engage in ideological work in a leading position. As a result, he was sent as ambassador to Canada, where he spent the next ten years and gained a good knowledge of Western political and economic institutions. In 1983, Gorbachev visited Canada, and the two of them met. It took a little mutual exploration, but eventually the two discovered that their views were close and they could talk openly. Both, independently from each other, reached the conclusion that the Soviet Union needed radical change. But Yakovlev's critique was far more radical by that time; unlike Gorbachev, he was far more progressed and practical in his thoughts on how to bring about change.

They became friends, and after his return to Moscow, Gorbachev insisted on Yakovlev's return to the Soviet capital and the Central Committee. The position he was offered and accepted was as head of the Marx-Engels-Lenin Institute. It was not exactly the most important power base, and Yakovlev's position at that time toward the official party ideology was negative. The attitude of other Soviet leaders was not one of great enthusiasm either—they simply ignored it. It would be difficult to find in their speeches a positive reference to Marxism-Leninism; they simply did not mention it. But Yakovlev went considerably further, and his attitude was one of total antagonism, even of hatred. He regarded Marxism-Leninism as a religion of hatred that had nothing to do with science.

How could a person with such convictions survive in the Politburo? Yakovlev later related that in the early days of perestroika, he could not yet speak the whole truth; one had to pretend and to lie. The others simply did not care one way or another. The policy of the party leadership was rooted not in deep ideological conviction, but in the interests of the *nomenklatura:* They were fools and cynics. He referred to the Soviet regime only as totalitarian—something that would have landed him in certain Western universities in deep trouble. He and some of his closest friends submitted to Gorbachev detailed plans on how to bring about real change. But Gorbachev, even though admitting that only a small revolution inside the party would bring about true change, argued that it was too early to do so.

Yakovlev left the Communist Party in 1991 and together with Eduard Shevardnadze, the foreign minister at the time, founded a social democratic party in competition with the Bolsheviks. The party existed for a few years but was not successful. The entrenched Communist Party apparatus was still quite strong, and while they did not worry greatly about the fate of Marxism-Leninism, they were rightly concerned about their position in society and their power. Furthermore, Yakovlev's energetic stand against chauvinism did not add to his popularity. After 1993 (he died in 2005), he did not play any significant political role but engaged in academic pursuits. He made many enemies and was attacked not just as an enemy of the party and the country, but even alleged to be a spy. However, his war record made him almost invulnerable. Among the party leaders of the time, he was virtually the only one who had not only fought for his country, but almost paid for it with his life. At his funeral, not one of the leaders of contemporary Russia showed up, which was not surprising. He had been sharply critical of the retreat from democracy under Boris Yeltsin and especially under Vladimir Putin.

THERE are differing versions of the beginning of perestroika and glasnost. According to one, Yuri Andropov had been persuaded of the need for immediate economic reform. But Andropov had virtually ceased to function by that time, and the next initiative came only after Gorbachev had taken over—the first law in May 1985 was a decree about the ways and means of overcoming alcoholism.

Not much activity was witnessed during 1986, partly because of excessive caution, but also because the plans to carry out perestroika were not ready. But in the meantime, the economic situation had deteriorated, mainly as a result of the decline in the price of oil, and immediate change became imperative. At the same time, domestic political conflicts (such as the clashes between Armenia and Azerbaijan) aggravated the situation. Through a series of laws beginning in the summer of 1987, the leadership began to dismantle the Soviet economic system.

Even earlier on, many opponents of reform had been removed from the Politburo and other leading party organs. It soon appeared, however, that it was much easier to push through the glasnost reforms than economic and social perestroika. Glasnost simply meant to limit the freedom of action of censorship—to give permission to publish *Dr. Zhivago* and other works that had been censored or banned and to stop jamming the broadcasts of foreign radio stations in Russian.

The policy of glasnost also found its opponents, such as a college teacher named Nina Andreeva, who in a full page article entitled "I Cannot Give Up Basic Principles" in the daily *Sovetskaya Rossiya,* defended the old system. But on the whole, glasnost had overwhelming support—from the left and liberal forces because it gave them much greater freedom to broadcast their ideas, and from the right-wing-nationalist camp for the same reasons.

But it soon appeared that perestroika meant not only greater freedom to publish novels but also action—in the economy, in domestic political life, in foreign policy—an end to the Cold War. It was difficult to think of a single field not affected by perestroika: It included relations with the satellites—the Communist countries of Eastern Europe and the Balkans. Past experience had shown that the hold of the Communist governments was not secure, and it was doubtful that these regimes would survive without heavy support from Moscow (and if they did survive, there was always the danger that they would be untrustworthy). Was the old policy to be followed, meaning that in an emergency military intervention could be taken for granted? Gorbachev and other Soviet leaders felt disinclined. Last, there was the nationalist ferment inside the Soviet Union. Despite all efforts over many decades, nationalist passions in the non-Russian republics had not been stamped out; on the contrary, with the strengthening of great Russian nationalism since the 1930s, nationalism in the non-Russian republics had received fresh impetus. This had happened in the past, and it began to happen again in the late 1980s, first and most sharply between Azerbaijan and Armenia.

If Andropov had thought it might be possible to carry out far-reaching economic reform while leaving the political system and other issues untouched, such assumptions were never put to a test. Gorbachev seems to have shared some of these illusions, but it did not take long to realize that such optimism was not warranted. These years, between 1986 and 1990, were years of optimism despite the dismal economic situation, not because great changes for the better had already occurred, but because there was at long last the promise of improvement, indications that there was a willingness to take action.

It soon appeared that of all the problems confronting the new rulers, the economy was the most difficult and complicated. The transition to a planned economy in the 1920s had not been easy, but it had not been entirely unprecedented; many countries had been compelled to adopt measures in this direction during the war. But a retreat from a planned economy toward a market economy was unprecedented at that time. It happened in China and Vietnam, but only in later years. Moreover, the situation in these countries was not really comparable to that in Russia, since per capita income in China and Vietnam was much lower given that the majority of the population was employed in agriculture.

True, Gorbachev and most of his advisers were not thinking in such radical terms. But gradually they understood that half measures would not save the country. They had inherited a situation that was untenable in the long run. In addition, they faced a sudden deterioration affecting Soviet industry and, to an even greater extent, agriculture. The flight from the countryside continued and even increased. The export of Soviet oil had not yet gained the magnitude of its later years, but it was of critical economic importance. And it so happened that income from the export of oil fell by 30 percent in 1985–86. This had an immediate effect on the country's budget and the availability of foreign currency, which in turn caused painful domestic shortages with respect to the commodities of mass consumption and imports needed for the functioning of Soviet industry and agriculture. The Soviet foreign debt had grown to $56 billion (as a Soviet minister later ruefully admitted, "We were in debt to about every country in the world").

But hardly anyone was thinking of privatization; Gorbachev seems to have believed in models of worker cooperatives, ideas that had been entertained for a while in Yugoslavia after Josip Broz Tito had left the Soviet camp. Thus the years 1986–89 witnessed a great many conferences inside the leadership of the Communist Party that passed many resolutions; the political monopoly of the Communist Party had not yet been broken, but there was no action. A powerful anti-Gorbachev faction emerged, demanding the preservation of the status quo, which eventually led to an anti-Gorbachev coup in August 1991, an event that led within a few months to his downfall (he resigned from his post as president of the Soviet Union in late December 1991) and the rise of Yeltsin—but it also led to the collapse of the old Communist Party.

If the Gorbachev years did not bring great economic reforms despite the acknowledgment that these were urgently necessary, they did bring "new thinking" (the official term used at the time in the conduct of foreign policy).

Only three years earlier, Gorbachev had been generally considered the most popular Soviet leader. What had caused the quick downturn? The disastrous economic situation played a key role, but probably even more important was the impression that there was no strong hand in the Kremlin. The country was unraveling by the time of the August 1991 coup, but all involved—politicians, the army top brass, and even the head of the KGB—lacked the experience to bring about decisive political change. Yeltsin had been Gorbachev's rival for years, but it was precisely at the time of the coup that his finest hour came, when from the top of a tank he addressed the crowd in defense of democracy and the reform party.

If the Gorbachev years did not bring the decisive far-reaching economic reforms that many said were urgently necessary, there certainly was a great deal of "new thinking" on foreign policy. It did not happen immediately after Gorbachev's election; he needed two years for the preparations—to familiarize himself with the most important issues and to gain support in the Politburo. Andrei Gromyko, still considered the great foreign policy expert, had the support of the old-timers, and they were against it. It is doubtful whether they could even have imagined any other policy they would not consider heresy. Gorbachev understood that a new foreign minister had to come from the party or government work, as remote as possible from Gromyko and his Foreign Ministry. Hence his choice of Eduard Shevardnadze, an intelligent man but with no experience in the fields of foreign policy and diplomacy.

Gorbachev built up a new team that shared the consensus that an understanding with the West had to be based on a halt to rearmament. Such a policy was most likely to gain support among the party leadership, because even these leaders understood that the burden of the defense budget had become too heavy. Precise figures of the size of the defense budget in that period are not available to this day. At the time, it was believed that defense constituted 8–15 percent of the general budget, but it is certain that it was higher, possibly even much higher than the official figures.

Perhaps the most important issue on the road to reducing Cold War tensions was Afghanistan. Soviet armed forces had been in that country since December 1979 and the war had not been going well. Furthermore, it had aggravated relations with China, which demanded a withdrawal of Russian forces as a precondition to a normalization of relations between the two countries. However, Brezhnev and his immediate successors could not bring themselves to adopt decisive measures. They could have opted for a Soviet withdrawal of troops, but this would have been interpreted (and rightly so) as a Soviet defeat. Or they could have bolstered the Russian forces in Afghanistan, but this would have increased tensions.

So the Afghan war continued during the 1980s like a wound that did not heal. (In a speech at a party conference in early 1986, Gorbachev called the war a "bleeding wound.") It is not known when exactly Gorbachev made the decision to withdraw, but by 1987 it became clear that the Soviets would leave the country. The only opposition came from the army leadership, but since the performance of the army in Afghanistan had not been impressive, they were not in a strong position to press their case. Shevardnadze suggested the maintenance of a small Soviet contingent in the country for an indefinite period, but Gorbachev overruled him. Soviet withdrawal began on May 15, 1988, and the last Soviet soldiers left the country on February 15, 1989, ahead of schedule. So ended a tragedy of errors that cost the lives of many soldiers and even more civilians. If Brezhnev's original decision had been a costly mistake, the American expectation that a victory over the Islamists was possible had also been a profound mistake, as it emerged a number of years after.

Important as it was, the ending of the Afghan war was not sufficient to bring about a radical change in relations with the West—an end, or at least a reduction, of tensions in the Cold War. Gorbachev's first contact with Western leaders had been in France and the United Kingdom in 1985; he had made a positive impression on François Mitterrand and Margaret Thatcher. Both recommended to the White House that Gorbachev's "new thinking" aimed at an end to the Cold War should be taken seriously. But he had not yet talked to President Ronald Reagan, the senior partner, except briefly and inconclusively in Geneva, also in 1985.

Reagan was the sworn enemy of communism and the Soviet Union; he had talked about the "evil empire" in a famous speech to an Evangelical meeting in 1983. Under him, relations between Washington and Moscow had sunk to an unprecedented low—would it be possible to reach agreement with him?

Alexander Yakovlev and his team had outlined the basic ideas of the new thinking in foreign policy, but how were ideas to be translated into a policy? The first major step in that direction was the Reykjavík meeting in 1986. This took place a few months after the nuclear disaster at Chernobyl, which from the Soviet point of view was another unmitigated disaster. But it could well be that as horrible as the consequences were, they had a positive effect on Russian thinking and perhaps also on American foreign policy makers. For, as no other event had done, Chernobyl added greatly to the feeling of urgency that steps had to be taken toward nuclear disarmament.

The Reykjavík meeting dealt mainly with "technical issues," such as whether land-based intercontinental missiles should be given priority or a cessation of nuclear tests and other points in the SDI (the American Strategic Defense Initiative) and the Soviet plans for reducing nuclear arms. There was a great deal of haggling, and in the opinion of Andrei Grachev, one of Gromyko's chief advisers and spokesmen, the conference was a failure.

Seen in retrospect, however, the conference was probably a necessary step toward the far-reaching changes that took place in 1989. At least both sides gained the impression that serious progress seemed possible, that both sides were eager to reach agreement. Relations had been frozen for so many years, it was unlikely that a thaw would suddenly take place and all major problems solved in one fell swoop.

Reykjavík was followed by Reagan's visit to Moscow in May 1988, when he declared in a speech in Red Square that he no longer regarded the Soviet Union as an evil empire. The breakthrough in relations with the West came as the result of yet another summit in December 1989, this time with George H. W. Bush on the Soviet warship *Maxim Gorky* near Malta. This led to a whole series of meetings relating mainly to arms control. In a joint communiqué, Gorbachev and Bush announced that the two superpowers no longer considered themselves enemies.

Western leaders (especially the Americans) had taken a long time to accept that the changes in the Kremlin were genuine and constituted a profound historical turning point in world politics. This is understandable in retrospect. For decades, there had been too many disappointments and setbacks, and Western leaders were afraid of yet another betrayal. For this reason, while there was the desire not to miss a historical opportunity, there was the wish to see first whether Gorbachev would deliver on his promises before making far-reaching concessions.

But after decades of freeze, events went into a faster gear and Western leaders were a little slow to react. In a well-known speech in Berlin, Reagan asked Gorbachev to go further and to open the gates. The Warsaw Pact was dissolved, suddenly the gates were open and the wall disappeared, but Western reaction was slow. For in view of the disastrous and constantly deteriorating economic situation in the Soviet Union, there was the danger that Gorbachev's days as leader were numbered, and no one could be sure that his successor would be equally ready to continue his policy. Gorbachev needed help, such as loans to confront the immediate domestic emergency, but no such help was forthcoming. Gorbachev felt frustrated and even betrayed. He complained to his advisers that when it had been a matter of going to war following Saddam Hussein's invasion of Kuwait, the White House had not found it difficult to find the billions to do so, but when facing a political emergency, they were either not able or not willing to make an effort.

Gorbachev did not understand that loans and other forms of help had to be confirmed by Congress or that the president did not have the power and resources to authorize such help on his own. Nor is it certain whether the White House would have been able to save Gorbachev (he resigned in December 1991). For by that time, the crisis was no longer primarily economic or financial in character; the whole Soviet system seemed to unravel, and there were doubts in Washington whether America could or should intervene to stop this process.

The anti-Gorbachev coup in August 1991 had failed, but his position had been greatly weakened. If the regime had somehow survived, it was primarily because of Yeltsin, who in the decisive hours had gathered support. Nominally, the Soviet Union now had two leaders. Gorbachev was still president of the Soviet Union, but Yeltsin had been elected president of Russia with 57 percent of the vote. In addition, Yeltsin now became prime minister. It seemed only natural that Gorbachev should resign as president of the Soviet Union, for the Soviet Union had virtually ceased to exist. It was replaced by the Commonwealth of Independent States, which consisted of eleven of the former Soviet republics. The Baltic republics had decided to declare their independence the previous year, and others followed suit in August and September 1991.

In the meantime, prices rose all over the country despite constant promises by the government that this would not happen. (Prices were eventually liberalized in January 1992.) How to put an end to a chaotic situation? The output of the Soviet economy had fallen by 11 percent during 1991, the deficit in the country's budget had risen by about a quarter, and a financial reform (fifty- and one-hundred-ruble notes were replaced by vouchers) had not brought any relief. The mood in the country was in favor of a market economy and privatization, even though no one knew what these radical changes really would mean and what effect they would have in practice. Yeltsin had appointed a small group of economists to prepare for the transition to a market economy, and this economic system became law in June 1992.

Everything happened very quickly now. But had the crisis been inevitable? More than ten years after, in an interview with the *Financial Times*, Anatoly Chubais, one of the two main architects of privatization, said that it had been a race against time. The pressure had been enormous, Yeltsin happened to be ill, and had the radical requirements not been pushed through, the Communists would have won the elections of 1996. History would have taken a different course.

All this may be true, as it was certainly a volatile situation in Moscow. In October 1993, there was another attempt to overthrow the government, by that time headed by Yeltsin. A ten-hour gun battle took place over the possession of the Russian White House, the seat of the government, and many were killed and injured. Yeltsin acted decisively. Within hours, the leaders of the coup were arrested. The National Salvation Front, which had launched the coup, was banned along with the Communist Party. (The Communist Party had been declared illegal two years earlier, but the Supreme Court had found this action illegal and revoked it: A political party, it argued, should not be banned because of the actions of some of its members.)

The whole story of what happened during these days of "voucher privatization" has not yet been revealed. The original idea underlying privatization was to get the economy going again, to make it more productive. But it was also hoped to attract foreign investors; Russia was joining the World Bank and the International Monetary Fund during this period. It is not clear how the public reacted to these sweeping innovations. In April 1993, the government received a vote of confidence in a referendum, but it is doubtful that the majority of the population understood what was going on in the country. Ownership of 130,000 of the country's medium- and large-sized enterprises passed into the hands of a small number of people, and the age of the oligarchs dawned. An account by Yegor Gaidar, the other architect of privatization, about the general situation at the time is certainly similar to the story provided by Chubais.

Gaidar was in a position to know. He had been minister of the economy and finance and for a while acting prime minister of the Russian Federation, after Gorbachev. He knew that the government was weak and that weak governments could not take the strong measures needed. He knew all there was to know about the postsocialist crisis that (as he wrote) was the result of long-term problems. It was rooted in the socialist model of industrialization and the profound disorganization of state finances, as well as the sharp decline in fuel prices. Writing some ten years later, Gaidar recalled that he'd thought it would take between three and seven years after the collapse for a recovery to occur: "This was the transformation period: The most important task of government in postsocialist countries at the stage of recovery growth is to create the preconditions for a transition from recovery growth to investment growth, based on the growth of capital investments into the economy and the creation of new production capacities."

After Gorbachev

The years after Gorbachev's resignation saw a great deal of turbulence, frequent elections and changes of government, and the adoption of a new constitution. Yegor Gaidar was succeeded by Viktor Chernomyrdin. During this period, a not-so-minor war (in Chechnya) and above all the disintegration of the Soviet Union took place. If any stability was preserved, it was owing to the fact that Boris Yeltsin managed to get himself elected and reelected president of Russia and that he succeeded in limiting the powers of the Duma (as the parliament was now called).

Gorbachev originally brought Yeltsin into the Politburo as an ally, but the alliance did not last long; Yeltsin was not a team player. The issues at stake were not ideological. Yeltsin had learned early on to steer clear of ideology, he had learned that much from the history of his own family since his own father had been a victim of the purges. His reputation was that of a boss—but as his biographer, Tim Colton, put it—a boss with a difference.

Born in the Urals, he made his career in a village near Sverdlovsk, the unofficial capital of the Urals. He was a man of great contradictions—charming yet very quarrelsome, a heavy drinker, and a person of little education. We do not know whether he ever consulted a psychiatrist. If he did, he would probably have been diagnosed not just as a very impulsive person but manic-depressive. On at least one occasion, he tried to commit suicide (the so-called affair of the scissors), or at any rate to create the impression of having tried to commit suicide. He was very ambitious yet the only person ever known to have tried to resign from the Politburo (twice). In extreme situations, he showed great bravery; in others, he hesitated and even gave the impression of cowardice. He hated the Communist Party, even though he had made his career in it.

He was in favor of a multiparty, democratic system, but in his political style, as a leader, he was anything but a democrat.

In background and character, there could not have been a greater difference between Yeltsin and the two men he had chosen to carry out the economic reforms that were long overdue. Yegor Gaidar and Anatoly Chubais were intellectuals and came from well-known *nomenklatura* families. Gaidar's father had been an army colonel and for many years was the defense correspondent of *Pravda*. Gaidar had studied economics and headed a little group of fellow specialists who had realized early on that the Soviet economic system was a failure and that only a transition to a market economy would save the country. Chubais's father was also a senior officer and later a philosophy lecturer at an army academy; his mother was a Jewish intellectual, but this was a period in which it was preferable to hide such blemishes.

Gaidar's career in government was relatively short. Yeltsin may have agreed in principle with the shock therapy advocated (and carried out) by Gaidar, but the transformation was painful, and he was unhappy with the immediate results. Gaidar had hoped to bring about financial stabilization, but in this he failed. He died relatively young, as much as he was attacked during his lifetime, he was praised after his death. According to the majority view, the only alternative to his policy would have been a civil war.

Chubais, on the other hand, managed to hang on for many years in senior government positions, but he was highly unpopular. After he left the government, he held several senior positions heading state corporations and private enterprises; he proved to be very successful attracting foreign capital for modernizing the Russian electricity sector.

Gaidar frequently expressed his conviction that there had been no alternative to the shock policy pursued by him and Chubais. The opinion was not, however, shared by all economists—even those of the liberal persuasion. Economists from the liberal Yabloko (Apple) party, for instance, believed that a more gradual transformation (the five hundred days project) might have caused less pain and would have had the same effect in the end.

While perestroika was essentially about the economy, political issues were preoccupying the leadership and the country at large—the transformation of the political system from a monolithic to a multiparty system, the disintegration of the old Soviet Union, the dissolution of the Soviet empire (above all in Eastern Europe), and the First Chechen War.

As supervision and control of the country from the center weakened, unrest spread in the outlying republics, first on a minor scale in Kazakhstan (December 1986) following the deposition of the first party secretary, an ethnic Kazakh, and his replacement by a Russian. This was succeeded on a wider scale by clashes (August 1987) between Azerbaijanis and Armenians. Local clashes mainly in the Karabakh region quickly turned into a wider confrontation as thousands, later on tens of thousands, of refugees from the disputed regions began to arrive in Azerbaijan and Armenia. Moscow hesitated to intervene militarily, and the proposals submitted by a research delegation from Moscow aimed at the improvement of living conditions did little to reduce a bitter national conflict. The clashes, pogroms, and deportations eventually turned into a civil war.

The Azerbaijani-Armenian conflict is mentioned here because it showed how Moscow gradually lost control. Next came the unrest in the Baltic countries, which was much less violent in character. Following the loosening or abolition of censorship, most of the action took place in the media. This led to a mobilization of the population. In all three Baltic republics, mass meetings took place in which hundreds of thousands participated, and "national fronts" came into being, all demanding independence. There were a few halfhearted attempts to suppress the separatist movements, but overall separation proceeded peacefully. The Lithuanian Supreme Soviet declared the independence of the country in March 1990, the Estonian a few weeks later, and Latvia voted in August in favor of independence. The Soviet government recognized their independence the following year. In March 1991, a referendum was taken on preserving the old Soviet Union. It may be interesting to recall that in elections that took place in December 1991, 90 percent of the votes in the Ukrainian referendum went for independence.

Yeltsin had announced earlier on that when the non-Russian republics made use of their right to leave the union, Russia could do so too. What might have induced him to make this declaration? Perhaps he thought that some republics would prefer to stick with the Russians. If so, it was a miscalculation. He also tried in a series of meetings to maintain a tie with the former Soviet republics by means of a looser federation, but it was not clear how this aim could be achieved. A treaty was eventually signed by all of them, with the exception of the Republic of Tatar and Chechnya. A collective security treaty was signed in May 1992, but Tajikistan and Georgia stayed out. Russia and Belarus signed an agreement on monetary union in January 1994, and a treaty about the fixing of borders was signed between Russia, China, Kazakhstan, and Kyrgyzstan in April 1994. More important was an agreement between Russia and Ukraine in May 1997 about the status of the Russian Black Sea Fleet—this concerned access to the Black Sea Fleet through Ukrainian territory.

The other treaties were of lesser importance, since the newly independent republics did not yet have military forces of their own. And the economic situation was very much in flux—the exchange rate of the ruble collapsed in October 1994. In these circumstances, what was the meaning of the existence of the Commonwealth of Independent States? Would Russia be able to impose its authority in the territories that remained after the secession of the republics? This seemed by no means certain. Chechnya expressed no desire to be part of the new entity and tried to break away; in December 1994, Russian troops moved into Chechnya.

The war that followed lasted until September 1996 and went badly from the Russian point of view. One observer wrote that it broke the back of the Yeltsin government; another called Chechnya the tombstone of Russian power. Seen in retrospect these were exaggerations, but it is easy to understand why such impressions were gained at the time. If the Russian army was unable to subdue the forces of the small Caucasian republic, it had certainly ceased to be a major power. The problems Russia faced in the region were not limited to Chechnya: There was unrest in Dagestan and elsewhere as well. Russian forces were ill prepared to fight a guerrilla war; they had been instructed for a long time to ready themselves for a world war.

If the First Chechen War ended in a stalemate, it was clear that the state of affairs created could not last, for the situation had not been stabilized—and stabilization had been the aim of the Russian move into Chechnya in 1994. While 70 percent of Russians called the First Chechen War a tragic event, 70 percent approved of the second war. For this reason, the Second Chechen War in 1999 (following an invasion of Dagestan by an "international unit" of Islamic militants) did not come as a great surprise. This time Russia was better prepared militarily as well as politically. The operation was envisaged not as a war, but as an antiterrorist operation, which lasted on and off until 2009. More important, perhaps, the international climate had changed. Whereas the First Chechen War had been universally condemned, the various Islamist terrorist activities in the 1990s in other parts of the world (particularly after the 9/11 attacks in the United States) created a climate of greater understanding for the Russian actions in the Caucasus. Furthermore, Russia in the Second Chechen War had a clear political aim—to defeat the separatist Aslan Maskhadov government and replace it with a pro-Moscow regime headed by Akhmad Kadyrov. In this, Russia succeeded; whether it would be a lasting success remained uncertain. The Islamization of Chechnya has continued, as have the lawlessness, border violations, raids, and other forms of violence, but on a lower level of intensity. It was a cruel war distinguished by massive hostage taking and the abductions of thousands who were never seen again. Quite often, it was impossible to say which side was the worst offender, and assigning guilt was not always possible. If it was clear who had taken more than a thousand people hostage (including 777 schoolchildren) in Beslan in North Ossetia, it was less obvious who was responsible for the 1999 bombing of residential buildings in Moscow, Buynaksk, and Volgodonsk.

The situation in Chechnya stabilized, but this was not the case in neighboring Dagestan. Russia was not loved in the Northern Caucasus, but it was feared. Even its bitter enemies had understood that there was no chance of gaining independence in the foreseeable future. The Northern Caucasus remained a wound that would not heal, but neither was there a danger that it would spread.

The Chechen separatists were too weak to press their demands with any success unless there was a major increase in Muslim political power in other parts of Russia compelling the central government to make major concessions in the Caucasus. For the anti-Russian forces depended on massive help from Islamist movements and states, and such help on a major scale was unlikely to come anytime soon. As long as the center was strong, Russia had nothing to fear from Chechen separatism, but it was also clear that the regime it had imposed in Chechnya could not be trusted in a critical situation.

Four years after he had become president of the Russian Federation, Boris Yeltsin had to engage in yet another guerrilla war—against the Supreme Soviet, in which the position of his political rivals, mainly old Communists, was still fairly strong. He tried to fortify his position in various ways, including a new constitution. But his popularity waned mainly as the result of the painful economic reforms that had become necessary. The way the war in Chechnya went also did not add to his popularity. Nevertheless, he decided to present his candidacy for a second term in office in 1996, much against the advice of many of his advisers and supporters. According to the polls, support for him had fallen to 3 percent, but his fighting instincts told him that he still could win. The main opposition candidate, Gennady Zyuganov, was uninspiring, lacking Yeltsin's common touch and appeal. Yeltsin had considerable resources at his disposal. Many of those who had grown rich as the result of the privatization policy were supporting him, and even some professional American public relations advisers were employed. Furthermore, Yeltsin promised to withdraw some of the most unpopular measures that the governments appointed by him had adopted. Some concessions were made to elderly people and some to students. The International Monetary Fund gave Russia a loan of $10 billion, the second largest it had ever given. Yeltsin promised he would end the Chechen war. Gradually, he caught up with Zyuganov, who had been leading him for a long time; in the end, Yeltsin received 54 percent of the vote and Zyuganov 41 percent. It was a victory, but not a very convincing one.

How to explain that after all the misfortunes generated by communism, the political party continuing its tradition was doing so well? (Both

Gorbachev and Yeltsin had left long ago.) One must look first at the many mistakes committed by the reformers—and the fact that there was really no reform party. People who had saved soon realized that they had been robbed of almost 99 percent of their savings; they had been given vouchers instead. No one knew what these vouchers were really worth, certainly not more than 15 percent of what had been taken from them. The opponents of reform were concentrated in the parliament. Yeltsin was ruling by emergency decrees, but the parliament curtailed and virtually took away his powers to issue such decrees. A new constitution, which had been favored by Yeltsin, did not help to break the stalemate that lasted for years. The liberal Yabloko party, headed by Grigory Yavlinsky, offered sporadic and halfhearted support for Yeltsin and the governments appointed by him. In its view, the Gaidar reforms were by no means a shock therapy, but rather superficial and sometimes contradictory. It was probably right in its assessment. But could a shock therapy as Yabloko envisaged it have been pushed through by a democratic government?

Yeltsin was at his best playing a double game in Russian relations with foreign countries. His rhetoric often fluctuated between open hostility when he was talking to a domestic public (blaming the West for most of the misfortunes affecting Russia) and a friendly and constructive tone when conversing with Western leaders such as Bill Clinton and Helmut Kohl, both of whom greatly liked him. Such double-dealing helped the Kremlin get financial support from the West, but not enough to have a decisive impact at home that would strengthen or at least stabilize Yeltsin's position. In the elections of 1995 to the sixth Duma—elections took place virtually every year at the time—the Communists emerged as the single strongest party, yet another warning sign. How to build and maintain a democratic system if the majority were opposed to it? The reformers won 109 seats, the anti reformers—Communists and "patriotic forces"—more than double that figure. (The difference between Communists and "patriots" had dwindled by that time). True, the Communists were generally for the old system whereas the Zhirinovsky party—the Liberal Democratic Party—was neither liberal nor democratic and agreed with the Communist attitude toward current problems.

Yeltsin managed a political comeback in the elections for the presidency the year after. The fact that Alexander Lebed (a general and his chief security adviser) had reached a peace agreement with the Chechens had certainly helped his election campaign. And 1997, the year after the beginning of his second term, was the best or at least the easiest during that difficult and painful period. Then, quite suddenly in March 1998, Yeltsin dismissed not just Viktor Chernomyrdin, but the whole cabinet, including Anatoly Chubais. The reason most often adduced was the ambition of the outgoing prime minister, who saw himself as Yeltsin's successor and acted accordingly. If so, the timing of the dismissal was less than brilliant, for it coincided with yet another economic crisis.

World demand for oil and gas had declined, and so had Russia's income from this source. The Russian market lost 60 percent of its value, and Yeltsin had to tell the Duma that the situation was alarming. True, things improved toward the end of the year, and 1998 witnessed a rise of 5 percent in the GNP. On the other hand, Yeltsin suffered another health crisis just at the time when stability at the top was needed more than ever. He had four heart attacks while in office, and in 1996, a bypass operation was carried out by Michael DeBakey, the Houston pioneer in this field; Russian doctors were doubting whether he would survive such a major medical procedure. He also had to undergo several other operations during these years, some carried out by Russian surgeons, others by foreign specialists who were flown into Moscow in great secrecy. He did survive the bypass without major complications, but he did not survive the political troubles of the late nineties and the attacks against him.

But commodity prices are notoriously fickle, and the recovery of early 1998 did not last. In August, the *Financial Times* published a letter by George Soros in which he recommended the devaluation of the ruble, as the Russian economy had reached the terminal phase of its meltdown. The advice was followed, the exchange rate was left to float, and the ruble lost half its value. The Duma voted to dismiss Yeltsin, but such resolutions were constitutionally not binding. Nor did an attempt to impeach the president have any success. However, by that time even Yeltsin's most faithful supporters among the oligarchs were afraid that the president would look for a third term (the second term was limited to four years). Such fears were unfounded, however, for popular support for the president had disappeared.

The International Monetary Fund was willing to bail out Russia yet another time, but it was also reaching the end of its patience—and resources. In this situation, in mid-1998 Yeltsin probably decided that he would have to resign and that another prime minister would be needed; for this, he chose a forty-six-year-old KGB operative named Vladimir Vladimirovich Putin. Putin was not well-known, not connected to any political party. Boris Berezovsky, Yeltsin's closest confidant among the oligarchs, had recommended him. While Yeltsin had not known him very well, Putin had apparently gained the president's support as a person on whose loyalty he could count. Putin had supported Anatoly Sobchak, his former boss and mayor of St. Petersburg, even after he ran into deep trouble and had to flee the country. It could well be that such a show of loyalty outweighed all other considerations in Yeltsin's eyes.

Yeltsin was hanging on to his job up to the last day of the year (and the millennium) when, several months short of the end of his second term, he announced his resignation. He expressed regret that he had not been able to make many of his dreams (and those of the Russian people) come true, and he recommended Putin to be his successor, for the time being as acting president.

It was the end of an era. For most Russians this was a ghastly time, and not just in terms of material deprivations. The crime rate was rising, as were corruption and many of the other negative trends that had been part of life in the Soviet Union. But Stalin and his successors could at least boast that the country had turned into a superpower, and this too was no longer true. Had perestroika really been necessary, and if so, could it not have been carried out in a less painful way? Why was the transition in China less painful and, as far as the economy was concerned, more efficient? The brief answer is that Russia was not China, it was not a multinational state, and by and large the Chinese perestroika had been limited to the economy, with no intention to introduce a multi-party system.

One of the aims of the architects of perestroika was to make the economy more effective: In most respects, this had been a failure. Another aim was to create a middle class, which would generate growth. A few people had become immensely rich during perestroika, and there was still much poverty; but if a middle class had come into being, it was certainly very different from the one in America or Europe. That there was a social stratum between the very rich and the very poor was beyond doubt—the number of Russians opting for foreign travel was just one indication out of many. In the Soviet days, such trips had been the privilege of a very few, not just for security reasons but because most could not afford it. Now masses of Russian tourists along with Chinese could be found not only in France and Italy, but at more distant and exotic places.

Russia had certainly become richer, but incomes of the many millions below the small group of oligarchs were still very low. Professionals in the private sector were often earning twice as much as those with equal ability and standing in the state sector. Such a situation was bound to invite corruption.

If there was a new middle class, how could it be defined? Did it consist of families with at least one car, computers, possibly a dacha (even if primitive)? There were indeed millions of such people in Moscow and St. Petersburg. (Income and the cost of living in the former was about 10–20 percent higher than in the latter.) Did a substantial middle class exist outside the biggest cities? The capital acted as a magnet, but life in provincial towns, such as described in Aleshkovsky's novel *Stargorod* was very different. As far as the countryside was concerned, the flight from the small villages continued; thousands of them ceased to exist. More than in any other country, everything was concentrated in the capital. Foreigners were not fully aware of this because most of them were concentrated in Moscow. It was a new edition of a Chekhovian situation as described in *Three Sisters:* The women had grown up in Moscow. Moscow stood for happiness. There was no life outside Moscow.

The political repercussions of these social trends were interesting and often contradictory. The intelligentsia was divided, many supported liberal causes, and the anti-Putin demonstrators of 2011–13 came mainly from the ranks of the intelligentsia and other middle-class sections, not from the poor and underprivileged. "Middle class" could not be defined by income only; education and other factors played a role. But there was at least equal support for the patriotic-conservative-reactionary camp from these circles. It was an unprecedented situation, sui generis, very Russian.

2 | WHO RULES RUSSIA?

WHO RULES RUSSIA? IS IT THE *NOMENKLATURA*, A NEW CLASS, THE *siloviki*? The term "*nomenklatura*" with regard to Russia was first used in a book by the Soviet dissident Mikhail Voslensky in 1970; Milovan Djilas similarly referred to a "new class" in his bestselling work, *The New Class*, which appeared in 1957. The *nomenklatura* did not claim to have any political, economic, or social precision. No one would claim that all (or most) members of the *nomenklatura* had political power. This was the domain of the members of the Politburo and general secretary of the party and those close to him. Leaders of the party and other important figures belonged to the *nomenklatura*, of course. But essentially it was an inchoate group of people with certain privileges, important in a society such as the Soviet Union, but not very significant politically. There were certain status symbols such as housing, car and driver, access to certain services. And at the very top, the possession of a *vertushka* (a special telephone) was a sign of belonging.

There was no doubt that the composition of the elite and its structure changed over the years. For instance, the average age of political leadership was in the forties in the 1920s, in the fifties after World War

II, and in the seventies in Brezhnev's day. Membership in the political party was a precondition, of course. Leading army commanders and secret police figures were included but were kept out of political decision making, and the same was true with regard to those in command posts in economic and cultural life.

The composition of the decision-making elite underwent basic changes as the Communist Party lost its preeminent position. Under Boris Yeltsin, the very richest people moved to the fore; under Vladimir Putin, KGB and former KGB senior staff attained leading positions in the country's leadership. This was an unprecedented process. In some regimes in history, the rich and superrich had attained positions of great political strength, and in military dictatorships colonels and generals had moved to the top. But the political police had never been in command, not in fascism and certainly not under any other political regime. Nor has it happened in other ex-Communist countries in Europe and Asia.

The Oligarchs

The rise to power of the oligarchs—and their frequent misfortunes and fall from grace—is a fascinating topic that has been (and will be) gone over in many studies. How did they amass their fortunes in such short a time? Basically through the takeover of assets belonging to the state at nominal or very reduced prices. No single answer can resolve all the questions surrounding this issue. However, in the present context our concern is with the extent of political power that has been in the hands of those who grew very rich as the result of privatization in Russia.

It all began with the decision to privatize the economy. No one knew exactly how to do this, but several astute individuals realized that state property was being sold or almost given away. Some were officials high up in government, including ministers and their deputies—Vagit Alekperov is now listed as the eighth richest person in Russia; he had been acting minister of fuel and energy. Others had no official position but close contacts with those in charge.

Of the oligarchs who made their fortunes under Yeltsin, only a few kept their status under Putin. Their ambition to play a role of political importance was a fundamental mistake and caused their downfall. It is difficult to understand how people who had grown up in the Soviet system could commit such a basic mistake. Was it unbridled ambition or the belief that with the end of communism anything had become possible? The cases of Boris Berezovsky and Mikhail Khodorkovsky, while best known, were not atypical.

Berezovsky, a talented mathematician (head of a department in the Russian Academy of Sciences), made his money first in secondhand car dealing, later became involved in the Russian media, and later still invested in a major oil company as well as Aeroflot, once the Soviet state airline. Subsequently, he went into the oil and gas business (Sibneft, now Gazprom Neft). These years of golden opportunities were quite violent. There was at least one attempt on his life by business rivals, and on another occasion, one of his deputies was assassinated. There were reports that he too had planned to do away with some business competitors.

At about the same time, his political career took off. Together with a number of other oligarchs, he financed the Yeltsin electoral campaign of 1996 for a second term as president. Owing to his close contacts with Yeltsin's daughter Tatyana, he entered the small circle of the president's closest advisers. Soon after Yeltsin's election, he was appointed deputy head of the Russian Security Council. In this capacity, he was (among other things) in charge of relations with Chechnya, one of the main issues at the time.

Berezovsky's ambitions brought him into conflict with many other oligarchs as well as politicians (such as Anatoly Chubais, who was in charge of privatization at the time). If his touch in business was more often sure than mistaken, he failed to see the dangers facing him and his group on unfamiliar ground. During Yeltsin's last two years as president, Berezovsky's position seemed unassailable. No important appointment to a senior government position was made without his recommendation. He and Roman Abramovich, another up-and-coming oligarch about thirty years old at the time, were the first to recommend Putin as prime minister to succeed Yevgeny Primakov, who (Berezovsky argued) was incapable of coping with the economy. Putin was resting at the time at a villa in Spain belonging to Berezovsky, and some prodding was needed. Putin knew, of course, that all prime ministers in recent years had failed. Moreover, Putin had no economic experience. Could he succeed where all others had failed? In the end, ambition prevailed and Putin accepted the job offered.

The Yeltsin era approached its end. This had been a lawless age during which the oligarchs could achieve, more or less, whatever they wanted—economically as well as politically. They could manipulate the president and had no reason to be afraid of the law. But Berezovsky should have realized that such a state of near anarchy would not last forever, for the prevailing system was incapable of coping with the constant crises facing the country. It was a situation in which the state or another strong force (perhaps the army) would eventually assert itself as a stabilizing factor. By recommending Putin, Berezovsky opted for the secret services. He and the other oligarchs had money and some influence through the media they owned, but they had neither a political party at their disposal nor another force that could translate into real power.

However, Berezovsky and most other oligarchs were not aware of their weakness. Instead of taking a backseat, keeping discreetly in the background, and perhaps withdrawing from active participation in politics altogether, Berezovsky launched a campaign against Putin after it appeared that the two did not see eye to eye on various issues. The Berezovsky media claimed that Putin had not shown true leadership in the affair of the *Kursk*, the Russian submarine that had sunk with 118 sailors on board. Putin had refused foreign help, which might have saved the vessel, and Berezovsky used this as a pretext to attack Putin for pushing through early antidemocratic political reforms—specifically, that governors were to be appointed in future by the Kremlin rather than elected. These criticisms were true or partly true, but they were bound to make an enemy of an erstwhile ally. Putin retaliated by nationalizing most television channels, which had been in private hands following privatization. This was tantamount to depriving Berezovsky of the only effective political weapon at his disposal. In addition, corruption charges were brought by the legal authorities against Aeroflot, in which Berezovsky was heavily involved.

This was the beginning of the end of the tycoon's career. Berezovsky was to be interrogated by the authorities but did not appear at the Moscow hearing. Traveling abroad, he refused to return to Russia, which as he argued in a letter to *The New York Times* was turning into a banana republic. The break between the two men who had once been skiing partners in Switzerland was now complete. The charges against Berezovsky were probably mostly correct. It is unlikely that any great fortune could have been amassed at the time without breaking the law. At the same time, the charges were clearly politically motivated. They could have been brought with equal justice against all those who had become rich during the Yeltsin era and, of course, also against the politicians and state officials who had accepted massive bribes. Whether it was an issue of not paying taxes or *raiderstvo* (taking over other companies by all means fair and foul), even involvement with the mafia—had any Yeltsin oligarch been entirely free of these practices? Berezovsky had failed to understand that under Putin, the balance of power was changing. It was not exactly a restoration of the rule of law, but it certainly qualified as a new interpretation by a new ruler.

Berezovsky was compelled to sell his stake in the Sibneft oil company—not to the state, but to Roman Abramovich, another oligarch and former ally who, politically far more astute, had joined the Putin bandwagon, collaborating closely with the new masters. Abramovich had also been involved in politics in the Yeltsin era. He had been a member of the Duma and a governor (of the poor Chukchen region in the far north). But under Putin he wisely shifted his activities from politics to soccer, a game in which he had a genuine interest. He supported a leading Moscow club and thus became known as a man far more interested in soccer than in politics. A fighter by nature, he was not reckless and knew that it did not pay to be petty in one's transactions. When he divorced his first wife, the settlement amounted to $300 million. This was a lot of money, to be sure, but no more than he had paid for one of his yachts. In this way, he kept out of trouble and on good terms with his master.

Some British lawyers benefited greatly from Berezovsky's exile in London as well as the presence of Abramovich. Both men were involved in many legal battles concerning the ownership of companies and several libel cases. Berezovsky was sentenced in absentia in Moscow as a member of a criminal gang, but he was winning the libel actions in the British capital. He bitterly attacked Putin and financed various anti-Putin activities. But it was a losing battle. It should have been clear to him that he could not prevail in a campaign against the head of a major power. There were allegations of assassination attempts by the Kremlin, but Berezovsky escaped them. Unfortunately, Alexander Litvinenko, a close associate (and a former KGB operative), was not as lucky: He was poisoned in London in 2006.

The *Siloviki*

These conflicts took their toll. Berezovsky became dispirited, lost a large part of his property, and committed suicide in March 2013. Prior to taking his life, he sent a letter to Putin (by way of his old colleague and current enemy Abramovich) asking for forgiveness for various "bad deeds" he had committed. This ending was symbolic of a historical trend that was taking place: the defeat by the *siloviki* of the oligarchs who had meddled in politics or, to be precise, in activities directed against Putin and his associates. The *siloviki* were willing to accept that the oligarchs were making large sums of money, spending lavishly, even taking much of their money out of the country. The *siloviki* were probably doing the same. But they were not willing to accept the political activities of the oligarchs unless they were undertaken on behalf of the *siloviki*, following their initiative and under their control.

The story of Mikhail Khodorkovsky need not be related in detail, since it was widely reported all over the globe following his arrest and long stay in a gulag. Born in Moscow and active in the Komsomol, the Communist youth organization, he followed in the footsteps of his parents, who were chemical engineers. He also worked for a while as a carpenter. None of the early tycoons had the benefit of a business or management education, a subject that did not exist in the Soviet Union; the first such schools did not come into being until the mid-1990s. A few studied international law and politics, but only a very few had ever been abroad. Many acquired their experience the hard way. Some of the older ones among them received their apprenticeship in the underground, illegal or semilegal "gray" economy. Most of them started at the very bottom. Mikhail Fridman, for instance, had been washing windows at the beginning of his business career. Roman Abramovich was a street trader, Vladimir Lisin, at one time the richest man in Russia, worked as a mechanic in a mine, Vagit Alekperov was employed on an oil platform in the Caspian Sea—a dangerous job if there was one. While still in his twenties, Khodorkovsky engaged in importing computers, jeans, and cognac, which brought him a small fortune. He established an early cooperative bank (Menatep), which went bankrupt. In between for a short period, he served as deputy minister of fuel and energy, which provided some useful contacts.

Khodorkovsky realized that he would need foreign capital to establish a truly major company. With the help of American investors, he acquired Yukos, at that time the biggest oil company in the country, valued at about $15 billion. The business practices used during those years, whether they involved declaring bankruptcy, attracting new investors, not paying taxes, or acquiring companies, were not only unethical but considered criminal by many. But they worked, and by the time he was arrested in 2003, Khodorkovsky had become the richest man in Russia, mainly as a result of the growth of the oil industry and its enormous profits.

Like Berezovsky, Khodorkovsky had committed the fatal mistake of getting involved far too deeply in politics, criticizing the government, and supporting the opposition. He became a major nuisance to those in power. Instead of acquiring soccer clubs or modern art or young mistresses, he argued openly with Putin on television, claiming that highly placed Kremlin officials had received many millions of dollars in bribes. In a first trial in 2003, he was accused of fraud and tax evasion; in a second trial in 2009, of money laundering and embezzlement. He spent eight years in a prison camp before he was given a pardon in 2013. Unlike Berezovsky, however, he was not broken but continued his critique of government policy while in prison and even managed to establish himself as a leading champion of democratic freedom and human rights. Given his record, this was no mean feat.

Few of the oligarchs of the Yeltsin era survived unharmed. Alexander Konanykhin, less known in the West, was only twenty years old when he established his first cooperative in building, employing six hundred workers. Soon after, he became one of the first brokers at the newly established stock exchange. It is not clear why he fell afoul of the authorities, perhaps because of his collaboration with Berezovsky. He fled to the United States, asking for political asylum because he claimed he faced assassination if he returned to his native country. His fortunes in America were mixed. In a court case he was awarded the highest sum ($33.5 million) ever given to an individual in a libel case, and in New York he was named Businessman of the Year (2004). But he also spent fifteen months in American prisons. His biography is titled *Defiance: How to Succeed in Business Despite Being Hounded by the FBI, the KGB, the INS, the Department of Homeland Security, the Department of Justice, Interpol, and Mafia Hit Men.*

Vladimir Potanin is an oligarch who survived unharmed. He served at one time under Yeltsin as deputy prime minister and also held other senior government positions. He is the head of a leading holding company, Interros, and his property is estimated at $12 billion to $13 billion. He kept out of politics after the Yeltsin period but served as head of countless nonpolitical government positions as well as contributing to museums inside and outside Russia and serving on their boards.

Vladimir Gusinsky, on the other hand, faced trouble early on in his career. His parents had lived in Moscow in a *kommunalka*, a single room that shares all facilities with several other families. He studied petroleum technology but was employed later as a theater manager outside Moscow. He made his considerable fortune as the owner of a bank and then started to buy up newspapers and television stations as well as companies engaged in movie production. His outlets criticized the government because of the war in Chechnya and other issues. He was arrested for the first time in 2000 but fled Russia, was subsequently stripped of his Russian citizenship, and acquired Spanish and Israeli nationalities. The Russian authorities tried to have him arrested and extradited through Interpol, but the European Court of Human Rights found that the Russian government's charges against him were illegal—in breach of the conventions for the protection of human rights. Gusinsky eventually left Israel and continued his business career in the United States.

Among the very few Yeltsin-era oligarchs to survive with life and property intact was Mikhail Fridman. His father had been a leading figure (and inventor) in the field of military technology. Born in Lvov, the younger Fridman studied steel production and metallurgy and began his business career while in his mid-twenties. Together with Swiss partners, he founded a company that later became the Alfa Group, with interests in banking and other fields. His property, estimated at $20 billion in 2008, fell temporarily to $6 billion the year after as the result of the world crisis, then increased again to $16 billion in 2013, which made him the second-richest Russian citizen.

Fridman was a notable contributor to Jewish cultural causes (the Genesis Philanthropy Group) as were, to a lesser degree, Gusinsky (who supported an Israeli basketball team for a number of years), German Khan, and Pyotr Aven.

Among the oligarchs of the Yeltsin era, more than a few were of Jewish descent, but there were also Muslims, including Alisher Usmanov, the very richest. But except those mentioned, the oligarchs were not active in Jewish life; on the contrary, they distanced themselves from the Jewish community or even, like Berezovsky, were reported to have converted to the Orthodox Church. Many were only partly Jewish with either father or mother being Russian Orthodox. In their propaganda, anti-Semites tried to make heavy use of these facts but, to their surprise, with relatively little effect. They had long maintained that Jews were ruling Russia, and repeating the old allegations was therefore bound to have only a limited effect, especially at a time when most of the oligarchs were losing much of their influence and money and some had disappeared from view altogether.

The list (Forbes 2013) of the richest oligarchs of the Putin era reads quite differently from the Yeltsin list

Alisher Usmanov	18 billion dollars
Mikhail Fridman	16
Leonid Mikhelson	15

Viktor Vekselberg	15
Vagit Alekperov	14
Andrei Melnichenko	14
Vladimir Potanin	14
Vladimir Lisin	14
Gennady Timchenko	14
Mikhail Prokhorov	13
Alexei Mordashov	12
German Khan	10
Roman Abramovich	10
Dmitry Rybolovlev	9
Iskander Makhmudov	8
Oleg Deripaska	8

The names in this list have been more or less the same for a decade, but the ranking tends to change from year to year and the figures given are rough estimates. At one time Lisin was heading the list; at another stage, Deripaska. As the result of the political crisis of 2014/5 the oligarchs are reported to have lost, so far at least, one quarter of their property.

It is difficult to establish where these billions are located. Of the above list, half, possibly more, are residents of other countries. For instance Usmanov, Abramovich, German Khan, and others reside in the UK, and Melnichenko lives in New York, Antibes, and Ascot. Much of the money has been taken out of Russia especially to northern (Turkish) Cyprus (which has no extradition treaty) and subsequently to London. The personal income tax rate in Russia has been very low since Stalin's days (13 percent), but conditions in the UK are considered even more favorable. While the attitude of the Russian authorities toward big business has been favorable, there seems to be a lack of trust—the fear that the funds in Russia could be seized, the owners arrested or killed.

Mention has been made of the lesson learned by the oligarchs with regard to getting mixed up in politics. Perhaps that lesson has been learned too well. When *Kommersant*, a newspaper belonging to a group headed by Usmanov published an article critical of the Putin regime and threw doubts about the honesty of election results, Usmanov immediately dismissed those who had permitted such criticism of the government. At the same time, he stressed the independent character of the newspaper. Usmanov's heroes since childhood have been the Three Musketeers, and he has been a patron of fencing as a competitive sport in Russia. But he understood only too well that even Athos, Porthos, and Aramis, had they lived in twenty-first-century Russia, would have known where to draw the line—and who could blame him? Usmanov no doubt also remembered his years in prison in his native Uzbekistan in the 1980s.

When the authorities wanted to establish another political party to prove the democratic character of the regime, they apparently had to invest considerable energy persuading one of the oligarchs, Prokhorov, to support such an endeavor. Who could blame him since such a project could easily get out of control with sham opposition turning into real opposition. Prokhorov left the party he had founded after a few months.

The older oligarchs were born in the 1950s, the younger ones in the following decade; most were in their late twenties or early thirties at the time of privatization. A few, such as Vladimir Potanin and Mikhail Fridman, came from families that had just made it into the lower ranks of the *nomenklatura*, but most of the others came from poor or relatively poor families. Some had already made a name for themselves in the academic world; most had studied scientific or technological subjects. About a third of the oligarchs made their fortunes in banking or holding companies, more than a third in metals and oil and gas. Not surprisingly, among the very richest were those active in the oil and gas industries. A few of the oligarchs acquired their money relatively peacefully and managed to keep out of the limelight, but most had to fight in protracted struggles replete with extortion, threats, and even murder. In the aluminum war alone about a hundred people were reported to have been killed. Roman Abramovich and Deripaska, whose close relationship with Putin has been noted, emerged victorious in this war. On this occasion, like others, the line between genuine business and the activities of the criminal underworld was difficult to draw. It is doubtful that the full story of these violent years will ever be written. If so, they could make the period of the American robber barons appear like petty quarrels in a kindergarten.

Did they enjoy their newly acquired wealth? Very few cases of retirement are known; the attraction and excitement of the world of business seem to have been overwhelming. Many established a second residence in London (which often became their first residence), some in America and Switzerland, but they continued to deal with their businesses from afar. Some acquired second and third passports—for instance, Timchenko, Putin's main financial adviser at one time became a Finnish citizen. This did not always help; Deripaska, for instance, was refused entry to the United States because of something that had happened in his past—well before the U.S. government imposed sanctions in 2014. Vitaly Malkin, another oligarch, was not permitted to enter Canada even though he traveled with an Israeli passport; there were accusations of money laundering as well as international arms trafficking. He had also tried to persuade American senators that Magnitsky, the Moscow lawyer who died in suspicious circumstances while in prison, was really a criminal.

They became major buyers of art, both modern and classical, whereas elsewhere, as in the United States, only the second generation of nouveau riche had shown such interests. The wife of one of the oligarchs owns a well-known art gallery in Moscow. Those who benefited most from this interest in art were contemporary British painters—such as Francis Bacon and Lucian Freud. Christie's in November 2013 sold a Bacon triptych showing his friend Lucian Freud for $142.4 million, a record price for a picture sold at auction. A few years earlier Abramovich had to pay Sotheby's $88 million for another triptych by the same painter. Usmanov, not interested in half measures, bought the whole collection of Mstislav Rostropovich the night before it went to auction. Over the years, Viktor Vekselberg has acquired the largest Fabergé egg collection. The eggs have become very desirable, and he opened a special museum to display his collection (the collection of Alexander Ivanov in the Fabergé Museum in Baden-Baden is also very impressive).

Russian art became both desirable and highly priced—Christie's had to pay Vekselberg $2.5 million in damages for Kustodiev's *Odalisque* after it appeared that it was of doubtful origin. The greatest private collection of Russian art is in the hands of Pyotr Aven, whose "second residence" is in a village outside London—he paid about $5 million for Konchalovsky's family portrait (1917). Konchalovsky was a fine painter, but he painted a lot, and until recently his pictures did not fetch high prices; thirty years earlier Aven could probably have bought the same picture for $20,000 or less. But thirty years earlier Aven was not yet an oligarch. The Melnichenkos are the proud owners of two of Monet's water lily pictures. This list could be made considerably longer.

Oligarchs have engaged in ostentatious spending, a matter that became the subject of many jokes, but also of scandals and bitter criticism. It certainly helped to make them unpopular as a group. True, all were eager to engage in philanthropic causes, but what they spent on them was a fraction of the enormous sums lavished on luxuries.

The authorities did not at first intervene, but a number of circumstances eventually compelled them to take action against some excesses. For one thing, most oligarchs' luxury spending on foreign residences, art, and yachts did not benefit the Russian economy. For another, the economic crisis of 2008 compelled many of them to retrench: Some saw themselves facing huge debts, with the result that employees of the companies owned by the oligarchs suffered even more. This led to social unrest and violence, which did worry the authorities. For this reason, the oligarchs were advised in no uncertain terms to maintain a low profile. After 2008, most took great pains not to be seen or heard except when spending money on good causes.

Government officials had also become rich—some of them immensely rich—but they had done so discreetly, such that no one knew exactly how great their fortunes were and where their money or investments had been deposited. According to Stanislav Belkovsky, a leading Russian investigative journalist, Putin, with $70 billion, could be one of the richest people on earth. (But such assertions can, of course, not be verified, at least not as long as Putin is in government.) Other journalists estimate that the wristwatches Putin has been wearing on some television appearances, Patek Philippe and others, are worth about $160 million. As the economic situation deteriorated in 2014, it became quite fashionable to attack the oligarchs and the system ("usury") that had made it possible for them to amass their riches. But the politicians leading this campaign had also benefited from the system, had grown rich, had no wish to change it and to give away their possessions. Spokesmen for the church also participated in the campaign, but the patriarch appeared on television wearing a wristwatch about as expensive as Putin's. These glaring contradictions between official propaganda and the actual state of affairs (the great and growing distance between the life of the rich and the rest) is a major weakness of the regime. It is bound to persist and to cause political tensions.

More billionaires reside now in Moscow than in any other city in the world. All over the globe, income inequality measured by the Gini coefficient (named after an Italian economist) and some other yardsticks has been substantially growing during the last three decades. In this respect the United States ranges at the very bottom of the developed countries. But if it is also true that the 110 richest Russians own about 35 percent of the country's GNP (as established by the Credit Suisse research department), and if, on the other hand, 93 percent of Russian citizens own less than $10,000, then the creation of a strong middle class has not been achieved as the result of privatization. The number of Chinese billionaires is somewhat greater than Russian, but not by very much. Moreover, the Chinese GNP is four times as large (eight trillion dollars) as the Russian, which at present is about equal to that of France and smaller than the Brazilian GNP.

Such a development is undesirable from both a political and an economic point of view. Is it possible to change and reverse this state of affairs? No doubt there are various ways to do so—for instance, by an income tax reform. But this might hurt the business interests of the political leadership and lead to an increase in the flight of capital from Russia. At any rate, the issue has not been high on the list of priorities of the Russian leaders, whose main concern has been to prevent wealth from becoming a major political weapon. In this, they have largely succeeded. But if inequality goes beyond a certain limit, it is bound to cause major social tensions, and the political leadership will be compelled to act. In the struggle between the *siloviki* and the oligarchs, the former prevailed totally and with no great effort. The oligarchs did not constitute a united front; more often than not they were competing with one another. Alliances between them were short-lived, and they usually lacked political instinct and understanding. They had political ambitions but no power base, such as a political party or close ties with the army and the security organs.

The *siloviki*, on the other hand, had an old school tie in common—their work in the KGB, at home or abroad. As Nikolai Patrushev said in a speech in September 2002, he had followed Putin as head of the FSB (the successor organization of the KGB), and the secret service had become the new nobility. They did their work not for money, but from a sense of duty—that is to say, patriotism and idealism.

The proportion of erstwhile KGB agents in Putin's inner circle has been estimated at about one-third, in the upper ranks probably higher. These are estimates, of course, because membership in "the organs" was until recently not considered a theme for public discussion. However, they had met socially as well as at work and had been indoctrinated that they were the very elite, the sword and shield of the system. The Chekists were the only honest, reliable, patriotic force, the only one that could be trusted implicitly.

They too suffered from certain handicaps. The KGB (formerly the Cheka and NKVD) had not always fared well in the past—in the purges of the 1930s they had been decimated. Two heads of the organs had even been shot. But it was solemnly declared (and often believed) that the bad old days were over and would never recur, that to serve in the organs was a great honor, a vital and patriotic duty—without the Chekists the fatherland would be in mortal danger, for it faced bitter enemies at home and abroad, scheming day and night how to hurt Russia and if possible to destroy it.

This kind of indoctrination was often effective. As a result of so many years of Stalinist rule, a mind-set of persecution had become deeply rooted in the country. Perhaps not all of it was believed, but enough to attract people to the organs both at the very top and further down in the hierarchy. The heads of the organs were mostly bureaucrats of average intelligence without much experience to deal with the world outside the Soviet Union. Yuri Andropov may have been the only exception, but he was ill when appointed and had no time to prove himself. The average operative often lacked a solid education; he was trained in a KGB academy or special courses to become reasonably competent in the language of the country to which he would be assigned. But this was often not sufficient to acquire the manners, customs, and social graces needed to move freely and inconspicuously in conditions so different from those he knew at home. Any successes experienced by the KGB were usually the result of good fortune. The reputation of the KGB was not too good in the 1970s and 1980s, and they were unable to prevent the downfall of the Soviet Union, which had allegedly been the work of its enemies abroad. For years, the KGB and its successors had invested major efforts improving and embellishing their image through novels, movies, and in other ways. The most successful by far was the Stirlitz TV series *Semnadtsat mgnovenii vesny* (*Seventeen Moments of Spring*, by Julian Semyonov, which described the life and actions of a Soviet agent who had infiltrated the Nazi security services at the very top and was therefore in a position to report even the most secret designs of the Nazis to his masters in Moscow.

This series was well produced and acted and became tremendously popular. It is regularly shown on Russian TV to this day. It became a favorite game of young boys all over the Soviet Union, who played Stirlitz. Stirlitz also made an appearance in other novels by the same writer. Semyonov, an alcoholic, died young of a stroke. He was a cynic who managed from time to time to smuggle in some doubts and even criticism of the regime in his novels. He knew that nothing even remotely like the Stirlitz saga had ever happened: It was pure fiction, exciting to watch but wholly unreal. There were other such attempts to embellish the record like the movie "A shot in the fog" but they were not nearly as successful.

Stirlitz had been the hero of anti fascism, in a "progressive, internationalist age." In the post-Soviet period another kind of hero emerged—not invented but real. The case of Nikolai Sergeyevich Leonov seems not to have been atypical. He had been high up in the KGB hierarchy, deputy head of the First Chief Directorate. He had the rank of a Lieutenant General and was head of the analytic department of the KGB. According to his biographer, over twelve years, he was never mistaken in his prognoses and analytic reports, truly a remarkable achievement. His anti-American activities were, as the biographer puts it, motivated by deep conviction and blessed by God. To give but two examples of how his predictions showed his deep understanding of world affairs: he classified South Yemen as the "most Marxist country" in the Middle East (since Leonov was not a Marxist, it is not clear whether this was a good thing or not) and announced that in Poland the prospects of communism were not very good. Such insights seem to have impressed his superiors as well as those who worked for him, among them Putin.

In 1991, he resigned from the organs in protest against the traitorous activities of its leaders. He became a member of the Duma, belonging to a Far Right party. In the following years, he was very active on behalf of these circles, mainly as a television personality. He also taught history at Moscow University. He became a practicing member of the Orthodox Church, sharing Archimandrite Tikhon as father confessor with Putin. In an interview, Tikhon called Leonov a man of exceptional honesty: "Meeting him several years ago was a real revelation for me."

Leonov had become a religious believer, but his new religiosity did not extend to the Jewish religion. He signed a letter to Russia's chief prosecutor in which he asked that steps be taken against the Jews in the light of the publication of *Kitzur Shulkhan Arukh*, a sixteenth-century book of Jewish law first published in Venice. The fact that leading Russian politicians such as Gorbachev and Yeltsin appeared traitors in the eyes of a man of such views can easily be understood. On the other hand, he too was a defector and traitor for having joined the Communist Party and the "sword and shield" of the Communist system, he must have accepted a certain ideology. Those he had initially joined could also regard his subsequent turn to "bourgeois nationalism and reactionary clericalism" as a betrayal.

Putin did not, of course, surround himself only with former KGB agents. According to both Russian and Western estimates, only about 30 to 40 percent of those in top positions were current or former KGB agents. In Putin's inner circle were others who had worked with him during his St. Petersburg years and elsewhere and on whom, he felt, he could rely. There were the Rotenberg brothers, for instance, who had been his sparring partners in karate, judo, and other martial arts. Almost all aspects of Putin's life and activities have been analyzed in great detail, but it may be little known that he has gained an eighth-degree black belt in karate and is passionately involved in martial arts; the impact of the techniques and rules of such sports on Putin's policy making have been neglected so far. Those who had achieved black-belt level also constituted a kind of brotherhood. Some oligarchs among those in the inner circle dealt with Putin's private affairs, while others became close advisers.

Some observers of the Moscow scene believe in the existence of an unofficial Politburo and claim that it resembles the Brezhnev Politburo during the *zastoi* (stagnation) period. The comparison with the Brezhnev era seems far-fetched, but the existence of a group of close advisers appears beyond doubt, even if unstructured and subject to frequent changes. According to A. S. Chelnokov (*Putinski Zastoi: Novoe Politburo Kremla*), it consisted in 2013 of the following:

Sergei Ivanov, a former KGB general, in charge of general administration. Putin knew him from his St. Petersburg days, when both worked for Anatoly Sobchak, the mayor.

Igor Sechin, formerly deputy prime minister, at present head of Rosneft.

Sergey Chemezov, of whom little is known except among the insiders. He is the head of a corporation named Gostechnologia, and his experience has been in the industrial field.

Gennady Timchenko, who is the money administrator (or consultant) of the group. Over the last twenty years, he has spent more time abroad than in Russia.

Yury Kovalchuk, co-owner of Rossiya, a Russian bank. He has a doctorate in physics, but his more recent experience has been in the fields of media and banking.

Sergey Sobyanin, the mayor of Moscow who succeeded Yuri Luzhkov (who after many years in his job was removed because he became too involved in conflicts of interest with Putin and the administration). He is also the head of a group of governors and other high officials representing the Urals and Siberia.

Vyacheslav Volodin, who hails from Saratov and has been subject to various accusations during his political career but always managed successfully to extract himself.

Dmitry Medvedev, a faithful stand-in for Putin. Whenever Putin served as prime minister, Medvedev was president, and vice versa. It is unknown how much real power he wields.

Next, the Politburo "candidates"—not yet full members, but very likely to be promoted. Leading the list are the following:

Sergey Shoygu, at present minister of defense. Originally from Tuva, the small Asian autochthonous republic that became part of the Soviet Union, he hails from a local *nomenklatura* family; his father was deputy prime minister. He is an excellent communicator, according to the polls the most popular Russian politician next to Putin.

Igor Shuvalov, who has served in a variety of senior government positions and been one of Putin's economic advisers.

Alexei Kudrin, a former finance minister, who has known Putin from the time both were serving in St. Petersburg.

Arkady Rotenberg, Putin's martial arts partner. He has a karate black belt and with a little help made his fortune in the oil and gas industry.

Alisher Usmanov, whose background is in metallurgy, especially the steel industry.

Roman Abramovich, who needs no further introduction.

This "Politburo," if indeed it exists, is a wholly unofficial body. Its members have never boasted of "belonging"; on the contrary, with the exception of Abramovich, they have tried to keep out of the limelight as much as possible. Some were promoted and others demoted, as is inevitable in such inner circles. But those who had belonged to the group were well taken care of and seldom dropped altogether.

It is fascinating to follow the process of the rehabilitation of the Cheka and the KGB. Glasnost, as the defenders of Russia saw it, had caused the demonization of those who had served as "the sword and the shield" of communism and the Soviet system. They were made responsible for the purges—the millions who had been sent to the gulag, the hundreds of thousands who had been murdered. But this was unjust because some twenty thousand Chekists had also been among the victims. This is historically true; the purges and the mass murder of the 1930s were Stalin's idea, not initiated by the NKVD. But the killing was still carried out by the organs, and Stalin too has by now been partly rehabilitated. As Putin has put it on various occasions, Stalin was a controversial figure. Some of Putin's underlings have cast Stalin in an even more positive light.

However, this demonization did not last long. The rehabilitation began under Yeltsin with a 1997 speech in which a "day of the Chekist" was announced, to be celebrated each year on December 20. Awards were to be given to books and movies restoring the good name of the Cheka/NKVD/KGB. Under Putin, these sporadic measures became a cult of state security. Those serving were called "the new nobility"; incorruptible, they were motivated not by material gain, but by idealism.

Some of those engaged in rehabilitation went even further and made those in the organs appear as modern-day saints. The Orthodox Church took a leading part in this campaign by sponsoring "spiritual defense" as one of its main endeavors. A new head of the KGB/FSB was given one of the highest orders of the Orthodox Church named after Dmitry Donskoy, who being a national hero had also more recently been made a saint. Whereas Dmitry was a historical figure who fought the Mongols and Tatars, the victor in the famous Battle of Kulikovo, Ilya Muromets, who has become something like a patron saint of the Russian organs, belongs to the realm of legends and folk culture. He is a great hero (*bogatyr*) involved in countless battles and he too has become a saint.

This collaboration between church and state in police work and espionage based on an elaborate ideological justification went much further than in czarist days. At that time the Okhrana was considered a necessary, even vital, part of the protection of the regime, but it did its work in the shade. There was no glorification of its agents. It was thought self evident: No justification was deemed necessary, and no publicity was sought.

Questions concerning the identity of those ruling Russia are bound to remain open for the time being. Putinism is an authoritarian regime, representing the interests of several groups in Russian society. The often-invoked "vertical power" structure simply means that orders are passed on from top to bottom, an obvious statement if there ever was one.

The identity of the supreme leader may be accidental. If Putin had not been appointed by Yeltsin, there would have been someone with a roughly similar background. His powers are not unlimited. There is again the cult of the leader and an obvious retreat from glasnost and democratic aims. "Sovereign democracy" is a synonym for such a retreat—not total, but substantial and significant. It means that the country is not ready for a Western-style democracy, perhaps never will be. In any case, it is not a political system wanted by most Russians, since it is not in the Russian tradition and in consonance with Russian values.

A little more than a century ago, Robert Michels, a German student of politics and sociology, published his thoughts about the "iron law of oligarchy." His ideas were interesting, but his political instincts (like those of some of his contemporaries who expressed similar views—Pareto and Mosca) were less than astute; all three sympathized with Mussolini. Michels, who had been initially a supporter of socialism, was concerned that even in democratic institutions (particularly in such institutions—trade unions for instance) an elite/oligarchy would eventually emerge and take charge.

Michels was referring not to billionaires, but to political leadership. Since then, various theories about the origin and function of elites have seen light, but none is applicable to Russia—the former Soviet Union. This is because the Russian situation is unprecedented and sui generis. Given Russia's history and traditions, it is unlikely that in the post-Yeltsin era a strong democratic movement would have emerged even if Putin had not been the choice of leader. But accident always plays a role, and Russia is not the only country to emerge from communism. Some have moved toward democracy; others (after promising beginnings) have moved away from it. It is banal to note that the situation in all these countries is very much in flux. But it is the only statement that can be made with any degree of conviction.

Much effort has been invested in attempts to define Putinism, and for good reasons. For if the leader who gave the system its name should resign or be forced to retire, it is likely that the new form of government will survive him, because it seems to conform with Russia's present needs and desires. It is a dictatorship approved by the majority, as long as the going is good. If this support should shrink, harsher methods of rule are likely to be introduced. In its present form, Putinism resembles more the kind of dictatorship that was (or is) in power in less developed countries—mainly in the Middle East and Latin America.

Putin's success rested (rests) mainly on two factors, above all the steeply rising demand for oil and gas and, correspondingly, a striking improvement in Russia's finances. This caused the emergence of a small group of megarich billionaires, the oligarchs. Inevitably, however, there has been a massive trickle down that has brought about a substantial rise in the standard of living of wide sections of society. These became the pillars of the support for Putin and his regime.

The other source of the success of Putinism was the unfortunate character of the transition from communism to some new form of rule based on a market economy. What should have been reforms leading to a democratic society became identified instead with chaotic political conditions and a kleptocracy. Putinism more or less successfully dealt with the former, strengthening the authority and power of the state. The new wealth enabled the Russian government to follow a patriotc (aggressive) foreign policy aimed at the retrieval of various parts of the Soviet Union that had been lost as the result of the collapse of 1989–91. At the same time, Putinism accepted the negative social and economic heritage of the Yeltsin era.

It had become customary to regard Russia after the breakdown as "Upper Volta equipped with nuclear weapons." But such comparisons were less than accurate, since Upper Volta had never considered itself a third Rome with messianic assignments to carry out, there has not been an "Upper Volta idea" comparable to the Russian idea, nor did it enjoy (as Russia did under Putin) the good fortune of the windfall of the oil and gas boom, which enabled it to play an important role in world affairs. These various circumstances make the Russian case sui generis. Comparisons with historical fascism may be correct and helpful in some respects, but not in others, and they cannot be indicative as far as coming events are concerned.

3 | THE PILLARS OF THE NEW RUSSIAN IDEA

The Russian Orthodox Church

ORTHODOX RELIGION ALWAYS PLAYED A CENTRAL ROLE IN THE history of the Russian idea. This is the case today and, in all probability, will be tomorrow. Christianity came to Russia from Constantinople, although there are various accounts concerning the origins. According to one, a Kievan prince sent a delegation to Byzantium in search of a suitable religion. They were deeply impressed by the Orthodox ritual practiced in the Hagia Sophia and recommended its adoption. It is more likely, however, that the Orthodox Church came to Russia by way of missionaries from Byzantium who visited the Greek colonies in southern Russia.

In the beginning, the church in Russia was under the guidance and control of the patriarch in Constantinople; with the decline and weakening of Byzantium, it became independent. The history of the Russian church in the following centuries is long and complicated, like those of other churches. It is a story of splits and reunions, of conflicts with the state and, more often, of collaboration. The church was heavily involved in politics. Many predicted that this would harm the church, but they did not prevail. The role of the church was clearly stated by Feofan Prokopovich, a priest and adviser of Tsar Peter the Great, in a book entitled *Dukhovny reglament* ("Spiritual Regulation"). It said that kings ought to be honored and obeyed. Those who opposed them, the monarchomachs, were sinners.

Up to the Russian Revolution, the church, or to be precise religion, had a considerable impact on all sections of society, including the intelligentsia. Under communism, the church did not fare well, particularly during the early years of the new regime, when churches were destroyed and churchgoers harassed. This changed to a certain extent during World War II, when Stalin tried to include the church in the common front against Nazi Germany, making certain limited concessions to church activities, always in the hope that young people would no longer be interested in religion and the church would gradually die a natural death.

This assumption was based on the mistaken belief in the continued attraction of Communist ideas. Therefore, Russian Orthodoxy continued to exist—a precarious existence for which a heavy price had to be paid. For it was not just infiltrated but virtually taken over by the organs of state security. No one could become a bishop, let alone attain a higher rank, unless vetted by the Politburo and the KGB. When the archives were opened for a short time in 1991, the bitter truth came out: Even the patriarch had been an agent. The patriarch in a speech confirmed this and delivered his *pater peccavi* on behalf of the church leadership and his own role. His argument was that concessions had to be made to survive.

Seen from today's vantage point, this is perfectly true. A case can be made in defense of the church's caving in. For the church did survive, whereas those who had persecuted it did not. The churchmen did not become Communists, but some of the former Communists found their way back to religion. In the post-Soviet national anthem, God and Holy Russia reappeared, whereas communism and the final struggle had vanished.

Was it not true that virtually all religions at one time or another had to make similar concessions in order to survive? The age of the martyrs had long passed, and it was unjust and unrealistic to expect modern churchmen to behave like Christ and the early Christian martyrs.

Such defense is true and yet not true. The pope kept silent during World War II when he should have spoken out, but he was not listed as a gestapo agent. Would Orthodox churchmen have been tortured and shot had they refused to become agents of the organs? Hardly. They would have suffered by not being promoted in the church hierarchy. In brief, the church survived, but its moral authority had been severely, perhaps fatally, diminished.

The political positions taken by the church after it regained its freedom did not show that a basic change in its thinking had occurred. It often took a line well beyond patriotism and nationalism, toward chauvinism. It had not become more tolerant vis-à-vis other faiths: Anti-Semitic outbursts, for instance, were tolerated. In 1993–94, new editions of the notorious *Protocols of the Elders of Zion* were published with the help of Father Ioann's diocese and his blessing (*po blagosloveniu*). Father Ioann (Ivan Snychov) was to become metropolitan of St. Petersburg and Ladoga—not an obscure priest but one of the highest positions in the church just under the patriarch. Twenty thousand copies were printed (these days, the average run of copies of Russian books is two thousand). While the Orthodox Church probably did not invent the *Protocols*, it was the most important agent by far in promoting the title. The most recent edition (2013) appeared with the benediction of the archbishop of Ternopol and Kremenets. Eight thousand copies were printed.

The patriarch (Aleksei) was under considerable pressure since a Moscow court had in the meantime declared the *Protocols* a forgery. This had been known for a long time: They were a nineteenth-century forgery possibly fabricated with the help of the Okhrana, the czarist political police. Their origins have not been conclusively proved to this day. They claimed in considerable if often ridiculous detail that world Jewry was planning to destroy Russia and rule the world. Interestingly, the *protocols* had not been a success in prewar Russia. Stolypin, a prime minister of impeccable right-wing credentials, had told the czar that they were a forgery. They became a success only after World War I, when some early Nazi militants such as the Baltic German Alfred Rosenberg, who had lived in Russia, began to make use of them.

Eventually, Aleksei did dissociate himself and his church from Ioann's propaganda activities, even though the metropolitan invoked God in defense of the forgery. The patriarch declared that the church was not racist. The interview appeared in a Russian newspaper—in English. It is doubtful whether the metropolitan really believed in the authenticity of the protocols, but as a propagandistic weapon, they seemed almost irreplaceable. Since then, several other nefarious conspiracies have been revealed, including "Barbarossa 3" in which foreign diplomats were accused of trying to undermine Russia from within. But the church seems not to have been involved in these affairs.

It would be unjust to make a church responsible for the thoughts and actions of some of its adherents. But it was more than that: The church's attitude toward other Christian faiths was certainly not ecumenical in spirit. Moreover, it was particularly hostile toward Catholicism and not much friendlier toward the Protestant churches, but only because these were considered less dangerous enemies. The Orthodox Church refused to accept the fact that millions of Russian citizens belonged to other religions; it wanted a monopoly in the field. In a letter to Boris Yeltsin, the patriarch complained about pseudoreligious and pseudomissionary activities, which caused harm to the spiritual and physical health of people, as well as to stability and civil harmony in Russia. Reform priests were given a warning to stick to the line prescribed from above. Furthermore, there were conflicts between the Moscow patriarchate and the Russian church abroad.

It is difficult to measure the depth and meaning of the religious revival in post-Soviet Russia. According to reliable opinion polls, only some 15 percent define themselves as atheists. Two-thirds of Russians thought religion should play a greater role in Russian life. But of these, only a tiny fraction said that it was trying to live according to Christian principles. And only 2 to 3 percent attended church services regularly. Earlier polls also showed that as in the Western world, more women than men declared themselves religious. It also appeared that religion had no significant impact on voting behavior. There are many inconsistencies, but this is true not only with regard to religious attitudes. For example, although a majority of Russians feel elevated when singing or listening to the new national anthem, only relatively few know the text of even its first lines.

In the subsequent two decades, many old churches were reopened and new ones built; more than twenty thousand priests were serving the faithful. Yet the impact of religion on the highly educated seems to have declined. In the late Brezhnev period, there was considerable interest in religion among young intellectuals. But such interest to the extent that it still persists has turned toward the teachings of more exotic beliefs (or superstitions), be it the predictions of Nostradamus or Madame Blavatskaya, who was a Russian occultist.

Mikhail Epstein called this phenomenon of the 1970s "minimal" or "poor" (*bednaya*) religion, a religiosity outside the church, sans temples, rituals, or doctrines. It refers specifically to the then young writers of this period such as Vasily Aksyonov, Bulat Okudzhava, and some of their contemporaries, or Joseph *Brodsky* in a later period. However, such free-floating religiosity is of little use to the state, for in contrast to official religion in the form of the Orthodox Church, it does not preach nationalism or loyalty to the state and its rulers.

This leads to the question of what has caused the decline in the attraction of the church even among the intelligentsia. There was a time (to give but one example) when Jewish individuals and whole families (the Rubinstein and Pasternak, for instance) converted, when Semyon Frank, a major religious thinker, believed that unless one belonged to the Orthodox Church, one could not fully identify with Russia.

In brief, the Russian Orthodox Church seems not to have been very successful among the intelligentsia. While perhaps not a fatal shortcoming from the church's point of view, it is still an interesting phenomenon. Once upon a time, even Lenin was worried about the church's influence among intellectuals. He had been convinced that religion, a historical phenomenon and anachronism, was incompatible with Marxism. But he refused to include atheism in the party program. He was disappointed when, after the failure of the revolution of 1905, some leading intellectuals turned away from Marxism toward religious or quasi-religious thinking such as expressed in *Vechi*, a collection of essays with a surprising emphasis on religion by a number of intellectuals formerly considered "progressive," even radical.

There had been a time when Russia was the home of an impressive array of religious thinkers, such as Vasily Rozanov and Vladimir Solovyov. The great Russian nineteenth-century writers—Gogol, Tolstoy, Dostoyevsky—were all heavily preoccupied with religion, and not always to the pleasure of the church, as in the case of Tolstoy, who was excommunicated. Solovyov was liked by the official church because of the central role of *sobornost* (the stress on the collective rather than the individual) in his thinking. What the church did not like was the influence of Hellenistic philosophers on his thinking and above all his ecumenism—the looking for common ground with Catholicism, which was anathema in the eyes of the church. (Solovyov was also an outspoken opponent of anti-Semitism and published a manifesto against what he considered a national disgrace. This too brought him into conflict with the church.)

Solovyov had a great influence on his contemporaries and the generation after—not so much the theologians, but the philosophers, writers, and artists. His story of the coming of the Antichrist was a powerful historical-literary essay, the tale of world conquest by some Asian power. Its impact was enormous; it was a contribution to the beloved Russian traditional belief in complicated and dramatic conspiracies.

Jews have not been lucky insofar as the attitude of the Orthodox Church is concerned, even on the highest level of intellectual sophistication. Georges Florovsky, perhaps the leading theologian between the two world wars, was a racialist and considered the castration of Jews; the attitude of Losev, another pillar of Orthodox theology, was not much more tolerant.

The leading theological thinkers of the next generation were Sergei Bulgakov and Nikolai Berdyaev. Bulgakov had been a radical in his youth, opposing autocracy and "false patriotism." He kept his distance in later life from chauvinism and other reactionary views, even though he did embrace Russian nationalism. But he envisaged a cultural rather than political nationalism, in contrast to the chauvinism sponsored by secular forces. He still remained suspect in the eyes of church authorities because of advocating certain unorthodox religious doctrinal views (sophiology).

Berdyaev was the religious thinker best known outside the Russian Orthodox Church. He too had been a radical in his youth, had been arrested and exiled for a few years. Berdyaev believed that Russia had a mission to fulfill. In his "Russian idea," he recalled that the Russian intelligentsia had been saddened by the depressing record of their country. Yet they had never given up the belief that their country had a historical mission and the day would come to say its word to the world. He did not elaborate, but the reference was clearly to true Christianity. Even Pyotr Chaadayev, the most severe critic of Russia of the nineteenth-century thinkers, had believed in the existence of hidden forces in the Russian people, forces that would eventually be released.

There is a world of difference between these religious thinkers and those of the present generation. It is not just a matter of the cultural level of the spokesmen or the fact that their pronouncements tended to be far more political than spiritual in character. They had been preoccupied with issues such as the czar's family and those serving him, who were killed by the Bolsheviks in 1918. In a political decision, the Romanovs were canonized following apparent pressure by the monarchists in the ranks of active church members. While this murder of a family, especially children, was a despicable act, they were not killed because of their religion and thus do not qualify as religious martyrs. The church authorities had therefore to think of some other justification, and the result was in no way convincing.

Generally speaking, the division between church and state has virtually disappeared. The church has remained a tool of the government, as in Soviet days. Its foreign political declarations could have come (and often did come) from the Ministry of Foreign Affairs or the general staff of the army or the police. These pronouncements, right or wrong, were outside the spiritual realm. There was nothing specifically religious about them.

There were strange occurrences within the church, and at times it appeared as if the patriarch had lost control: There was the case of the high Orthodox dignitary in the Duma whose assignment it was to defend church interests in the Russian parliament. But he converted to Islam and devoted most of his time trying to show that Rothschild (not the CIA) had been responsible for the Arab Spring, which was highly undesirable. There was another high Orthodox churchman who alleged that the church was dominated by a homosexual lobby, which tried to influence it in this direction.

There have been fairly constant attacks against the godless West by the Moscow church, but also by Putin. Putin has declared that many Euro-Atlantic countries have moved away from their roots, including Christian values. Russia, on the other hand, appears as the defender of traditional values against an assault by the West, a staunch defense being the only way to prevent Russia from descending into chaotic darkness.

Patriarch Kirill has repeated Putin more or less verbatim on various occasions. And Archimandrite (Chaplain) Vsevolod has attacked church-state separation as a fatal mistake by the West, a monstrous phenomenon that has "occurred only in Western civilization and will kill the West." Then, as one moves further down the hierarchy, the declarations by churchmen become even more strident. Among the 1,350 pieces of advice to believers on how to defend themselves against occult evil forces is one question: Which books are most displeasing to Satan? The answer: Books written by the saints.

The belief in satanism is a specific Russian feature going back to pre–World War I days, and the Russian media reports from time to time about the existence of satanist groups. Most recently, in 2008, eight youngsters between seventeen and nineteen were arrested near Yaroslavl and charged with having consumed four other young people.

Neo-paganism has had a certain following in Russia as well as in the Baltic countries and elsewhere in Eastern Europe since the 1980s. But it has not been a factor of any political importance. In Russia, it is split into many small sects. Some take their inspiration from the ecological movement, praying to the sun, to the moon; others worship the earth and other deities. Yet others are openly neo-Fascist, engaging in occasional acts of violence such as burning churches. Many celebrate the summer solstice. They take their inspiration from the folk peasant culture of pre-Christian days. But since very little is known of that age that is authentic, many of the customs and rituals recently adopted belong to the realms of fantasy, invention, and forgery. According to some reports, their number has grown in recent years; young people in the cities bored or even repelled by the Orthodox Church have been looking for something more exciting and/or original. But these reports about a growth in numbers may well be exaggerated. None of the neo-pagan groups has so far lasted for long, and at the present time they apparently stand no chance in competition with the deeply rooted and well-entrenched Orthodox Church. Given the highly conservative character of the Orthodox Church and its limited appeal to young people, this could change in the future, and the Orthodox Church may well share the fate of other faiths—namely, a decline in the number of the faithful practicing religion. But this could take considerable time, and it is by no means certain who will benefit from a development of this kind.

In the meantime, the Russian Orthodox Church mainly fulfills a political function supporting the government, particularly in the field of anti-Western propaganda. It is striking to observe the changes that have taken place. In 1880, on the occasion of the unveiling of a monument in Moscow honoring Alexander Pushkin (under Stalin, the location of the monument was changed), Fyodor Dostoyevsky was invited to give the speech in honor of the poet. Dostoyevsky was deeply religious, and while not exactly a Slavophile (their time had passed), he was very much in their tradition. The speech, made in a state of ecstasy and generating more ecstasy among the listeners, became the event of the year, if not of the decade, and was widely discussed. Toward the end, Dostoyevsky said:

> Yes, the Russian's destiny is incontestably all-European and universal. To become a genuine and all-round Russian means, perhaps (and this you should remember), to become a brother of all men, a universal man. . . . Oh, the people of Europe have no idea how dear they are to us. . . .

It is not easy to imagine a speech of this kind 140 years later. Dostoyevsky would not be arrested—those days have passed. But the organizers would regret having invited him, and there would have been considerable booing. The church would not have excommunicated him, but he would have been given a warning not to repeat such unsuitable, false, almost blasphemous statements. And next week's *Zavtra,* the leading periodical of the extreme Right, would have charged him with incredible naïveté bordering on treason.

Leading Thinkers of the Russian Right

Scanning the pages of Wikipedia (Russian version), the reader may come across the picture of a handsome man, not in his first youth, carrying an RPG antitank weapon. On another page, the same man appears in front of a tank, carrying a Kalashnikov submachine gun. Clearly a person not to be trifled with. A Russian officer, perhaps, or a leading figure in the field of arms construction, perhaps an arms collector or a man with many enemies? Far from it: He is a philosopher, and since the scene is South Ossetia and the time about 2008, chances are that he isn't Martin Heidegger, either. His name is Alexander Gelyevich Dugin, and he is no ordinary philosopher. What tanks or aircraft does he want to destroy or disable? It is a long, complicated, and fascinating story.

There has been since the 1980s a plethora of groups, mainly in Moscow, of young people influenced by and imitating Nazism. Similar groups have appeared in other European countries, but their emergence in Russia is probably more striking and more difficult to explain. It was no doubt partly the result of the declining attraction of communism during the Brezhnev era. But considering the record of German occupation in Russia, the war crimes, the enormous damage inflicted, and the millions of Russians who perished, it is difficult to understand how young Russians could be influenced by an ideology that considered them subhuman, even if one takes into account the urge of young people to shock their elders or recognizes that this generation has not experienced the German invasion and occupation and that all they know about fascism is second or thirdhand. Be that as it may, the fact remains that there were many such groups, even if short-lived. It is equally surprising that the reaction of the authorities was mild, much milder than the treatment of the democratic dissidents.

Some of these groups were more "cultural" than political in character, such as the skinheads, imitating certain Western fashions. Others, however, were heavily political, such as a variety of small national Bolshevik parties. These were usually banned by the government but after a while reappeared under a new name. There was a National Salvation Front which lasted for a few years and then fell apart. Some of these groups made no secret of the fact that they were very close to the Nazis, displaying Nazi symbols and shouting Nazi slogans. Others, more moderate, accepted some of the Nazi ideas and practices but rejected others. Some have lasted for a longer time than others have who survived for a few months only. Lastly, there was always a certain amount of genuineness to these groups; some were undoubtedly genuine and spontaneous, but there were doubts about the genuine character of others, which might have been sponsored or at least helped by unknown forces. Such cases had occurred on the right-wing scene before, during and after the revolution 1905. There might have been a repeat performance in the 1990s.

The philosopher carrying the RPG had belonged to one of these groups in his youth but became eminently respectable in later years. Among a recent list of Russia's leading thinkers, Alexander Dugin figures quite highly. He is preceded by the patriarch (6) as well as Eduard Limonov (10), Nikita Mikhalkov, the famous filmmaker, Mikhail Leontiev (24), Zakhar Prilepin (31) and perhaps a few others. But such lists, usually based on the frequency of television appearances, have more to do with entertainment value than with political impact. Seen in this light, Dugin figures quite highly, even though those in the West who have made him Putin's brain may be exaggerating. He even appears, albeit under a different name, in a bestselling novel of the post-Soviet era: Pelevin's *Chapaev and the Void* (*Chapaev i pustota*) in which the main characters discuss geopolitics, neo-imperialism, and neo-Eurasianism with great passion. Pelevin is known for his interest in Buddhism, but the political debates described in the novel take place in a mental home.

Some of his contemporaries believe that he is a unique star, a man of immense historical learning, one of the greatest ideologues of our time.

Born in 1962 in Moscow, the son of a general in military intelligence, Dugin joined during the last years of the Soviet era a small group of young people imitating the German SS and became their leader. It is not clear whether the romanticism of heroism was the main attraction (it could hardly have been German patriotism) or the element of decadence and sadomasochism that has frequently been observed among postwar non-German admirers of the SS. But at some point he left that group and moved on to Pamyat, the foremost anti-Semitic organization at the time. In 1992, however, he withdrew from Pamyat (or was excluded) and subsequently made his living providing "geopolitical expertise" and appearing on various private radio stations. His politics at the time were national Bolshevik, but he had also become an adviser to the president of the Gosduma, the Russian parliament.

In 2002, Dugin became almost overnight known to a wider public, founding his own political party, Evrazia. In 2009, he was made a sociology professor at Moscow State University but continued to work as an adviser to the president of the Russian parliament and other highly placed politicians. Although he was bitterly opposed to Yeltsin and his administration, he entered the orbit of the Putin government and was in growing demand as an expert on a variety of subjects. This was a man who could always be relied upon for some new ideas. He also became a television star. (Some of his appearances are now accessible on YouTube.)

Among his many books, the most widely read is probably an encyclopedic survey (more than six hundred pages) of conspiracy theories. Dugin's inclinations were always toward mysticism and metaphysics, and it is not known in how many of the conspiracy theories he believes. His work is in great demand; his readers will find all they need to know about Count Dracula and Leo Strauss, the famous neo conservative, about Sakharov (a "leading mondialist") and the "liberal totalitarian ideology," about Apollo and the many anti-Russian crusades in the past, about the Project of a New American Century and the "metaphysics of the occult war." The reader may not have known that Khrushchev was an Atlantic agent and Gorbachev a double agent, but he will find details here.

Dugin's books and journals appeared in a publishing house he founded. He seems to have enjoyed the political and probably also the financial support of various official institutions. (According to some reports, it came from military intelligence.) He introduced to Russia the views of leading European neo-Fascist thinkers such as Julio Evola and the extreme New Right such as Alain de Benoist as well as some more obscure thinkers such as René Guénon, Jean-François Thiriart and the French Romanian writer Jean Parvulesco, of whom few in Russia had ever heard. He also disinterred some of the German pre-Hitlerian thinkers such as Lanz von Liebenfels. Later yet he seems to have realized that young Russian patriots would not mount the barricades inspired by Parvulesco, that the primitive anti-Semitism of Pamyat was unlikely to attract the political support of the masses, let alone the intellectuals needed for a political movement, and that for a Russian movement, of the far Right, some Russian antecedents were vital, not just some obscure foreigners. He found these in nineteenth-century Russian anti-Western theorists such as Konstantin Leontiev and Nikolay Danilevsky.

It appears, however, that the more counterintuitive they are, the more interested in them he became. But the sum total never makes sense, not even as disinformation. His work is in great demand, yet his thinking is difficult to follow because of its rapid ideological changes, the contradictions in his views, and his tendency to bring in topics that are unrelated to politics (such as the second law of thermodynamics).

In his early days, he seemed to have embraced neo-paganism, but in 1999 he suddenly joined the Orthodox Church—the young believer joined the church of the old believers. On many issues he has frequently expressed contradictory views. This is true for instance with regard to China; early on he seems to have excluded China from his geopolitical purview but included Japan, which would be in contradiction to all "geopolitical laws," Japan being an island. But later on, realizing the growing importance of China, he seems to have adjusted his views. That a member of the extreme Right should not like Jews goes without saying, but Dugin never pronounced radical anti-Semitic views. On the contrary, he expressed considerable interest in the kabbalah because of its mystical character, and he also seems to have sympathized with the most extreme elements among the supporters of Israel. This brought him into conflict with the less sophisticated anti-Semites on the Russian right who had not the slightest interest in the kabbala, or any other Jewish books unless they admitted ritual murder.

He denounced the xenophobic propaganda of extremist right-wing groups, which (he claimed) was causing "great damage to the national cause," and became a passionate advocate of Eurasianism, the movement preaching Russia's mission in the East and need to cut itself loose from the West and Western influences. He also discovered the teachings of Lev Gumilev, in particular Gumilev's expansionist theories of ethnogenesis and passionarity, and inclination to give him the benefit of the doubt, even to admire him. Yet in truth his work consisted largely of ideological assertions for which there was no proof. There was no great difference between him and certain Nazi ideologues such as Hans Güenther except that in his case the favorite races were not Nordic but nomadic. He became a great supporter of various theories of a past age and incorporated them into his own Eurasian brand of geopolitics, which has been his main cause during the last two decades.

Dugin has moved in and out of various political parties such as Rodina and founded a new party sponsoring Eurasianism including a youth organization promoting Eurasian ideas. His attitude to the authorities has changed no less than his ideological beliefs. He sympathized by and large with Putin ("a true Eurasian man") but has criticized him occasionally for being too cautious (or too slow) expanding the Russian empire and regaining the territories that had been lost. But as the general mood in the country became more right-wing and Putin's policy more aggressive, Dugin became more closely identified with the authorities. He invited Putin to join the leadership of his "international Eurasian movement." The invitation, needless to say, was ignored but still appreciated.

Among those who have taken the trouble to follow Dugin's writings, some think him a political chameleon and others believe that he is a case of genuine, honest, and infectious confusion with an admixture of showmanship and hysteria. The constant factors in his ideology are antiglobalism, antiliberalism (this being the most important ideological plank), anti-Americanism, the occult, Eurasianism, geopolitics, the presence of secret forces shaping world politics, and the dissemination of the myth of Russian great power. These are accompanied by imperialist, racialist Aryanism and occult beliefs that are expressed in a euphemistic way and whose scope remains unclear, these beliefs do have consequences.

But what consequences? And are these ideological extravaganzas, often contradictory, really needed? It is doubtful whether a single German in the 1920s and 1930s became a Nazi as the result of reading a book by a Nazi leader, and this was true even with regard to Hitler's *Mein Kampf.*

Two important Russian influences on Dugin's thought and on other ideologues of the Russian Far Right were Konstantin Leontiev and Nikolay Danilevsky. Leontiev is difficult to categorize, with his deep belief in mysticism and his even deeper pessimism, which sometimes proved to be prophetic: He predicted a great revolution in Russia in the twentieth century, instigated and carried out by the Antichrist. Dugin was particularly attracted by Leontiev's belief in an "Eastern orientation," which was the result of his hostility to Western influences on Russia. It probably helped to induce Dugin's turn to Eurasianism, which was to play a central role in recent years.

Nikolay Danilevsky spent many years in the Russian consular service in the Ottoman Empire and was greatly intrigued by Byzantium and its influence on Russia. A scientist by training, Danilevsky became famous mainly after the publication of his book *Russia and Europe.* He was probably the most radical of the anti-European thinkers of his time. In his younger years, he had belonged to a circle of intellectuals in opposition to the political regime of the day (Dostoyevsky was another member). He claimed that between Russia, Germany, and the Latin countries there was an abyss that could not be bridged. He also promulgated a theory concerning the development of cultures, highly speculative in approach, that evoked some interest in his lifetime.

These two influences on Dugin were by no means the only ones, but they were significant. And their reach was more widespread than might be imagined.

The situation resembles in some ways the one facing Hitler when he appeared on the Munich scene soon after World War I. There existed several societies such as the Thule Society propagating views close to Hitler's own thoughts and some of the latter-day Nazis belonged to it. But Hitler did not think much of it, even ridiculed it, and quickly dissociated himself from this society. He thought these sects ineffectual because they lacked the common touch, and their ideology was far too complicated. Instead of concentrating on some essential points and constantly repeating them, they engaged in what Hitler considered esoteric issues of no particular interest to the masses. The same was true with regard to Alfred Rosenberg, a Baltic German who also became a member of Thule. He had helped bring the *Protocols of the Elders of Zion* from Russia to Germany.

Rosenberg's book *The Myth of the Twentieth Century* was considered second in importance only to *Mein Kampf.* But Hitler never read it and Göring called it a swindle. Goebbels ridiculed him and thought him a man of no consequence, even an idiot. His magnum opus was sold or distributed in later years in a million copies but it is doubtful whether many read it. For with its fantasies about race and blood, Marcionism, Catharism, and "negative Christianity," it disregarded the elementary tenets of political propaganda.

If Dugin did better than Rosenberg, it probably was because of television. Dugin was far more widely read than Rosenberg was, and he impressed the semiliterate. But on TV he was compelled to concentrate on essential points, which was not necessary in his books. In his television appearances, he had to drop the references to Guénon, Evola, and Parvulesco, and similar obscurantists. Unlike Hitler, he was not out to be the head of a mass party—he was preaching to the intellectual elite, such as it was after many of the best and brightest had left the country. There were few left in the humanities who were aware of modern intellectual currents.

Dugin has often collaborated with other right-wing ideologues (most of them TV hosts), such as Mikhail Leontiev and Sergey Kurginyan.

(Mikhail Leontiev is said to be Putin's favorite commentator, while Kurginyan was active in the world of theater.) He came to join the Putin camp without any reservation; on one occasion, he declared that only the mentally ill would not do so. Then, in May 2014 following an "emotional interview," Dugin was suspended from his position in the Department of Sociology at Moscow State University. His friends from the far-right periodical *Zavtra* used the opportunity to argue that being a philosopher, he should not have been in the department in the first place. There were also discussions about his mental state in general on this occasion.

Dugin by no means had a monopoly in the anti-Western, antidemocratic field. After the breakdown of the Soviet Union, a small encyclopedia would be needed to name all the groups and their spokesmen active in this field.

There is Maxim Kalashnikov, for instance (not the inventor of the famous submachine gun). Born Vladimir Alexandrovich Kucherenko in Turkmenistan, he grew up in Odessa and studied history and economics in Moscow. He is the author of many books (*The Broken Sword of the Empire, Moscow: The Empire of Darkness, The Battle for Skies, Inferior Race, The Übermensch Speaks Russian, Do We Have a Future?*) that became bestsellers, and he was invited to the Kremlin by President Dmitry Medvedev for a discussion of his ideas—some of them sensible, some extreme, and others belonging to the realm of psychiatry rather than political analysis.

The following general picture emerges from studying these books: Kalashnikov is sometimes called a conservative (as a member of the Institute of Dynamic Conservatism in Moscow), but this is inaccurate. He admires both Stalin and Hitler. Ten years ago, he predicted the imminent collapse of the United States and the white race in general. According to him, Russia has the chance to achieve a great comeback, because its collapse occurred early on and it may learn from the experience.

There are two major preconditions for his vision of Russia's comeback. First, a new Russian person has to be created. Its present mentality is hopelessly stupid since it is not even aware of its own self-interest. It is ill and cannot be cured; it will go under and disappear unless a new race of Russians comes into being. Therefore, there must be a new nation, a new race of supermen and superwomen. At this point Kalashnikov enters territory, which is not quite new—the Nazi project of *Ahnenerbe* that aimed at creating a new Nordic race. He says that much can be learned from the German experience of the 1930s. But time is of essence, how to create a new race within a few years? This question is left open.

Second, all this should be done secretly, including the new race, the new economy, and the new Soviet Union, or the dark forces will sabotage it. Behind the façade of the state, there will be another, real state, and the same will apply to all the other important institutions, such as the army, police, economy, and so on. As Kalashnikov sees it, these parallel institutions will be able to accomplish what the official ones cannot—by performing illegal actions not limited by civil rights and other such considerations. They will be able to take the money away from the oligarchs using psychological and other methods. The oligarchs will not even realize what is happening to them. Control over the financial sector will again be in the hands of the state. Will the secret state be more honest, will there be less corruption? This Kalashnikov takes for granted, perhaps because it will consist of members of the new race of supermen genetically programmed to be not only more intelligent but also less corrupt. In this way, a new Russia, a new nation, will emerge.

While Alexander Dugin's thinking stresses his brand of geopolitics, Kalashnikov's emphasis is on modern technology, which can achieve just about everything. He is a great believer in innovation—Stalin was a great innovator; so were Lavrentiy Beria and Adolf Hitler. In one interview he spoke of himself as a Stalinist, but in another the following exchange occurred: "The media quote you having said, 'I am not a Communist, I am a Fascist.'" His answer: "I am a follower of Konstantin Leontiev, and I was attracted by Nietzsche. I highly estimate Stalin and believe that much of value can be learned from the German experience in the 1930s."

In 2014, Kalashnikov became somewhat more pessimistic. His most recent work is entitled *The Collapse of the Putin Regime: Darkness at the End of the Tunnel*. He still does not like the Anglo-Saxons ("They have always been the sworn enemies of the Russians: All our history shows this"), considering them cold, hypocritical, calculating, clever, and cruel.

But the real point of the book is that not only will Putin's Russia crash, but everything, everywhere, will go to pieces—the economy, society, the entire social fabric.

Like Dugin, Kalashnikov is considered an original thinker, although many of his ideas have been shared or preempted by other thinkers of the Far Right. There was, for instance, the prediction that the United States would break up in 2010. According to Igor Panarin, a KGB analyst who later became dean of the Russian Foreign Ministry academy for budding diplomats, the state of California will be part of China, Texas will be part of Mexico, and so forth. And Nikolai Starikov, a popular television presenter who specializes in historical documentaries, put virtually all the professional historians to shame by solving many of the great mysteries of the twentieth century. For example, he proved beyond any shadow of doubt that the February and October revolutions in Russia and the November revolution (1918) in Germany had been organized by British intelligence, with the possible support of the United States and France. Their goal in World War I was to force the two powers to bleed each other out and eventually spark revolutions there. And when Hitler—who was actually a British agent—was egged on by Churchill and Roosevelt to attack the Soviet Union during World War II, it was fortunate that Stalin was there to stop him.

Finally, during the days of the fighting in eastern Ukraine in the summer of 2014, the Russian media discovered and built up another hero: Igor Strelkov, a man of action and a patriotic thinker at the same time. Born Igor Girkin in Moscow and currently about forty-five years old, Strelkov was a reserve colonel in the Intelligence Department of Russian military intelligence who had been fighting in a number of battlefields, including the former Yugoslavia, and became the highest-profile rebel leader in eastern Ukraine. According to a manifesto written by him, he called his fighters an orthodox army, proud to serve not the golden calf, but our Lord Jesus Christ. He has been described as a deeply religious person: For instance, he demanded a ban on using swear words on television and in daily life. But he was also accused of the murder of several thousand Bosnians, the disappearance of many Chechens, and the execution of several Ukrainians. The Strelkov phenomenon is interesting for a number of reasons: He accused Putin and other leading figures of the elite of acting indecisively in Ukraine and predicted that unless they mended their ways, they would ruin Russia and be swept away. These tensions seem to point to a deeper conflict among radical circles in the army, especially the GRU, the army intelligence, and the slightly more cautious *siloviki*—former KGB officers ruling Russia at the present time.

Eurasianism

According to some sources, the term "Eurasianism" was first used by the German polymath and world traveler Alexander von Humboldt early in the nineteenth century. It is (together with *geopolitika*) the single most important component of the new Russian doctrine. Its origins can be traced back a long time, but its updated version—namely, neo-Eurasianism—is quite different in character. Contemporary proponents of Eurasianism favor Nikolay Danilevsky's interpretation in his classic *Europe and Russia*, which more or less pioneers the idea that there is no universal human culture, no common values, and that between the German and the Slav world in particular there is an abyss. Danilevsky had a considerable influence on Konstantin Leontiev and some others. But he is of limited use to the neo-Eurasians because they are preoccupied with America, want Germany as a partner, and envisage a future Eurasia reaching from Dublin to Vladivostok. Danilevsky would have been horrified. The early Eurasians were concerned about "Europeanization"; those of today fear Americanization.

Eurasianism originally emerged among Russian émigrés in the early 1920s; its first major doctrinal statement was a 1921 collection of essays entitled *Exodus to the East*, which repeats the thesis of the unbridgeable divide between Russia and the West and even the bitter enmity between them. But there is nothing about America and Atlanticism, about liberalism and democracy, the subjects that are of paramount importance to the neo-Eurasians of today.

The best brief summary of its aims can be found in an article by Caspar Meyer titled "Rostovtzeff and the Classical Origins of Eurasianism," published in 2009 in a journal dealing with ancient history and archaeology:

> Their program envisaged the Bolshevik regime as a temporary but necessary cataclysm paving the way to a pan-Eurasian ideocratic state. The vast ecological zone of Eurasia conditioned its dispersed inhabitants to rally under a central authority and periodically to restore a timeless steppe empire in changing historical guises. The Russian empire was a natural successor to the Mongol empire of Genghis Khan and tended, like its predecessor, towards antagonism with the "Romano Germanic" West. Post-Bolshevik Russia would be the ultimate manifestation of the Eurasian "geopolitical destiny" and its leadership should logically be entrusted to those who recognized the country's essence and providential role.

The 1920s were the heyday of Eurasianism; after 1929, the movement fell apart. Many continued to believe that Russia was a country and a culture sui generis but were less enthusiastic about the purely Asian origins and influences. Some Eurasians, especially the younger ones, turned pro-Soviet and even pro-Communist, more for sentimental than ideological reasons. Some even turned Soviet agents of influence in Western Europe or cooperated with the GPU/NKVD, which did not save them from execution or the gulag after they returned to the Soviet Union. The story of Sergei Efron, not known in full detail to this day, is perhaps one of the saddest. A young officer in the White Army (of Jewish origin), he had met Marina Tsvetaeva, the great Russian poet, on the Maximilian Voloshin estate in Crimea and fallen in love with her. They later married. Efron helped Soviet intelligence kidnap a White Russian general in Paris. He had to flee to the Soviet Union but was arrested there and executed after a member of his family stated in evidence (having been tortured) that Efron was a Trotskyite spy. Tsvetaeva committed suicide soon after.

Prince Mirsky (Dmitry Petrovich Svyatopolk-Mirsky), who had been in exile in the United Kingdom, also disappeared soon after his return to Russia; the date and circumstances of his death (probably 1939) are not known. The well-known British historian E. H. Carr may have been involved unwittingly in his sad fate. A sympathizer with the Soviet Union even though a critic of Marxism, Carr met Mirsky in a Moscow street and, glad to see an old acquaintance from his London days, approached him and tried to engage him in a conversation. Mirsky pretended that he had never met Carr before, but apparently without much success. The story is mentioned here to show the massive political naïveté of the Eurasians. Earlier on, some of them had been taken in by a maneuver of the Soviet organs, in which they were made to meet some members of "the opposition" inside the Soviet Union who in reality were agents of the organs.

The major figures among the early Eurasians eventually went to the United States and became professors at leading universities. Trubetskoy died at an early age in Vienna soon after the Anschluss. Shortly before his death, he had published a book condemning racism and chauvinism ("pseudonationalism"), similar in outlook to his essay condemning chauvinism fifteen years earlier in the original manifesto of the Eurasians. This caused his arrest for a while by the gestapo.

Why Eurasia? There is no obvious answer except that some Russians were offended because Europeans had not received them as equals and that perhaps they did not like all aspects of European culture—if there was such a thing in the first place. If Eurasians had argued that Russia was like a third force different from both Europe and Asia, this might have been the starting point for an interesting debate. Anything more sweeping was bound to lead them away from historical truth. The origins of Russia were not in Asia, but in Europe. Eurasianism was the updated and adjusted Russian version of imperialism in other countries—of Lord Milner's "constructive imperialism," of Jules Ferry's idea that the higher races have to take care of the less fortunate ones, and of the German equivalent of the 1890s. A hundred years later, such arguments were no longer suitable, but it was still true that the purpose of expansion was not altruistic. Underlying it was the desire to restore to Russia its national mission, its great-power status, and this in modern conditions could be achieved only through some form of alliance dominated by Russia. It meant, among other things, the upgrading of the reputation of Genghis Khan and Batu Khan, the Golden Horde, and various other khanates.

The invasion of Asia by the Russians had begun in the sixteenth century. The Cossacks went beyond the Urals to explore the conditions for hunting and trapping. Ivan Grozny (the Terrible) had sent them, and the venture commanded by Yermak Timofeyevich had been organized and financed by a wealthy merchant family, the Stroganoffs. Very little is known about this venture; all we know about the expedition is based on various annals that are dated several decades after the event and may not be true. If the reports are true and if Timofeyevich's little army counted 840 men and if they all went on foot and only a few were armed with rifles, it was certainly a remarkable undertaking considering the distances they covered—within a few years, they had reached what we now call the Bering Strait. (Vitus Bering, an officer from Denmark serving in the Russian army, undertook a number of expeditions in the 1740s and was also the first to explore Kamchatka more or less seriously.)

Few Russians went to Siberia in those years and for a long time thereafter, except for criminals and political prisoners, who did not go there of their own free will. The big cities beyond the Urals were founded only in the nineteenth century (Vladivostok in 1860); Khabarovsk (Khabarovka at the time) was established as a military outpost, as was Vladivostok, a naval base. In brief, the settlement of Siberia and the Russian Far East took place not that long ago, and it was part of the general imperial expansion during the nineteenth century.

Seen in this context, the Russian colonial expansion to the East was neither better nor worse than the expansion of other imperialist powers. It could perhaps be justified because the Russians brought progress to these parts of Asia—Marx, it will be recalled, made this argument with regard to the progressive character of British rule in India. But the kind of argument that was acceptable in the nineteenth century is altogether out of place in our time.

According to legend, the tribes living in Russia had invited Rurik and the Varangians to come and rule them because otherwise there would have been chaos (this is known in Russian history as *Prizvanie varyagov*), but even legend does not tell us whether the Russians were invited to Siberia. Against this background, it seems that the fascination with the East had to do with certain short-lived cultural fashions among the Russian intelligentsia, but this too came by way of Europe. Empress Catherine the Great was enthusiastic about the East; she learned about Asia when she visited Crimea. These fashions beginning in the eighteenth century were not limited to Russia. They were equally pronounced in western Europe—in the form of chinoiserie or interest in Japanese art. (The prominent painters Nikolai and Svetoslav Roerich went to India and virtually became Indians.) It was also the time when the academic study of the Orient came under way—the schools of Rosen, Bartold, Oldenburg, and others—few of them of Mongol origin.

The next wave of preoccupation with Asia occurred during the "silver age" of the symbolist poets around the turn of the twentieth century, the generation of Alexander Blok and Andrei Byely. But they were not blind admirers; they were afraid of an Asian apocalypse. The symbolists were influenced by Vladimir Solovyov, who had written about the danger of Pan-Mongolism and thought of the contemporary East that it had much more to do with Xerxes than with Christ. They agreed with what Tennyson wrote at the time:

> Better fifty years of Europe than a cycle of Cathay.

No one doubted that Russia at one time had been exposed to Asian influences; to give but one example, the Russian word for money (*dengy*) was of Tatar origin. (The German word for interpreter [*Dolmetsch*] comes from the Tatar, but what far-reaching conclusions should one draw from this?)

Nikolay Karamzin wrote somewhere that the khanates one way or another created great Russia and also the concept of autocracy (and the very name "Karamzin" is probably of Asian origin). But all this had taken place a long time ago, and as far as Russian culture is concerned, what had been the impact of the Golden Horde on the golden age of Russian culture in the nineteenth century? Thousands of Russian intellectuals and writers and artists went to Europe, but who went to Asia?

The language of the intellectuals was not Mongol or Tatar, it was not even Russian. The great scenes in Russian literature were written in

French. The opening of *War and Peace* and quite a few pages thereafter were in French. Tyutchev grew up in a home in which only the servants spoke Russian, and in later life, too, his spoken French was better than his Russian. Ivan Turgenev spent most of his adult life in France.

But the Russian composers wanted to be different from the West. When the great Five, the *moguchaya kuchka* (the "mighty handful"—Mily Balakirev, Alexander Borodin, César Cui, Modest Mussorgsky, and Nikolai Rimsky-Korsakov), wanted to find an authentic Russian identity, they borrowed heavily from Eastern motifs (or what they thought were genuine Eastern tunes), which produced "Scheherezade," "Islamiye," and "Antar" (set in Arabia).

Orientalism had also to do with the aims of contemporary Russian foreign policy, of course. Just as Pavel Milyukov, the liberal, discovered the importance of Byzantium for Russia, the Eurasians, having witnessed the failure of Western political patterns in their country (and the defeat of the revolution of 1905), cast their eyes farther east. Just as there had been a Japanese cultural fashion in France two hundred years earlier, there was an Indian fashion in Germany after World War I—everyone was suddenly reading Rabindranath Tagore, and leading writers such as Hermann Hesse were preoccupied with Indian topics such as Siddhartha. India had a second coming in the West at the time of the students' revolt of the 1960s and 1970s. In Russia and later in the Russian emigration, the fashion was political rather than cultural.

But the political fascination focused on an East (and an Asia) that was largely imaginary. Even the most ardent Eurasians did not start visiting Asia, let alone establish their residence there. They did not study Chinese or Urdu, let alone Arabic, and immerse themselves in the civilization of these countries. To the Eurasians, the steppe was of cardinal importance, but how many (or rather how few) of them had ever been in the steppe—the grasslands, the prairie of Russia beyond the Urals—for any length of time?

For most of them these were metaphysical grasslands, an imaginary world, not a reality. One should never underrate the importance of mythology in politics and history, but now that neo-Eurasianism has become a political force—and could be of even greater importance in future—it is essential to remember from time to time the origins of that movement in a world of fantasy.

Neo-Eurasianism, the movement headed by Alexander Dugin and some like-minded ideologues, came into being in Russia in the 1990s and is now a political movement, not just a cultural trend. But Dugin too got his original inspiration from neo-fascism in France, Belgium, and Italy, not in the grasslands of Transbaikal. There is Pan-Turanism in Turkey and similar groups in a few Central Asian countries, but they do not constitute a world movement—the differences among these various branches, their interests and agenda, are too striking.

The first wave of Eurasianists in the 1920s developed their ideas because they were disappointed by Europe. They belonged to the party that had been defeated in the civil war, and they were looking for an ideological way out of the dilemma in which they found themselves. It was unthinkable that they would give up on Russia. But how to find a common denominator for Russia's future and their own?

About the current Russian government and those supporting it, it can be said with only a little exaggeration that "we are all Eurasians now." This has to do in part with their aversion toward Europe, which (they feel) rejected them, but it is also a reflection of the immense popularity of the ideas of Lev Gumilev.

The son of the great writer Anna Akhmatova and another poet shot by the Bolsheviks in 1921, Gumilev was the Russian Spengler, widely read, a flawed genius. In several books and many articles, he tried to prove the Asian and nomadic origins of his native country. For the German Oswald Spengler, the future belonged to the young people such as the Germans and the Russians; for Gumilev, the Mongols were the young people. His unorthodox views landed him in prison and the gulag more than once. His ideas were sometimes very interesting, often highly original, at other times far-fetched and clearly wrong. He claimed to be scientific in his approach. But when he announced in an interview "I shall tell you a secret—Russia will only survive as a Eurasian power" (in the periodical *Socium*, 5, 1992) this was hardly a scientific statement that could be either proved or disproved.

Gumilev antagonized the Orthodox Church with this Asian approach and alienated the ultranationalists (because his views denigrated Pan-Slavism), who called him a Russophobe. He also offended the Jews with his comments on Jewish history in the Middle Ages, a subject that admittedly did not belong to his fields of expertise. But his reception in Kazakhstan and among other non-ethnic Russians could not have been more enthusiastic. A university was named after him, a statue of him was erected in Kazan, and his portrait appears on a stamp issued by the Kazakh postal service.

Neo-Eurasianism came into being following the fall of communism and the Soviet Union. We witness now an interesting repeat performance of what happened in the 1920s: Toward the end of that decade, the generation of the founders of Eurasianism was squeezed out of their leadership positions, which passed into the hands of younger, pro-Soviet militants. They are usually described as "left wing" but were in fact pro-Russian rather than Marxist, let alone Communist. Their endeavor was to find a common platform for the young officers who had fought in the White armies of the civil war—and the Soviet Union. They believed they had found such a platform in patriotism/nationalism, which had to be dressed up in Eurasian garb. Their assumptions were not that far off the mark, because the general trend in Russia was away from internationalism toward nationalism. But they did not appreciate the time factor—it would take considerably longer than they assumed, and few of them would live to see their dreams fulfilled. They were not the only émigré group to recognize this trend correctly. Others did, like Ustryalov's *Smena vekh* and the *Young Russians* of Alexander Lvovich Kazembek which gravitated toward fascism. Those who made the mistake of returning to Russia too early had a sad fate. Those who waited a bit longer, until the 1960s, were at least not sent to the gulag. (Kazembek returned to Russia in the 1960s and got a minor job—he worked for the Moscow patriarchate). By the end of the 1920s, the Eurasian movement had ceased to exist. The Communists had taken over their journal, but after a while they no longer had any use for them.

The present-day similarity with the first wave of Eurasians consists in the following. After the collapse of the Soviet Union, the patriots needed a new doctrine. As one of the thinkers of the Russian Right wrote in *Zavtra*, the weekly organ of these circles: An elite without an ideology is a danger. And it is true that a self-respecting political movement needs an ideology: Interests alone are not enough. What could it be in post-Communist Russia? Dugin had tried fascism in his younger years, but this was not such a good idea, even if suitably dressed up. And old-style conservatism, as the experience of other countries had shown, was not sufficient—it was unexciting, even boring. Dugin looked at the experience of the antidemocratic, antiliberal European New Right. They had some ideas, but none really successful. Not one of these groups had managed to become a mass movement or at least gain a position of real influence.

At this point, Eurasianism was rediscovered as an eminently suitable ideological plank. It was patriotic/authoritarian, antidemocratic, nationalist; it was above all suitable for a "revisionist" power trying to regain the territories that had been lost. It was anticapitalist—that is, against the oligarchs—but not too much so. It was sufficiently vague to accommodate people and groups with difficult views in politics and the world. Suddenly everyone discovered Eurasianism—the old/new Communism Party, Vladimir Zhirinovsky, and even Putin, who also said that he was a Eurasian. But Dugin had been first in the field. Perhaps Eurasianism was not sufficient and loans had to be made from fascism and populism. But this could be done without going too far in this direction—after all, there was no systematic cult of the leader, no single state party. Eurasianism in the context was not entirely meaningless, but it could always be interpreted in various ways. Names and terms did not mean that much—the Nazi Party from beginning to the end had been the NSDAP, meaning the National Socialist German Workers' Party, even though workers had been weakly represented in comparison with other classes. But what did it matter?

This is not to suggest that the "Eurasia" concept was fraudulent. Some no doubt sincerely believed in this kind of mythology; others liked it because it could be interpreted in so many different ways. It opened the way to alliances with other parties and forces in Europe. "Conservative" and "neo-Fascist" had their drawbacks. "Eurasian" was far more neutral and had very few; it could attract about everyone. In the 1920s

Eurasianism acted as a bridge for the acceptance of the Soviet Union without necessarily believing in Marxism-Leninism. At the present time it could serve in a similar capacity, accepting the policy of the current government, conservative or ultraconservative. Inasmuch as the foreign policy of the new Russia is concerned, the presentation of Russia as a Eurasian power could facilitate closer relations with Turkic people, perhaps also with the Far East. Russia would be one of several powers in a great coalition based on close economic and political collaboration.

At this point, the difficulties of such a strategy become manifest. A coalition of this kind makes sense from a Russian point of view only if Russia plays the leading role. For this is its historical mission: Russia taking second place alongside a Turkish group of states or as a satellite of China is unthinkable. But why not a coalition of equals? Because the differences in outlook and interest are too great and the dynamics of world politics do not follow the laws of equality. Both with regard to the size of its population and its economic power, Russia is not in a strong position compared with the potential members of a Eurasian coalition. It does not even have a monopoly with regard to the possession of nuclear arms.

It could be different if there were a major threat, a common enemy, and the neo-Eurasians have been trying hard to present America and the West in general as an enemy. But Europe has become gradually weaker, and as American foreign policy has trended toward a withdrawal from world politics and from the Atlantic to the Pacific, the neo-Eurasians will be in desperate need of an enemy and will have great difficulty finding one.

What remains of the Mongolian Empire as a model? Its attitude toward religion, perhaps? The Orthodox Church would not be at all happy. Or the belief that the history of the nomads is exemplary for the future of unifying the destinies of peoples and nations? Europe may be in poor shape, but whichever way one looks at it, it is not clear what the Eurasian past has to offer Russia in the twenty-first century.

Given the present Russian fascination, official and unofficial, with Eurasianism, Asia, and above all Siberia, one should have expected great efforts on the part of the Kremlin to strengthen its ties in Asia. In

2014, Putin appointed a general to act as his special representative to deal with the needs and development of the regions beyond the Urals. But by and large there was the impression that they had been neglected, which led to widespread resentment and even a form of Siberian separatism. Anti-Kremlin demonstrations erupted in places such as Novosibirsk, and there was a belated recognition in Moscow that rapid action was needed. Thus, a new front suddenly opened and new problems were facing the Kremlin in a place where it had been least expected.

Russian Geopolitics

The term "geopolitics," coined in or about 1898 by the Swedish geographer Rudolf Kjellén, was originally a synonym for political geography with some additional thoughts borrowed from political philosophy. It was different from other aspects of geography, such as physical geography. However, within a short time the term assumed specific meanings varying greatly from country to country and according to the political outlook of those using it. Kjellén, a member of the Swedish parliament, was active in politics. He was pro-German, and his main work was written in German. The general idea of geopolitics was in the air. Friedrich Ratzel, a German professor, was a cofounder of the new school; his *Politische Geographie* appeared in 1897. Alfred Mahan, a flag officer in the U.S. Navy, was another early writer on the subject; he first published his *Influence of Sea Power upon History* in 1890. Halford Mackinder's *Britain and the British Seas* appeared in 1902. And Karl Haushofer, the most famous exponent of the German school, was at the time an officer of the Bavarian general staff. His works appeared somewhat later, but his ideas were also formed at about the same time or soon after.

Geopolitics was a latecomer to Russia; in czarist Russia, there was no great interest in the subject, and under communism it collided with the official ideology of Marxism-Leninism. Marxism was about the economy, not about geography. Geopolitics is a term often indiscriminately used (and misused) and has therefore given rise to many misunderstandings. In some ways it merely stated the obvious—that geography had an impact on politics. Today, especially in the United States, it is often used as a synonym for "geography" (geography is a subject not normally taught in American schools and only in relatively few universities). For this reason, caution is called for when "geopolitical" is used in common speech or writing. More often than not, it is meaningless, simply a fashionable term.

The impact of the teaching of geopolitics on nazism has frequently been exaggerated; it did not noticeably influence Italian fascism. This is known to the present writer from personal experience. He went to school in Germany after nazism had come to power. Geography was one of his favorite subjects. It was fashionable at the time and heavily infused with geopolitics. But there was little specifically Nazi in what we were taught. The journal of the group, *Zeitschrift fuer Geopolitik*, was interesting and contained news and comments about foreign countries not normally carried by the German media. There was nothing "Fascist" about geopolitics; the subject was almost unknown in Italy under Mussolini.

True, the idea of *Lebensraum* (need for space) was part of Nazi doctrine, but it had its origin elsewhere, mainly in Hans Grimm's novel *Volk ohne Raum*. However, Hitler (for whom race was more important), Goebbels, and Göring did not have a particular interest in the subject or use the term "heartland." Only Rudolf Hess (who was Haushofer's assistant in Munich for a short time) used the expression, and he defected in the middle of the war. While Haushofer was serving on the army general staff, he was not bellicose in his writings. When World War II broke out, he became depressed because he feared its outcome. Haushofer, in brief, was never quite persona grata in the Third Reich; his wife was of Jewish extraction, and his son, Albrecht, who cooperated with the opposition to Hitler, was executed toward the end of the war. Haushofer's politics were conservative rather than Nazi.

Later additions to geopolitics such as *Lebensraum* or the theories of Halford Mackinder (about the heartland: "Who rules East Europe commands the Heartland. Who rules the Heartland commands the world island. Who rules the world island commands the world") were more than dubious; Mackinder was a man of many parts—one of the early directors of the London School of Economics, a member of Parliament, and the first to reach the top of Mount Kenya. But this specific obiter dictum is useless. The same is true with regard to Mahan's belief in the vital role of coal stations (for ships), the need for which was overtaken by technological progress.

But after the breakdown of the Soviet Union, geopolitics found a new home in Russia. According to present-day geopolitical colleagues from the European Far Right, "It is the merit of the gifted [Alexander] Dugin, something like a one-man think tank. . . ." He is conversant in all the major European languages, erudite in the antiliberal and esoteric heritage rescued by the New Right from the postwar memory hole, and above all an uncompromising, metapolitically prolific opponent of the United States, the citadel of world liberalism and thus the principal source of evil in our time.

If geopolitics has spread in Russia in recent years, so have differences of opinion among the geopoliticians. The heads (often nominal) of the various Russian geopolitical institutions are usually retired army or air force generals such as Leonid Ivashov, with a sprinkling of intellectuals (such as Vadim Tsimbursky) and some former diplomats. Dugin's "fourth political theory" has been criticized by some of his geopolitical colleagues for going too far in dismissing the importance of the race factor. Some Russian geopoliticians admire F. William Engdahl (a not very well-known American German journalist living in Germany), who has been called "wise" and a "genius"; this professional anti-American maintains that all coups and revolutions in the world have been instigated and engineered by the CIA. Several conservative Russian geopoliticians stress the conflict between the Christian West and radical Islam, whereas others believe there is no conflict because the West long ago surrendered its Christian foundations.

Natalya Narochnitskaya, a former Russian diplomat (at the United Nations), is heavily involved in geopolitical activities, being to the far right of the political spectrum. She advocated a return to the Soviet model—shorn, however, of Soviet ideology, it should be replaced by the Orthodox Church, which in turn should play a leading role in Soviet/Russian politics.

Leonid Savin, on the other hand, believes that Russian Christian Orthodoxy does not offer a panacea, either. While he concedes the church is a "thesaurus of wisdom," he seems to doubt the depth of the religious attachment of many believers who in fact go to church only twice a year, at Easter and Christmas.

Savin is editor of the journal *Geopolitika* and is heavily involved in the Euro-synergic school of geopolitics. As chief coordinator of the Eurasian movement, he worked closely with Dugin and on various occasions emphasized cybergeopolitics—apparently a reference to the impact of technological developments on politics. In an interview in 2013, he tried to clarify the aims of his movement and his own views about the world situation. The primary goal of the Eurasians, he maintained, is to establish a multipolar world order of five or more centers of power. Unfortunately, Europe at present pursues pro-Atlanticist policies. Islam as he sees it is no threat to Russia because the Muslims have been well integrated. He sees good prospects of a Moscow-Berlin axis; Germany became attached to Washington because America during the Cold War used very black propaganda and induced the fear of a Soviet invasion. But this has now been overcome. He discovered a lot of Asian elements in Germany, specifically in Bavaria, which some centuries ago was settled by the Avarians. Perhaps Bavaria will find the road back to its Asian origins?

What of China? Hundreds of millions of Chinese face some forty million Russians (not all of them ethnic Russians) east of the Urals. Savin knows that some Russians and Europeans describe China as a possible enemy, but even though some border incidents have taken place, China has no interests in this part of the world. China will focus on Taiwan and the islands in the Pacific, and its satellites' geopolitical attentions will focus on this, not on Siberia and the Far East. It will need support from Russia and others—an interesting case of wishful thinking prevailing over geopolitical realities and common sense.

What of the situation inside Russia? As Savin sees it, the key problem for Russia is a neoliberal group inside the Kremlin. Putin has the support of certain people who want more radical action against corruption, Western agents, and so on. The masses do not believe in the pro-Western opposition's ideas of democracy and human rights. Mikhail

Khodorkovsky, Sabin reveals, is a friend of Baron Rothschild—and we all know what this means. The knowledge of Russian right-wing radicals about the location of the major fortunes in the contemporary world is out of date by about a century; they seem not to subscribe to Bloomberg and other sources of information.

Subjecting this current Russian literature to critical analysis, the question arises: What has this farrago of nonsense to do with geopolitics?

Geopolitics is about political geography, land power, and sea power and their dichotomy, about space and Pan- regions and the strategic domination of certain specific areas. It has nothing to do with neoliberalism and the Orthodox Church, not even the CIA and the KGB. It deals with the ideas of Kjellén, Ratzel, and Haushofer and perhaps the attempts to apply them to the modern world, if this is possible. It does not deal with Rothschild and Khodorkovsky, not even with Putin.

In brief, this kind of "geopolitics" is not geopolitics but merely the appropriation of a name: It is a case of misguided theory building. The intention was presumably to show and to prove that the "Atlanticist" sea powers are liberal-democratic and therefore evil, and that land power is conservative and therefore religious, patriotic, and good. It wanted to show that land power is entitled, indeed obliged, to expand until it reaches its natural borders, whatever these might be. For this purpose, today's geopoliticians might as well have borrowed a theory from organic chemistry or the second law of thermodynamics, as indeed Dugin has done on occasion.

Confabulation?

For some considerable time, the element of fantasy has been strong (and growing stronger) in Russian political literature—not only at the popular level. How to explain this? Where did it originate, and how important is it in the general context of the new "Russian doctrine"? Extreme, even fanatic, statements directed against "the enemy" can be found at almost all times in many countries. There is nothing specifically Russian about it. But if the statements or theories are demonstratively false, even absurd, more often than not they will not be rejected. How to explain this?

Joseph Goebbels, the Nazi minister of propaganda and an accomplished practitioner in this genre, is a prime example for the deliberate fabrication of falsehoods. The head of police in Berlin in the years just before the Nazi takeover was a Jew named Bernhard Weiss, a former army officer and a career official with moderate views. Goebbels launched an all-out campaign against him, turning him into a demonic figure, highly dangerous, incredibly cunning and devious, aiming to destroy everything in his way. When friends pointed out to Goebbels that Weiss (whom he had nicknamed Isidor) was a perfectly harmless bureaucrat, he laughed and said, "Do you think I am not aware of this?"

This is a typical example of a cynical approach. But not all statements, ideas, and theories that are manifestly absurd are deliberately fabricated and cynically exploited as part of a wider propaganda campaign. Some, as in contemporary Russia, are genuinely believed for reasons that have been insufficiently investigated. *The Protocols of the Elders of Zion* was a product of deliberate fabrication, and the same is true with regard to the doctors' plot in Stalin's last year. But both the *Protocols* and the story of the Jewish doctors-assassins were believed by many, and why they believed is apparently not an easy question to answer.

There is a widespread tendency (not specifically Russian and not invented there) to believe in occult, hidden forces as the real shakers and movers in world politics, whereas those about whom we read and hear in the media are merely their puppets. Some Russian ideologues believe (or pretend to believe) that the real struggle in world politics is between two parties—the Rothschild party and the followers of the Rockefellers. According to the more learned followers of Lyndon Larouche, for instance, it is a bitter fight between factions on a higher philosophical level: the Aristotelians and the neo-Platonists. But it is not made clear where they keep their money—certainly not in present-day Greece. There has been in recent years a close cooperation between the Russian extreme Right and the Larouchans (recent example's are Sergey Glazyev's "On Eurofascism," in *Executive Intelligence Review*, a Larouche organ, and a Glazyev is an adviser to president Putin; for another Glazyev interview with Dmitri Simes see *National Interest* June 27, 2014).

This belief in the hidden hand and the evil forces tends to be particularly strong in times of great upheaval, such as after World War I and the Russian Revolution (events of world historical importance that could not easily be explained)—and following the disintegration of the Soviet Union, a similar event with enormous consequences. How could it possibly be explained that a great power that had been established forever—*naveki* (as the then Russian anthem said)—that seemed invincible, had suddenly collapsed? The obvious approach for investigating this issue would have been to look for internal, domestic reasons; something must have been wrong with the very foundations of the system. But this would have been too easy—and also too painful, because many had believed in the system and had been convinced that the foundations were solid. Hence the overwhelming temptation to look behind the obvious, to look for hidden forces, the secret machinations by occult, outside forces intending to destroy the Soviet system.

This search for the culprits took various forms. One was the search for a master plan, the so-called Dulles doctrine. This was the outline of overall CIA strategy authored by Allen Dulles in 1945 and aimed at destroying the Soviet Union. The strategy was simple but ingenious. It envisaged not a war or warlike action, but the destruction of the country, the state, and the nation from within by undermining and corrupting the cultural heritage of the Soviet Union and the moral values of the Soviet nation. Soviet writers, actors, and filmmakers were to be influenced to spread violence, depravity, alcoholism, addiction to drugs, shamelessness, cosmopolitical views, corruption, hatred among the various nationalities, and general distrust, to mention but a few factors involved.

It should have been clear from the beginning that there was something suspect about "the Dulles master plan." In 1945, there was no CIA and no Cold War. Dulles was not in a leading position, and since he was not a Russian expert, no one would have expected from him a grand strategy paper on what to do about the Soviet Union. Soviet cultural life was not his field of specialization. Furthermore, Soviet cultural life was strictly regimented by Stalin and Andrei Zhdanov and various other censorships.

They would not have permitted Boris Pasternak to peddle drugs and Anna Akhmatova to advocate pornography and alcoholism and preach violence. To anyone even vaguely familiar with Soviet cultural life, the whole scheme must have appeared preposterous.

Some students of the Soviet scene have tried to trace the origins of this document. As mentioned earlier on, certain phrases seem to have been taken from Dostoyevsky (*The Possessed*): "We shall make use of slander, drunkenness, we shall corrupt the young." The alleged master plan appeared in the 1960s and 1970s in political novels by some minor Soviet writers—Nikolay Yakovlev, Dold Mikhailik, and Anatoly Ivanov. But in its present form, it got its start only in 1993, when Metropolitan Ioann of St. Petersburg and Ladoga (Ivan Snychov), in a message entitled "*Bitva za Rossii*" ("The Battle for Russia"), gave it his blessing (perhaps even authored it). This church dignitary quoted Dulles (and even made him a general):

> By sowing chaos in Russia, we imperceptibly replace their values with false ones, which will force them to believe. How? We'll find our accomplices, helpers, and allies in Russia herself. In a series of episodes, a tragedy, grandiose in scale, will be played out: the demise of the last unbroken nation on earth, the final irrevocable extinguishment of their national self-consciousness. From art and literature, for example, we'll gradually exterminate the social element. We'll retrain artists, discourage in them the desire to depict the world, and examine those processes taking place in the masses of the people. Literature, the theater, and the cinema will all proclaim the basest of human feelings. We shall use all our means to support and promote those so-called creators who will hammer into the people's consciousness the cult of sex, violence, sadism, and betrayal, in a word—immorality. . . .

In brief, the triumph of Satan.

The late metropolitan continued in this vein: "We shall create chaos and confusion in the workings of the government." He dealt in considerable detail with the notorious anti-Semitic tract *The Protocols of the*

Elders of Zion, of which he was a sponsor, noting that some historians did not believe in the authenticity of the Dulles plan. He also attacked the Catholic West, which succumbed to vanity and the false glory of worldly greatness and fell away from the universal fullness of the true Orthodox. He referred to the cynicism of "enlightened Europe," which was simply beyond words. But always he returned to the *Protocols.* While admitting that its history was rather murky and that he was far from qualified to judge whether it was a forgery or not, he did not shrink from fully endorsing its message, because all that happened over the eighty years that passed since it first appeared confirmed this message.

The Dulles document, then, appears as a modernized version of the *Protocols,* endorsed and/or quoted with approval by a whole array of prominent Russian citizens, including Vladimir Volfovich Zhirinovsky, head of the Liberal Democratic Party of Russia (LDPR); Nikita Mikhalkov, one of Russia's most distinguished filmmakers; Sergey Kara-Murza, professor of chemistry and political commentator; and Sergey Glazyev, another well-known political figure. Even though it is by no means an extreme case of political confabulation, the Dulles master plan has been adduced in some detail because it helps to understand the readiness with which forgeries have been accepted as gospel truth in contemporary Russia, first by extremists only, but subsequently also by sections of the establishment.

The Stalinist system came to Russia eighty years ago, and with it the frequent belief in manifestly untrue assertions. This practice has been more pronounced during some periods, less so in others—denounced on various occasions by experts, but never fully rejected. If in recent years there has been increased sympathy, even a certain longing, for the Stalin period in Russian history, it should not be surprising that this includes the readiness to believe manifestly untrue assertions.

According to ISIOM and other leading Russian public opinion polls, almost 50 percent of Russians took a positive view of Stalin in 2008–09, and the number has certainly not gone down since. This does not mean that criticism of Stalin has become illegal or that all aspects of Stalin's rule are considered desirable. But an excess of anti-Stalinism is frowned upon by the authorities, and the schoolbooks have been adjusted accordingly. What it does mean, then, is that certain psychological attitudes that were prevalent in the Stalin era have again become acceptable.

This includes the belief in conspiracies in order to explain past and present events. But this mind-set alone cannot account for the present day's penchant. How to explain the fact that deliberate falsehoods are often genuinely, sincerely believed?

This fascinating phenomenon has been observed and described by neurologists, psychiatrists, and psychologists for a long time and is known as "confabulation." It was first described in 1889 in amnesic patients by a leading Russian psychiatrist, Sergei Korsakoff (1854–1900), and is known in contemporary medicine as the Wernicke-Korsakoff syndrome. The issue has been intensively studied in recent decades, when medicine and psychology became increasingly interested in problems of memory. To give a recent clinical example:

> On a Monday morning in a home for the elderly, a nurse in Cologne, Germany, asked the 73-year-old Mr. K about his weekend. "Oh, my wife and I flew to Hungary and we had a wonderful time" he replied. The nurse paused, for Mr. K's wife had passed away five years earlier and he had not left the home in months. Was he trying to impress her? More likely Mr. K. was confabulating, a phenomenon in which people describe and even act upon false notions they believe to be true. (Maria Dorothea Heidler, "Is Your Brain Lying to You?" *American Scientist*, March 2014.)

Research on confabulation has shown that there are various types, that confabulators present their stories in great detail, usually with absolute conviction, and will not be made to reconsider their narrative if faced with rational argument. Those engaged in confabulation research also found that it was frequently caused by some form of brain damage resulting in a deficiency of vitamin B_1. (Korsakoff first thought that alcoholism was the most frequent cause.) But on the whole there has been no unanimity with regard to the causes of this condition, probably because it has appeared as the result not of one specific injury or disease but of a variety of causes.

The literature about confabulation is extensive, but not of much help in accounting for the many cases of political confabulation. It is unlikely that the late metropolitan of St. Petersburg and Ladoga and the many others who have been peddling the Dulles doctrine and similar conspiracy theories have suffered from a vitamin B_1 insufficiency. Some undoubtedly knew better but presented their narratives anyway to disseminate their ideas. Others may have believed that their theories or doctrines may have been correct only in part, just enough to circulate them with impunity. Or they may have believed that even unproven theories might have had a grain of truth to them—enough, at least, to offer them up to an eager public. In any case, there is a striking similarity between clinical and political confabulation: the deep conviction of the confabulators that they are speaking the truth, the elimination of doubt where doubt is called for. And to repeat: This is by no means a specific Russian phenomenon. But it has become particularly widespread in Russia, where it has been embraced not just by the more gullible and less educated section of society, but by sections of the intelligentsia, trained not to engage in blind belief, but to use a critical approach. Political confabulation is certainly a phenomenon deserving much wider study and Russia might be one of the best places to do so.

4 | PUTIN AND PUTINISM

THERE IS NO *WHO'S WHO* IN RUSSIA SO FAR. BUT IF THERE WERE one, the entry for Putin would read approximately like this:

PUTIN, Vladimir Vladimirovich b. Leningrad, October 7, 1952. Father, Vladimir Spiridonovich, d. 1999, served in World War II, severely wounded. Grandfather Spiridon was a chef who on several occasions cooked for Lenin and Stalin. Mother, Maria Ivanovna, was a factory worker. Had two brothers, both of whom died very young. Poor family, lived in a *kommunalka* (communal apartment shared by several families). We have it on the authority of Vera Gurevich, Putin's favorite elementary school teacher, to whom he remained attached for many years, that the mother was a "very nice person, kind, selfless, the soul of goodness." Putin remembers that in the 1990s when on the St. Petersburg City Council, he went to Israel as a member of a delegation. His mother gave him a baptismal cross to get it blessed at the Lord's tomb: "I did as she said and then put the cross around my neck. I have never taken it off once." Attended school number 193 in Leningrad; known for rowdy behavior. Demonstrated early interest in sports, mainly judo and sambo. Attended Leningrad State University, graduated 1975 from the Law Department, following completion of thesis on most favored nation in international law. Member of Communist Party since 1972. Joined KGB 1975. Worked first in Counterintelligence Department, later monitoring foreigners and consular officials in Leningrad. Was stationed in Dresden, Saxony, 1985–90. No reliable information about the nature of his job in East Germany. Recalled to St. Petersburg 1991, worked in administration of local university. Resigned from KGB August 1991 with rank of lieutenant colonel. Head of Foreign Relations Department, St. Petersburg Mayor's Office, 1991–96. Moved to Moscow 1997, various appointments in state apparatus, became first deputy chief of presidential (Yeltsin) staff, May 1998. July 1998, head of FSB, one of several successor organizations to KGB. August 1999, first deputy prime minister, appointed prime minister of Russia seven days later. July 1983, married Lyudmila Shkrebneva; divorced 2013. Two daughters, Masha and Katya; insist on privacy, live under assumed names. Remarried 2014, Olympic gymnast Alina Kabayeva.

So much for the early career of the man who was to become Russia's ruler for many years. It was a successful career. He had acquired a reputation as an eager, hardworking, reliable official, showing great loyalty to his bosses—first Anatoly Sobchak and later Boris Yeltsin—but was known only in a small circle of bureaucrats. Soon after first meeting him, Yeltsin expressed his wish to see him as his successor. When Putin became prime minister in 1999, even a year later (in May 2000) when he succeeded Yeltsin, he was still not well-known. There is reason to believe that he was not interested in publicity at this stage in his career. Not long after, most of Russia knew a great deal about him—even that the president's Labrador retriever was named Koni and how he looked and that he was barking whenever Putin's nickname was used.

Putin's KGB training had taught him the advantages of facelessness. However, he certainly had opinions of his own and also a working style that have all been described and analyzed over the past ten years in dozens of biographies and political critiques published in Russian, English, and other languages. In addition, the recollections of Putin's supervisors and teachers in the KGB training school are of interest. One of them, a retired colonel, remembers:

> I can't say he was a careerist. But I do remember I wrote about some negative characteristics in his evaluation. He was somewhat withdrawn and uncommunicative—which could be considered both a positive and a negative trait. I also recall a certain academic tendency. I don't mean he was dry, he was sharp-witted and always ready with a quip. Putin was a steady student without slips. There were no incidents. There was no reason to doubt his honesty and integrity.

When Putin became president, Russia was in dire trouble. Neither the state nor the economy was functioning. A great deal of personal ambition and/or patriotism was needed to aspire to the leadership of the country in these circumstances. Not being an economist, Putin was probably not fully aware of the gravity of the situation, but he must have known much in view of his senior positions in the years before. For his prime minister, he appointed Mikhail Kasyanov, who later became a sharp critic of his regime. Kasyanov carried out important and successful reforms in the economic field (taxation, fiscal reforms, customs). Inflation was reduced and the economy grew during his term of office by about one-third.

However, he disagreed with Putin's style of governing, arguing that separation of powers had been abolished and replaced by the "vertical power" principle, which meant that all important decisions were taken by the government; neither parliament nor the judiciary had a say any longer. There were allegations of fraud against Kasyanov, but the same was true with regard to Putin; it is difficult to think of a single Russian politician of that period or in the years after who did not come under suspicion. Kasyanov joined the opposition after his resignation in 2004, but he did not enjoy much popularity, and his political career came to an end.

Kasyanov was succeeded by Mikhail Fradkov as prime minister;

this cabinet included two well-known liberal economists, German Gref and Alexei Kudrin. They pursued a sensible policy but did not last long.

The beginning of Putin's presidency was not auspicious. Three months after his appointment, in August 2000, the *Kursk* submarine disaster occurred. *Kursk* was a nuclear-powered cruise missile submarine, and it went down in the Barents Sea. Putin was on holiday at the time but did not immediately return to Moscow or visit the scene, nor did he accept offers of help by foreign countries. But he emerged unscathed from this affair, just as another disaster did not harm him: the 2002 terrorist attack, when 130 people were killed in the ineffectual attempt by Russian Special Forces to release hostages in a Moscow theater. This was an attack by Chechens in the Dubrovka Theater in Moscow. It occurred during the performance of a musical based on Veniamin Kaverin's *The Two Captains*. The Special Forces pumped a poisonous agent into the theater's ventilation system, which caused the deaths of many. Nevertheless, Putin's popularity did not suffer. Perhaps it was realized that it would be unjust to attribute the blame to him personally. Perhaps it was the feeling that Russia needed a strong hand, a leader, that the authority of the state had to be reestablished, that the country should follow a more assertive, nationalist foreign policy—and that under Putin it would get what was needed.

Above all, it was Putin's good fortune that the price of oil and gas was rising; without this, none of his policies could have been carried out. The price of a barrel of oil in Yeltsin's days (1994) had been about $16. In 2002, it was $22; in 2004, $50; and in 2008, $91. It has remained at this level for five years. From 2001 to 2007, the economy grew on average 7 percent a year. By 2006, the Russian GNP was double what it had been at the end of the Yeltsin period. Russia could repay all its debts, a new middle class came into being, pensions were doubled—in brief, almost everyone benefited from this prosperity, which was attributed not to good fortune, but to the wise and efficient leadership of Putin. It was one of the most striking cases of good luck in modern history.

Putin's outlook on the economy had been formed in all likelihood by his years in Germany—the West German example, to be sure. He was in favor of a market policy within limits, insisted on a great measure of state control and supervision, and firmly resisted any attempt by the oligarchs to wield political power. Those disobeying the new rules, such as Mikhail Khodorkovsky and Boris Berezovsky, found themselves in a gulag or in exile. Furthermore, a new group of superrich was emerging, such as Genadi Tymshenko, who were personally known to him and on whose loyalty he could implicitly count.

The new rulers of Russia were not the oligarchs but former colleagues of Putin from St. Petersburg and from his KGB days. They also included some senior military and police officials, some specialists, even a few "liberals" (in the early days), and all people who could be trusted. The leadership style was strictly authoritarian. Perhaps a quarter or a third had a KGB background. Their part in the government may even have been higher, since an organ background was usually not widely publicized. The case of Mikhail Fradkov, Putin's second prime minister, is of interest in this context. Very little was known about him when he was first appointed except that he had been active in the field of foreign trade. However, after his resignation as prime minister in 2007, he became head of Russian foreign intelligence, and it is unlikely that such a position would have gone to someone without prior experience in the field.

Most of those serving in the highest echelons became wealthy, but to what extent, from what sources, and where their money was eventually located were state secrets of the highest order. There were certain rules—no ostentatious spending, for one (sometimes the wives suddenly became the main breadwinners of the family). A great amount of literature appeared on this subject, some probably exaggerated (Putin was on occasion described as the richest person on earth), but it seems certain that no one left a senior position in the government destitute and in need of social security.

Putin was now the president, yet little was known about his opinions. Was he at heart a reformer, sympathizing with the liberals, or a conservative? Did he want to change the country, or did he see as his main priority calming the country and bringing tranquillity after many years of unrest? It would have been unrealistic to expect from a KGB graduate the democratization of Russian society. But would he accept the changes that had taken place under Gorbachev, or would he reintroduce a strict authoritarian regime moving more and more toward the right, based on a conservative reactionary worldview? Would the emphasis of the new regime be on domestic or foreign policy? These and other basic questions were left open for a considerable time. There were contradictory indications, but by about 2005 the impression gained ground that the conservative and nationalist impulse was strongest. Those working closely with him and willing to share their impressions thought of him as a patriot, very cautious, playing his cards close to his chest, not given to trusting people except perhaps a very few with a background similar to his own. He has apparently never believed in socialism, let alone communism. He certainly seemed not to think that Russia was ready to move fast (if at all) on the road toward democracy.

His hero at the time was Yuri Andropov. But Andropov did not think highly of the Russian nationalists in the organs over which he presided. Putin, on the other hand, while not a member of this faction, was more inclined to listen to them; he was attracted by nationalist political leaders and thinkers of czarist Russia and by some of those who left Russia after 1917. Paradoxically, at this time, support for Putin was weaker in the organs than in other sections of the state and society. It is not known why this should have been the case, and it probably has changed since, particularly with the Second Chechen War. Putin distrusted foreign governments, which is not particularly surprising, since he had been trained for this job.

Much has been written about "the faceless Putin," his masculinity, his activity in the field of judo and other sports. He has appeared on comic strips and in thrillers, and he has been shown kissing a sleeping tigress and a sturgeon and also as the father of the nation and confronting a major economic crisis. His approval rating has been consistently high, at times skyrocketing to 80 percent and even higher. The state-controlled media played a decisive role in this rise in his popularity.

One could think of some other twentieth-century leaders who reached similarly high approval and even enthusiasm and became the object of a cult. But it is also true that Putin admirably fit the role of a leader as wanted by many Russians at the time. Democratic institutions were not in demand, but the country wanted a leader exuding strength and self-confidence. Most Russians have come to believe that democracy is what happened in their country between 1990 and 2000, and they do not want any more of it. There never was democracy in Russia except perhaps for a few months in 1917, hence the deep-seated distrust and aversion, the belief that democracy is the state of affairs in which a few people get very rich and the rest remain poor or get even poorer.

After many years of uncertainty and chaos, Putin must have appeared like a knight in shining armor, not to the intelligentsia, but to much of the rest of the people. Perhaps he was not the ideal hero. But he was certainly preferable to what they had been exposed to in the recent past. Television was of great importance, but even massive doses of television would have found it impossible to sell to the public the old Leonid Brezhnev or Konstantin Chernenko in the role of a savior. Whether the Putin breakthrough will have a lasting effect, whether it will manage to carry out the basic structural changes that the country needs to survive and be a success in the twenty-first century, remains to be seen.

We shall have to return to this issue when dealing with the prospects of Russia. Kissing the sturgeons and the sleeping tigress may strengthen for a while the mood of optimism in the country; it may induce a feeling that Russia is no longer a weak country surrounded by strong and dangerous beasts, but a strong state surrounded by weaklings. But this optimistic mood will be of limited duration. It will not take Russia any nearer to a democratic order; it may not even be conducive to carrying out the economic reforms so badly needed. It will probably not help Russia to produce more children. If the demand for oil and gas had not grown and the price risen dramatically, Putin would have been a dismal failure. But he was lucky, and given the unfortunate history of the country and the mood of the people, Russia simply was not ready for someone like Alexander Yakovlev or anyone leading it toward an order that was not authoritarian.

The terrorist attacks in the Caucasus and by Chechens in 2003–04 tested the Putin regime. The gravest setbacks were the assassination of Akhmad Kadyrov, Russia's partner as the Chechen president, in May 2004, and the Beslan siege, when 330 people, mostly children, were killed in North Ossetia, in another botched rescue operation. However, after many more terrorist attacks, Moscow succeeded in imposing its rule on the Northern Caucasus, with the younger Kadyrov succeeding his father. But a high price had to be paid not only by way of financial subsidies; the northern Caucasus largely lost its Russian character and became an Islamic enclave.

In 2004, Putin was elected president for the second time. On the home front, the assets of Yukos, a giant oil company, were seized. Its owner, Mikhail Khodorkovsky, was arrested in 2003 and sentenced to nine years for tax evasion and other crimes. The sentence was extended in a second trial; he was released only after considerable lobbying in 2013. Khodorkovsky had failed to understand the changed balance of power in Russia, arguing publicly and contradicting the president. He had been one of the richest people in the world; according to estimates, after leaving prison and the gulag, he was still left with a fortune on the order of up to $200 million.

The years 2006–07 witnessed tensions with Russia's neighbors such as Ukraine, Georgia, and the Baltic countries. Dmitry Medvedev became president in 2008, with Putin as prime minister—the beginning of a tandem arrangement that enabled Putin to play a leading role in Russian politics well beyond the two-term presidency stipulated by law. Also in 2008, Russia went to war with Georgia for a few days, resulting in the loss of South Ossetia and Abkhazia, which became "independent."

There was a limited thaw in relations in 2009 with the United States, but it did not last long. Relations with European countries and Russia's neighbors did not improve, and there was a slow but systematic curtailment of freedoms, of civil and political rights on the domestic front. The state took over or brought pressure on the media, and Putin's victory in the elections for presidency with 63 percent of the vote for him in March 2012 did not therefore come as a great surprise. Medvedev again served as prime minister. Some Western commentators had believed that Medvedev presented a moderate alternative to Putin in both domestic and foreign policies, but this assumption proved to be mistaken. He had been chosen precisely because he was not pursuing a policy markedly different from Putin's, nor did he have apparent ambitions to present an alternative.

During Putin's third presidency, there was a considerable hardening in Russian domestic and foreign policies (such as the incorporation of Crimea in 2014). Demonstrations by members of the new middle class and the intelligentsia against "thieves and crooks" created the mistaken impression of the emergence of a strong opposition, but this was a misreading of the situation. Support for Putin's nationalist policy resulted in approval rates that were higher than ever. His aggressive anti-Western line strengthened his position at home. As a commentator put it: As long as the price of oil and gas was high, the government was not in serious danger.

The style of the government was autocratic, though officially the term "vertical" was used. It meant that orders were given from above and not to be questioned, let alone contradicted. This ensured that no time was wasted in discussion, but it did not ensure effective government. Promises were made to combat corruption, the plague that has affected Russia since time immemorial.

Various social programs were announced. But in reality, little (if anything) was achieved in the fight against corruption, although occasional use was made of charges of corruption to defeat or at least weaken political enemies. Certain social programs were not carried out or achieved only in part, which led to open complaints on the part of Putin.

Putin had three chiefs of staff during most of this time. The second, Vladislav Surkov, who held this position from 2004 to 2011, was the most talented by far. Surkov began to work for Putin in a lower capacity in 2000. A Chechen from his father's side, he had grown up in an entirely Russian surrounding. He was the man of ideas, complementing Putin, whose interest in the subject was limited to certain basic attitudes such as patriotism/nationalism. To a large extent, he provided the ideology of the regime, including the idea of limited democracy (sovereign—or managed—democracy). According to insider reports, Putin kept him always at a distance, since Surkov came from the world of business (or public relations, to be precise) and had no organs background.

Surkov also seems to have been slightly more liberal than others in this group, not too enthusiastic about Putin's harder, more dictatorial line after 2010. At the time of the mass protests in 2012, he went on record as saying that "the protesters included some of the best people in our country," which cannot have pleased the conservative majority in the leadership. He was less successful trying to establish a youth organization of the ruling party called Nashi (Ours), a job that may have been imposed on him. However, even after his dismissal he continued to work in various capacities and special assignments for the Kremlin. The record shows that Putin was a believer in rotation of this kind, not to leave officials for too long in their job, but not to drop them altogether unless they had been disloyal. He realized the danger of creating a growing group of disgruntled people.

Surkov was too clever, did not hide it, and was therefore somewhat suspect to the bureaucrats who constituted the great majority in the top echelons of the Kremlin. He could make use of Alexander Dugin (with whom he later quarreled) as well as with Gleb Pavlovsky, an erstwhile dissident who had made his peace with the "organs." But in the end, he seems to have had too many ideas for his boss.

Surkov was preceded by Alexander Voloshin, who later became head of Norilsk Nickel, one of Russia's leading corporations. Surkov's successor was Sergei Ivanov, one of Putin's KGB former colleagues who had also acted as a deputy minister of defense. Putin apparently thought him less erratic.

Putinism

What is Putinism? A great amount of mental energy has been devoted to finding an accurate definition, as so often happens when a new regime appears. But it has not been a very successful enterprise: Putinism is state capitalism, a liberal economic policy, but also a great amount of state intervention—almost total interference when important issues are concerned. It is an autocracy, but this is nothing new in Russian history and is almost mitigated by inefficiency and corruption. There is a parliament, but the opposition parties are not really in opposition. There is a free press, but the freedom is limited to small newspapers and the criticism must not go too far. There is a constitution, but it is not the best guide for the realities of contemporary Russia. (There was a Stalinist constitution in 1935, allegedly the most democratic in the world, but it had nothing to do with the practice of Stalinism.) It became a matter of sad irony and many jokes. Historians know that each system especially each extreme political system, is different and often unique. The quest for a Russian new political doctrine is particularly unique because there were few transitions from Communism and each was different, be it in China, Vietnam, or Eastern Europe.

Many close observers of the Russian scene believe there is no great demand at present for a new ideology and very little interest in the subject. If people quarrel, it is about finances—about their income, their investments and profits, and how best to improve their interests—not about ideological questions or dialectical materialism.

This is not to say that those who run the country care only about their investments. The fact that they have become billionaires does not disqualify them from acting as patriots and desiring to live in a powerful country that is a major player in world politics. Patriotism may be modified but does not necessarily disappear with wealth and a high income. To paraphrase Karl Marx, the financial infrastructure may still have an impact on the ideological superstructure and the policy pursued. The new nobility has a vested interest in maintaining the status quo, and patriotism can be quite useful in this context.

As indicated by Andranik Migranyan, a spokesman of the new regime, they want strong state power, not chaos. Under Putin, the state has regained its traditional function, recovered its effectiveness over its own resources, and become the largest corporation responsible for establishing the rules of the game. It may be an autocratic regime, but it needs the assent of its citizens.

There might be no elaborate Putinist ideology, but there is a document that was prepared by a think tank established by German Gref in 1999, just prior to Gref's appointment as minister for economic development. Approved by Putin, it constituted a platform for Putin's election campaign and has been quoted since on various occasions. It opened by saying that Russia is passing through the greatest crisis in its history and that all its resources, political, economic, and moral, have to be enlisted so that a united country will be able to overcome it. The country needs a new feeling of mission, a new Russian idea. This new Russian idea should be the basis of the state policy—of *gosudarstvenost* and of solidarity.

The country did not become Fascist, even though it moved in that direction. There is a parliament and several political parties, but they constitute a loyal opposition, voting with the government on all important issues. There was a parliament, it should be recalled, also in Germany after 1933 and also in most Communist countries. Jean-Jacques Rousseau argued that democracy is possible even in the absence of opposition parties, but not many students of politics would agree with him.

There is also a free press, as long as the writers do not go too far criticizing the authorities, and the newspapers (or television stations) reach only a small audience. If opposition newspapers or radio or TV stations become too influential, they are closed down or their ownership changes hands. In this way, a façade of democracy is maintained.

The most important component in the new ideology is nationalism accompanied by anti-Westernism. The origins of this intense anti-Westernism are not entirely clear; anti-Americanism did not exist before the Cold War to any significant degree. But from an eminently practical perspective, it has to do with the necessity of the FSB, the successor organization to the KGB, to justify its existence, budget, and policy. For unless Russia is protected against its dangerous, powerful, and devious enemies, the country will be destroyed again. Hence the need to maintain this enormous and costly security apparatus headed by the new nobility of the country. These in briefest outline are the basic tenets of belief in the thinking of this new class.

What of the Putin cult? It is not really a permanent feature in Russian history—after all, no czarist minister ever became the object of such adulation. A vodka was named Putin, as were a milkshake, a lollypop, ice cream, a brand of kebab, and a frost-resistant tomato. Perhaps he had asked for it with his bare-chested adventures in Siberia and Tuva. Perhaps it happened because he was looking so much younger and moving faster than Brezhnev and his immediate successors. The country obviously needed such a person. In the city of Yaroslavl not far from Moscow, a group of women had to be detained in a psychiatric clinic because of their uncontrollable passion for the man in white overalls (so as to resemble a bird) flying in a hang glider with the cranes in Siberia. It would not have happened to Stalin, Khrushchev, or Brezhnev.

Who will succeed Putin one day? Half a dozen names have been mentioned. Obviously the successor will have to belong to the new "nobility." He will have to be capable but not too much so in order to avoid outshining his predecessor. He will have to be considered loyal to the leader who appointed him and trusted to pursue his policy. Among those mentioned, Sergei Shoigu is perhaps the most popular. He is not an ethnic Russian (but neither was Stalin), and his religious background is Buddhist, but he is believed to be a hawk in foreign politics. Dmitry Medvedev has served as a stand-in for Putin in the past; he is not believed to be a very forceful leader, but this circumstance could work in his favor inasmuch as he will not be suspected or feared. Others mentioned in this context include Sergey Sobyanin, the Moscow mayor. However, if Putin should postpone his retirement by years, a younger candidate may emerge with greater chances than any of those mentioned.

5 | STALIN AND THE FALL OF THE BYZANTINE EMPIRE

Public Opinion Poll: Russia, 2013. Statement: Stalin was a wise leader who brought the Soviet Union to might and prosperity.

Completely Agree	14.8%
Mostly Agree	32.0%

Great Historical Figures, 2012:

Lenin	37%
Marx	4%
Peter the Great	37%
Pushkin	29%
Stalin	49%

MORE THAN SIXTY YEARS AFTER STALIN'S DEATH, RUSSIA HAS YET TO come to terms with his legacy. At the time of the Twentieth Party Congress with Nikita Khrushchev's famous speech, many thought that this stage had been reached or would be very soon. But far from it: There now is a *Stalin Encyclopedia* (Moscow: Eksmo, 2006) that tells us there is no conclusive proof that Khrushchev killed him, together with Lavrentiy Beria or alone or with about any member of the Politburo or his family except perhaps Vyacheslav Molotov. Poor man, whatever his gigantic achievements, he seems to have been surrounded by enemies and traitors. Far from blaming him for engaging in too many purges, we should be sorry that "the father of the people" had not been more watchful, that he was not able to evade those who succeeded in killing him before he had carried out the great reforms he still had in mind.

But why should these issues matter now, more than sixty years after his death? The Soviet Union of which Stalin was the great leader does not exist anymore, nor does the Communist Party of which he was for so many years the general secretary. Yet the debate continues. Stalin the great purger has been purged—and reinstated. And the process of reinstatement continues, with no end in sight. It continues because a great leader shapes to a decisive degree the character of the country, and until this continuity is broken, the debate is bound to continue.

WITH the possible exception of Hitler, it is difficult to think of a political leader of a major country in modern times who was less suited for such a mission. Stalin was unattractive; he had neither charm nor charisma, was not particularly intelligent or distinguished by great foresight. Most of the great endeavors in which he engaged failed, some in his lifetime, others after his death. Those that succeeded owed their outcome to the competence of others. Yet this man was characterized as follows in a private letter that was not expected to be read by anyone else:

> Stalin appears to be the greatest human being of our era. We do not find in the history of mankind a similar example of the greatness of one person, of depth of popularity, of reverence and love. We ought to be proud that we are his contemporaries and his collaborators, however minute our part in his actions. How often do we forget—and this goes particularly for the young generation—that we breathe the same air he does—that we live under the same skies. How often do people shout "Dear beloved Stalin"—and then they turn to their own affairs and behave meanly at work or in their relations with others. Coexistence with Stalin demands from

> his contemporaries boundless purity and devotion, belief and will, moral and social heroism.

This was written on the occasion of Stalin's seventieth birthday in 1949 by a leading composer of popular music. One of his songs, which carried the refrain "There is no other country in the world in which people breathe so freely," was for many years the signature tune of Radio Moscow. The composer who wrote these lines was bound to know that in virtually every family of his acquaintance, someone had been "repressed," to use the euphemism of later years, that the person about whom he wrote was one of the greatest mass murderers in modern history and one of the greatest liars. Yet he referred to "boundless purity" and "moral and social heroism."

Stalinism has been analyzed against the background of the general zeitgeist, the great enthusiasm, the backwardness of the country, the naïveté of the enthusiasts, the dangers luring from outside, and so on. But once all allowances have been made, how to explain the cult after the truth about Stalin had become known—in small part after the Khrushchev thaw; in far greater detail following glasnost, when impeccable witnesses such as historian Dmitri Volkogonov had the opportunity to research Stalin and his period in great detail; after biographical and autobiographical accounts were published, along with novels, movies, and documentaries about the Stalin period? Why is it still so difficult, often impossible, to speak the truth about Stalin?

Memorial, a historical and educational society, was founded in January 1989. It collected source material on the victims of Stalinism. Owing to its initiative, the Law on Rehabilitation was passed in 1991. However, much of the financial support came from outside Russia.

There was and is by no means unanimity in this respect. Stalinism had its ideological defenders, and there were many who benefited from Stalinist policies. Originally, support for Stalin came from Communist hard-liners, but within a few years they were joined by circles and individuals—mainly Russian nationalists—who had not been among Stalin's early defenders. As critics of Marxism-Leninism, they had been among Stalin's enemies. But as time passed, their perspective changed radically. Under Stalin, the Soviet Union gradually became a superpower, which was a source of great pride to Russian patriots. With the collapse of the Soviet Union, the status of Russia in the world diminished. This was what ultimately counted. Marxist-Leninist doctrine had been a transient phenomenon, and "proletarian internationalism" had been quickly discarded and forgotten, but superpower status had been a matter of enormous pride and its loss a tragedy—certainly in the eyes of Russian nationalists. For them, the great challenge and mission was to regain such status. True, Stalin had not been an ethnic Russian, but he had become an honorary Russian who had identified with them and had done all he could to enhance their cause.

Few Russian nationalists would identify with every one of Stalin's actions, but the good things (they believed) he did outweighed by far his failures and mistakes. In the circumstances, it is historically wrong to emphasize Stalin's failures. He is an inalienable part of Russian history.

What were Stalin's great achievements? Above all, of course, that under his rule the country greatly expanded and became a superpower. He built a powerful, modern industry and made agriculture efficient. Owing to his wise and efficient leadership, the Nazi invasion was defeated. Owing to his iron fist, the many plots against the Soviet Union came to nothing.

Certain of Stalin's achievements are no longer mentioned—for instance, that owing to him as much as to Lenin, the great October Revolution was victorious; or that owing to his assistance to Trotsky, the Reds prevailed in the civil war. Most Russians believe they would have been better off without revolution and civil war.

What of the other achievements? As for the expansion of Russia, czarist Russia was more successful in this respect. The czarist empire included Finland and most of Poland; the Soviet Union no longer did. The great strides in industry and agriculture? During Stalin's rule and for many years after, the Soviet Union was lagging behind the developed countries. The price in suffering was tremendous for whatever progress was made. Stalin was a disastrous strategist in the beginning of World War II. He ignored numerous warnings about the Nazi attack, and as a result, the number of Soviet soldiers killed and taken prisoner was enormous. If the Soviet Union was successful later in the war, it was mainly because Stalin interfered less with his marshals and generals. The Soviet Union defeated Nazi Germany, as Russia defeated Napoleon. But the czar still did not become the greatest military leader of all time. The price that had to be paid for all of Stalin's achievements was staggering—with regard to the number of people killed and sent to the gulag. The political system that came into being was a brutal dictatorship based on primitive, mendacious propaganda and repression as well as an unprecedented cult of the leader often bordering on the ridiculous—Stalin as the greatest genius ever born, the greatest saint, as well as the greatest hero.

One example among millions is an article about Stalin commenting on a picture by Fyodor Shurpin, which was awarded the state Stalin prize in the late 1940s. The painting depicts Stalin on a bright, early morning walking in the vast collective farm fields with high voltage power transmission lines in the distance. He is wearing a white tunic with his raincoat over his arm. His exalted face and his whole figure are lit with the golden rays of springtime, and his whole figure is lit with the golden rays of sun. One recollects verses that the people's poet Dzambul wrote on Stalin:

> Oh Stalin, the sunshine of springtime is you. He walks confidentially towards the new dawn. The image of Comrade Stalin is the triumphant march of Communism, the symbol of courage, the symbol of Communism, the symbol of the Soviet people's glory, calling for new heroic exploits for the benefit *of* our great motherland, in this image are immortalized the features of a wise, majestic, and at the same time amazingly modest and unpretentious man who is our beloved leader . . .

From the records it is known that Stalin visited a village once in his life and this was before collectivization.

This, then, was the spirit and the style of the time. It was this style that made Mikhail Prishvin note in his diary that "Pravda is the worst liar the world has ever known." Prishvin was not a political scientist or even particularly interested in politics. He was a beloved author of children's books, but he knew the difference between truth and lies. And he knew that *Pravda* was his master's voice.

Ultimately, the house Stalin built did not last; it came crashing down after his death. It is said in his defense that this was not his fault but the responsibility of his incapable and traitorous successors. However, these successors were chosen and trained by him. Whichever way one looks at it, Stalin cannot escape responsibility.

After the demise of the Soviet Union, the restart of the Stalin cult began in earnest with articles and books by Yuri Zhukov in *Komsomolskaya Pravda* and Vadim Kozhinov in *Nash Sovremennik* and *Molodaya Gvardiya,* journals of the "Russian party" that had enjoyed a certain amount of freedom even during the 1980s, although Yuri Andropov as head of the KGB had taken a dim view of their opinions.

According to Kozhinov, Stalin was really a Russian nationalist, even though he regarded himself as a faithful Marxist-Leninist. However, at the same time Stalinism was not a specific Russian phenomenon, "powerful global forces transformed Stalin into an omnipotent leader." In other words, foreigners were responsible for the cult. Some of the Russian Right went further: Stalin's aim had been to purge the party of the "internationalists," and this was all to the good. And last, there were the protagonists of the anti-Semitic explanation. According to them, Stalin was merely a puppet in the hands of the Trotskys and Kaganoviches.

During the 1990s the defense of Stalin continued, albeit in a lower key, but it went into higher gear after the turn of the twenty-first century. The new master in the Kremlin was of the opinion that the "demonization of Stalin" had gone too far. Statues of Stalin were erected again in various cities. With some exceptions, books about the period of repression were not to be published. The main exception was Solzhenitsyn, whose bona fides as a Russian nationalist could hardly be doubted. During an interview, Putin asked, "What is the essential difference between Cromwell and Stalin? Can you tell me? No difference . . ." But Putin should have known that there were certain differences. True, what Cromwell did in Ireland had been defined as genocide by some historians.

But it did happen a few centuries earlier, at a time when humanitarian standards were not those of the twentieth century. And even if one ignored human lives and rights, there was that small matter of loyalty, of which Putin has reportedly always been a leading proponent—loyalty for instance toward one's colleagues. There was a public discussion whether Stalin should be honored at the Kursky metro station in Moscow. At the same time, opinion polls were showing that almost half of the population took a positive view of Stalin and his policies.

True, on one or two occasions Putin said that Stalin (and his whole era) was controversial, that not all his deeds were admirable. After all, Stalin had given orders to murder twenty thousand of Putin's colleagues from the NKVD/KGB, the famous sword and shield. Did this count for nothing? And Medvedev went on to mention totalitarianism and a closed society, implying that at least some of the policies of the time were no longer desirable. But generally speaking, the impression was gained that each year anti-anti-Stalinism became louder, more pronounced, and more official. At a history teachers' conference in June 2007, Putin announced the preparation of a textbook that according to reports was to present Stalin as a cruel but successful leader acting rationally; terror was an instrument of development, and the aim had been to instill in young people a feeling of pride in their homeland.

A little later, in July 2009, it was announced by the Ministry of Education that Solzhenitsyn's *Gulag Archipelago* would become required reading for Russian high school students. However, teachers were free to choose from a list of some forty books covering the Stalin period.

According to a variety of polls, there was a growing opinion that the debates about Stalin and his historical role were of interest mainly to intellectuals and historians, not to the public at large. However, as far as publications were concerned, there was a clear majority of the anti-anti-Stalin school of thought. As far as the government was concerned, the main assignment was to promote a sense of pride in one's country, and for this reason a one-sided anti-Stalin line would not do.

The impression was created that during the Putin period there was a steady process of re-Stalinization. A stream of books claimed that Stalin's purges and many of his so-called excesses had been justified, that most political leaders of the time had betrayed Stalin, and that but for Stalin's energetic, decisive actions just before and during World War II, the Soviet Union would have been defeated.

Some argued that the so-called purges (the mass arrests and executions) had in fact been instigated and carried out not by Stalin, but by his enemies. The anti-Semites among these writers claimed that it was the work of the Jews. Once the Jews had been removed from the NKVD/KGB, the purges ceased.

Stalin had been a paranoiac, his paranoia was infectious, and the aim of this new literature was to show that his fantasies had been justified. He was convinced that those around him in the Politburo and the security apparatus were at best simple-minded, trusting, and naïve people unaware of the fact that the world was full of enemies and that without a leader like him, the country would be lost. He was irreplaceable. This paranoia reached its limit during the last year or two of his life with the "doctors' plot," when he claimed that the physicians treating the leading politicians and generals had tried systematically to kill their patients; apparently, no one in the Kremlin from Andrei Zhdanov and Alexander Shcherbakov onward had died of natural causes. Most of the doctors happened to be Jewish, and Stalin apparently planned to arrest all or most Jews in Russia and deport them to some faraway place in the Soviet Union.

The general tendency of this new wave in apologetic literature was to justify whatever Stalin did. Some of the authors were professional naysayers who doubted or opposed anything that had been stated by others. Others, professional or semiprofessional historians, tried to provide more sophisticated theories to justify Stalin's mass murders.

It made a great deal of difference whether these books were the private fantasies of sensationalist writers intending to shock their readers, whether they were forgers or confabulators or genuinely convinced that their fantasies were correct, or whether they were true Stalinist believers out to make their fantasies the official party line in the years to come.

All these various motives could be found among the Stalin apologists. It is not surprising that there should be such apologists; throughout history, the most far-fetched, unlikely statements and theories have found their believers. And the more emotional or political the motives, the greater the temptation to to swim against the current.

The decisive issue was whether the authorities would accept these findings as the basis of a new party line, but there was no clear answer; the authorities made it clear where their sympathies lay, but they still could not bring themselves to sanction the Stalinist version.

As time passes, the importance of the Stalin issue is bound to decline. Even now the issue is of little importance to the younger generation. Nevertheless, it remains a matter of concern, for Stalin is indeed part of Russia's history, and if its rulers believe that the truth about this part of the history of their country cannot be revealed because it would have a detrimental effect on patriotic education—if, in other words, pride overrules truth—this raises troubling questions about the character of such a society. The history of all nations, especially its beginnings, is shrouded in myth, but there is a difference between the question of whether Romulus and Remus ever existed and consciously opting to cover up the crimes of a particularly evil dictator and the society he created. What is one to make of a people who find it impossible to see the difference between truth and falsehood, between a monster and a saint?

The Fall of an Empire

Stalinism is one of the issues bedeviling the emergence of a new doctrine of Russian society. It raises the question of truthfulness in history in general and what kind of heritage the new Russia would like to emphasize and base itself upon. Another widely discussed issue has been Byzantium, in particular the reasons for the fall of the empire.

Why this question should be of such importance is not immediately clear. According to the Eurasian nationalist school of thought, the Byzantine heritage had much less of an impact on Russia than the Mongols and Tatars. Nevertheless, empires do not last forever, so it becomes a matter of interest to explore both why Byzantium lasted as long as it did and what caused its downfall.

In January 2008, Russia's main TV channel aired a documentary entitled *Gibel Imperii* (*The Fall of the Empire*), produced by Archimandrite

Tikhon (Shevkunov). Born in Moscow in 1958, Tikhon serves as head of the Sretensky Monastery, an Orthodox religious seminary in Moscow. He has been reported to serve also as Putin's spiritual adviser but refused to answer questions concerning this in interviews.

Father Tikhon originally trained as a filmmaker and graduated from the leading institute in the field. As for the circumstances of his conversion and becoming a monk, it says in his autobiography that he belonged to a group of students who were dissatisfied with the intellectual poverty and lack of attraction of Communist ideology and engaged in spiritualist experiments with a Ouija board. The group to which he belonged tried to converse in one of its sessions with Nikolai Gogol, the famous Russian writer. Gogol (or his ghost) duly appeared, angrily upbraided the students, and told them to swallow poison as soon as feasible. Frightened, the students consulted a priest the following day, who told them that they had obviously been victims of some tricksters—if they were truly interested in religion, they should study it seriously. This Tikhon did, with creditable results.

The documentary starts with a paean on Byzantium. It stretched from Gibraltar to the Euphrates and lasted longer than any other empire. Its jurisprudence was monumental; its engineering and architecture were unrivaled; its financial system was superb. Its capital city's wealth was incalculable, while its beauty and elegance amazed the European barbarians who happened to visit it. All this at a time when crude, ignorant, and primitive Scandinavians, English, French, and Germans engaged in one thing only—robbing and stealing. On the basis of robbing and looting the treasures of Constantinople, European banks began to spring up and the monstrous modern lending system was established—the famous capitalist system with its inevitable lust for profit. The first significant Jewish capital was the result of speculation in Byzantine relics. The barbaric West became the civilized West only after having taken over, stolen, destroyed, and swallowed up the Byzantine Empire.

But this was only the beginning. Byzantium gave up control over its trade and finances to its foreign "friends" from the West. The West subsequently lured Byzantium to join all kinds of Western unified trade organizations. Byzantine capital was flowing to the West, and Byzantine traders became bankrupt or dependent on the West. By the time the empire realized what was happening, it was too late to do anything.

Sixty years later, Byzantium attempted to recover its lost glory, but to no avail. The emperor who strove to restore power (Andronikos) was brutally murdered, and Byzantium became "the evil empire." As time went by, this image would continually be pulled out for use from Western ideological arsenals. Evil contact with the West brought to Byzantium oligarchs and corruption. Cultural contacts generated a Western fifth column. Young people went abroad to study, with predictable consequences.

All this unfolded at the beginning of the epoch historians call the Renaissance, which the author regards as an unmitigated evil. The first to give in to these foreign influences was the intelligentsia, "the worldwide creation of a nationalistic, Hellenist, Greek, pagan ideal." Thus the story continues to the bitter end: "The elite sacrificed higher ideals for the sake of practical advantages. The soul collapsed in a great nation. It had given the world grandiose examples of flights of spirit but now reigned in that nation unbridled cynicism and squabbles."

Describing the final death agony of Byzantium, the narrator concludes: "The vengeful hatred of the West towards Byzantium and its heirs continues to this day. Without understanding this shocking but undoubted fact, we risk not understanding not only the history of long-gone days, but also the history of the twentieth and even the twenty-first century."

This documentary was repeatedly shown on the first channel of Russian television, and it was widely discussed for about three months. The judgment of most, but by no means all, historians was negative; both sides agreed that the documentary was really about contemporary Russia, not Byzantium. Political and literary critics were also divided; a majority disagreed with Father Tikhon's conclusions.

The screening of a documentary of this kind on Russia's main TV channel shows that a significant part of Russian public opinion did indeed believe not just that the West was deeply hostile to Russia and everything it stood for, but that such hostility was so deeply rooted that nothing Russia could do would possibly affect it. The aim of the West, therefore, was bound to be the destruction of Russia, and it would only wait for an opportunity to do away with the eternal enemy. If this was the case, was it not the duty of Russia's leaders to take care that such a situation should never arise?

The production of a documentary of historical interest by a filmmaker/monk, however well connected, was not the only indication of a prevailing sentiment. There have been similar endeavors on various levels of sophistication. One other worth mentioning is Mikhail Yuriev's bestselling novel *Tretya Imperia* (*Third Empire*).

This is a massive (620 pages) fantasy written by a leading businessman who was also a member of the Duma. It deals with the visit to Russia by a young Brazilian sociologist at some not very distant future date. By that time Russia has swallowed Europe, China, and more or less the rest of the world. After it had been clarified that American Special Forces had been responsible for all terrorist attacks inside Russia, the Kremlin retaliated in Chicago and Ohio; there were twenty-five hundred victims in Chicago, more in Ohio.

But this was not all: Following some warnings, Russia dispatched several nuclear missiles to the Nevada, Utah, and New Mexico deserts; for humanitarian reasons, these little-populated areas had been chosen. America had to pay $1 trillion in compensation for holding on to Alaska. Even before, in 2014, Russia had left all international organizations and ended all obligations under international treaties. Inside Russia, Ukraine had ceased to exist, for the Ukrainians had all become Russians. The parliament had been abolished because it was no longer needed. The country was ruled by an emperor.

It could be argued that fantasies of this kind are not worth serious discussion. Father Tikhon's documentary, for instance, was not endorsed by the Moscow patriarch, and other highly ranking church dignitaries announced that Tikhon's views did not express the opinions of the Orthodox Church. There have been in recent years strange occurences among senior church dignitaries. One of them, Vyacheslav Polosin who had been head of the Duma committee in charge of religious affairs, converted to Islam and has since then devoted much of his energy to proving that the Rothschilds and George Soros had instigated the Arab Spring, which in his view was a very negative phenomenon. Another leading dignitary went public with the allegation that among the church leadership was a very powerful lobby trying to prevent anti-gay legislation. (If true, the lobby was singularly ineffective.)

Given the troubling scenarios conjured up in *Third Empire*, one would have expected the author to build a deep underground shelter in his house far from the center of Moscow or to retire to some South Sea island. Instead, Yuriev moved to the United States, arguing that business opportunities are better there. Of course, this could be the case, but it raises questions concerning the sanity of writers and publishers in the Russian capital as well as the genuineness and depth of their patriotism. Why take seriously a television documentary by a mere archimandrite—not a very high rank in the church hierarchy? After all, Mr. Putin is known for his pragmatism; neither he nor his colleagues would be swayed in their political decisions by utopian or dystopian fantasies.

Such arguments may have sounded convincing in 2008 and 2007, when the two works in question were first offered to the public. Unfortunately, as time passes one feels slightly less certain in this respect.

6 | DEMOGRAPHY

ANY DISCUSSION, ANY SPECULATION, ABOUT RUSSIA'S FUTURE HAS TO begin with a focus on demography. And unless it is known, however roughly, how many human beings will live in the territory in ten, thirty, or fifty years from now, such a discussion will be meaningless, or it will lead not to one conclusion, but to several.

It is believed that in the eighteenth century, after the death of Peter the Great, some five million to six million people lived in what was then Russia. The first and only ("imperial") census took place in 1897; it took years to prepare, was undeniably thorough, and concluded that the number of people living then in the Russian Empire was 125 million (16 million in towns, the rest in the countryside).

According to Russian nationalists of the extreme variety, there would be six hundred million people living in Russia today were it not for the fact that since 1897 a series of major disasters—World Wars I and II, the civil war of 1918–19, and Communist rule (including starvation following the agricultural policy of collectivization, the Stalinist mass murders, and the gulag)—adversely affected population growth. The actual number today, they claim, is only 142 million.

But disasters cannot by themselves account for this decline: Consider, for instance, the declines in birthrate and the size of the population in the 1990s, a period that experienced no wars, civil wars, mass purges, or violent social upheavals.

Since our task in the present framework is to focus on the future of the country, not its past, it must be questioned whether in addition to a general population decline, the country's low population density—Russia's paltry 8.6 people per square kilometer offers a striking contrast to the European Union's 112 and the United Kingdom's 246—will jeopardize its ability to maintain its current territory, let alone recover the territories that were lost following the fall of the Soviet Union. It could be argued that the climatic conditions in northern Russia, Siberia, and the Far East are such that its population density will never be similar to that in Europe. On the other hand, global warming and technological development may bring about totally unforeseen changes in population growth.

Present projections by outside commentators vary considerably; while all agree that there has been an improvement from the 1990s, none is excessively optimistic about the future. According to the most recent Russian calculations on current trajectories, the country's population, absent immigration, is set to shrink by almost 20 percent from one generation to another. The survival rate for men is now sixty-five years; for women, seventy-six. This compares with seventy-seven years for men and eighty-two years for women in Germany. There is general agreement that alcoholism is the single most important factor accounting for the much shorter life span of men. Under Gorbachev, an effort was made to combat alcoholism, but it had no lasting effect. Commentators have noted that Sweden had a similar problem with alcoholism but managed to overcome it by the action of civil society. Why? Because it had a social state serving the population, a national state that defined itself in terms of the individual and his or her rights, and a legal state able to regulate life with the help of laws. Russia has been deficient in all three respects.

The United Nations Population Division projections suggest that depopulation in Russia will continue. The pool of Russian women entering their twenties will shrink rapidly over the next decade, a result of the baby crash in the 1990s. And at just 1.7 percent, Russia's current reproduction rate is woefully insufficient.

These negative figures will have immediate political consequences. Russian military forces will face a shortage of recruits, especially ethnic Russians. And Russia may experience a serious decline in the number of college graduates; in the 1990s, Russia still accounted for about 9 percent worldwide, but this will have dropped to 3 percent by 2030, according to projections. The fact that budget allocations for education have also decreased in recent years probably contributes to this trend.

Another moderately pessimistic view reaches the conclusion that Putin's natalist policies (encouraging Russian women of childbearing age to have more babies) may be partly responsible for the slight increase in birthrate and population in Russia. Nevertheless, it remains true that by 2040, the number of Russians aged twenty to twenty-nine will be half that of today. While the decline of Russia seems inevitable in the long run, it may take longer than frequently assumed.

A question that has been discussed for some time is whether pronatalist policies can reverse depopulation, specifically in Russia. The historical evidence is not clear: Natalist policies were tried in Russia in the 1930s (when there was a sudden, substantial fall in the birthrate), and again under Stalin after the war, it has been tried in Nazi Germany but also more recently in many European countries especially in Scandinavia following the research and initiative of Gunnar and Alva Myrdal.

Such policies can take various forms such as making abortion difficult. In Nazi Germany in 1944 it became a crime of capital punishment. Earlier on in 1941 the production of condoms was stopped. Positive measures have been more frequent such as extending parental leave and financial incentives. Again, the Nazi example has been the most radical, but more in theory than in practice. Hitler and the other Nazi leaders believed that the place of the woman was at home, giving birth and taking care of children. But Nazi economic policies, especially rearmament and wartime exigencies took millions of women away from home to work—mainly in industry. The fact that women received signs of distinction (the "Mother Cross" starting with the third child) had little if any effect and the financial awards were minuscule.

Studying the Russian experience through investigations in 2013, Serafima Chirkova reached the conclusion that, in the short run, the changes in Russian family policy had a significant positive effect on the second birth: the probability of a family's having a second child increased by 2.2 percent on average. According to the 2007 family policy reforms, the "maternity capital" concept was introduced. There was a minimum benefit of 40 euros for the first child and 85 euros for the second child. The experience in Scandinavia was similar; in the Nordic countries provisions are also made for keeping the place of work for some considerable time after pregnancy—up to three years. In Russia maternity leave consists of twenty weeks, usually ten weeks during, and ten weeks after birth.

However, these conclusions apply for the time being to the short term only—and to the probability of having a second child. Whereas in Russia a higher birthrate is needed to prevent depopulation. In other words, natalist policies can slow the process of depopulation but not drastically reverse it.

If the depopulation of Russia has not been more extensive, it is the result of immigration, and this will probably be true in the future. Most of the history of immigration to Russia dates back to the eighteenth century when the empress Catherine (herself a German princess born in Szczecin) induced German settlers mainly from southwest Germany to settle in Russia; most of them became known as the Volga Germans. A first office dealing with migrants from Central Europe was established in 1763—it was probably the first of its kind in the world. The immigrants of recent years come from the Central Asian republics once part of the Soviet Union and from the Caucasus. Their exact number is unknown, although they account for some 8 percent of the Russian GNP. According to the World Bank, some twelve million foreign workers are employed in Russia, only about one million legally. If Russia were to deport many of them and to refrain from keeping its gates at least partly open in the future, this would be a heavy blow to the Russian economy and negatively affect the demographic structure. For this reason, Putin has opposed steps aimed at drastically reducing their number.

However, the presence of so many millions has caused friction in a country that, like many others, is not known for welcoming foreigners with open arms. "Russia for the Russians" is the slogan chanted by thousands of Muscovites, and this, despite economic needs, is also the policy of the government.

Putin has been dealing with the topic of "law-abiding migrants with desirable characteristics" in a number of articles and speeches—all of them in favor of assimilation with Russia. As he sees it, the multicultural project rejecting the notion of integration through assimilation has failed. Multiculturalism resulted in the formation of closed national and religious communities that not only refuse to assimilate, but do not even adapt. He expressed astonishment that neighborhoods and entire cities in the Western world where generations of immigrants are living on welfare do not even speak the language of the host country: "There can be just one outcome for such a social model—xenophobia on the part of the indigenous population which understandably seeks to protect its interests, jobs, and social benefits from the foreign competitors."

Putin said that historical Russia was neither an ethnic state nor an American melting pot, where everyone was one way or another an immigrant. Russia developed over centuries as a multiethnic state in which there was mutual adjustment, mutual understanding, and unification of people through families, friendship, and work, with hundreds of ethnicities living together on the same land. The core, the binding fabric for the Russian future, was the Russian people and the Russian culture that united them. There was a Russian cultural dominance flowing not only from ethnic Russians, but from all carriers of this identity regardless of nationality. This was the cultural code that should be nourished, strengthened, and protected—mainly through education. Putin also referred to the American (Western) cultural canon, the hundred books that should be read by every self-respecting student, and suggested a similar project for Russia:

> We need a national policy strategy based on civil patriotism. Any person living in our country should not forget their faith and ethnicity. But before anything else he must be a citizen of Russia and be proud. No one has the right to put ethnic and religious considerations above the state laws.

This in barest outline is Putin's vision of integration on which Russia's future is to be based; strong institutions are a precondition to that end. It is, as commentators have noted, a trumpet call not only for the dominance of Russian culture, but for patriotism and a strong state. At the same time, there have been warnings against chauvinism and other exaggerations.

Putin's observations about the shortcomings and difficulties of multiculturalism can hardly be denied; the successes of anti-immigrant movements in the United Kingdom, France, and other European countries in recent years provide clear evidence to this effect. Nor can there be any doubts with regard to the greatness of Russian culture. The difficulties arise once one moves from the realm of what might be desirable to realities. With all the respect and sympathy for Russian culture, ethnic and religious groups may prefer their own traditions, customs, culture, and way of life. In other words, they may accept assimilation only up to a certain point. They may prefer a commonwealth, a loose alliance of states, to the existence of one strong state as envisaged by Putin. Putin invokes pride, but not everything that happened in Russian history can instill pride within ethnic and nonethnic Russians alike. The experience of the Soviet Union over seventy years has not been positive. The moment the strong state disappeared, the Soviet Union fell apart. It can be endlessly discussed whether this was a good thing or bad, whether all the independent states that emerged are viable. In brief, certain interests and ambitions will have to be overruled by others; there will have to be coercion. And the question is how much of this is compatible with democratic norms. This emerges perhaps most clearly when considering the status and ambitions of Muslim minorities in Russia, to which we shall turn next.

Russian Islam

Islam is "Russia's fate"—thus predicted Alexey Malashenko, one of Russia's leading experts in the field. His pronouncement gained attention at a time when fighting was going on in the Caucasus. Fighting there still continues in some parts, and it probably will not cease entirely in the foreseeable future. But Russian Islam remains an issue of paramount importance.

The Russian encounter with Islam goes back many centuries; in certain parts of the country, it predates the meeting with Christianity. For a long time, much of Russia was under Tatar rule. But despite such coexistence, Muslims were largely regarded as alien in Russia. The Tatars over the years became familiar. They took care, after all, as superintendents of many houses in Moscow. And who would not be enchanted by Aida Garifullina (a native of Kazan), by her looks as much as her voice. A generation earlier, Muslim Magomayev (1942–2008) was one of the most popular tenors in the Soviet Union and Russia.

The Muslims in the middle Volga region, Kazan, and vicinity were a shining example of peaceful coexistence. Nor was it exactly a depressed region. Average income, especially from industries connected with oil and gas, provided a standard of living higher than that in many other parts of Russia except its capital. However, the Russian attitude toward Muslims from other parts of the country, especially the Caucasus, remained negative.

Inasmuch as foreign relations were concerned, the Muslim countries ceased to be of much interest after the disintegration of the Ottoman Empire. Muslim countries (Turkey, Iran, the Arab world) were not considered much of a threat, but also not much as potential allies against the West. Past experience after World War II had not been encouraging from Moscow's point of view. There was Pan-Turanism, and the Iranians too tried to gain a foothold in Central Asia, but they were not very successful and therefore not considered particularly dangerous. This changed somewhat when Russian security services became aware of the activities of radical preachers (usually called Wahhabi in Russia) from the Arab world. They were active above all in Central Asia and caused the rise of extremist (and terrorist) activities in Muslim communities. But such information barely reached the general public. A somewhat greater impact had a certain literature highlighting the growing importance of Islam in Europe and in Russia as a result of the demographic growth of these communities. One widely read novel by Elena Chudinova, *The Notre Dame de Paris Mosque*, describes France following a Muslim takeover; it starts with a public stoning at the Arc de Triomphe. In the field of nonfiction, a study such as *Islamizatsiya Rossii* (*The Islamization of Russia*, by Golubchikov and Mnatsakanyan [2005]) ought to be mentioned. It concludes with four scenarios, none of them very happy.

There are about twenty million Muslims in Russia. There is no exact figure because of the presence in Russia of millions of "guest workers," most of them illegal, from the Central Asian republics. Muslim communities in Russia are concentrated in three regions—the Caucasus, Moscow, and the middle Volga region. The Central Asian republics were overwhelmingly Muslim, but they seceded from Russia when the Soviet Union disintegrated.

The conquest of the Caucasus took many years and inspired two generations of Russian writers, from Alexander Pushkin and Mikhail Lermontov to Leo Tolstoy. Lermontov had called a fellow officer a *gorets* (Muslim highlander), which, considered an insult, led to a duel in which Lermontov was killed. Alexander Griboedov, one of the leading Russian writers of his day and a diplomat, was sent on a mission to Persia; he was killed by a fanatic mob in Tehran. The Slavophiles such as Aleksey Khomyakov wrote occasionally on Islam, but they were not really well informed, and much of the writing was speculation. Academic institutions for the study of Islam, centered in Kazan, came into being in the late nineteenth century.

Resistance against Russian rule continued on a local scale, but it was suppressed by the central authorities without much difficulty. Examples include the Central Asian rebellion of 1916, when about one-third of the Kyrgyz people fled to China, and the Basmachi campaign after the Bolshevik takeover, which lasted almost seven years. There was the widespread impression among Western observers in the 1930s that the Soviet government, whatever its other shortcomings, had succeeded in solving what was then known as "the national question." This proved to be a mistake; the Central Asian and Caucasian republics opted for independence when the Soviet Union disintegrated. They all seceded, even though some of them remained in various respects dependent on Russia. As for the smaller autonomous republics within Russia, they too would have preferred independence but were too small and poor to exist as viable bodies. Chechnya was subdued in two protracted wars, and an uneasy modus vivendi was achieved in Dagestan.

In Chechnya, the Kadyrov clan remained in power, but sharia replaced Russian laws, and the little country became one of the world's most repressive regions. The Russian government was willing to accept this as well as the exodus of most of the Russian population and far-reaching Islamization, provided Chechnya accepted Russian overlordship. The situation in Dagestan was similar except that there it did not turn into an all-out war. Violence became a permanent feature, albeit on a lower level. Despite Islamization, the ruling clans in both republics remained "traitors" as far as the opposition was concerned. However, militarily the opposition had been defeated and was no longer in a position to engage in major military or terrorist operations. In 2009, the Kremlin declared that counterterrorist operations on a major scale in Chechnya had ended; five years later, Moscow established a new Ministry for Caucasian Affairs.

It remains to be seen whether those representing Moscow's interests in Chechnya and Dagestan can be trusted. Their desire for greater freedom of action, if not full independence, remains undiminished. However, as long as the central government is strong, their chances of obtaining greater concessions from Moscow are small. If the hold of the central government should weaken, their loyalty cannot be taken for granted. Even at the present time, contacts between the local pro-Russian authorities in Dagestan (and to a lesser extent in Chechnya) and the more radical opposition have been reported. Moscow's man in Dagestan is Ramazan Abdulatipov, who followed a very hard aggressive line with some success. Even so, about fifty to sixty people are killed monthly in terrorist incidents.

It is impossible to say whether he will be successful in the long run—as usual in such conditions, much depends on the presence or absence of a few capable and loyal leaders and on the Kremlin's willingness to give substantial financial support to Dagestan. But at a time of economic stagnation, there is considerable resistance to providing such help, for it will mean cuts in other parts of the Russian budget.

How strong is the influence of the Islamists—the radical Muslims standing for secession and, if need be, violent struggle? According to certain information, it is far stronger in the Caucasus than in the other Muslim concentrations. But even there the evidence is so widely divergent as to be meaningless. It ranges from assertions that there are no radicals to claims that everyone is a radical. According to some elections in Dagestan, the Communists emerged as the leading party, which, if correct, probably had less to do with political/ideological issues than with the personality of the candidate standing for election (who likely belonged to an influential clan and picked the party as a platform that would give the most freedom of action).

The strongest Muslim trend in the Caucasus was Sufism for a long time, and in many regions it still is. Radical missions have been carried out by the Salafi movement rather than a political or religious party and by the Hizb ut-Tahrir (more in Central Asia than in the Caucasus). This is an organization founded in Arab Jerusalem in 1953, active in some parts of the world such as the United Kingdom, but hardly in existence in others. They demand the abolition of present-day borders between Muslim states and the establishment of a single entity—the caliphate. However, generally speaking, a considerable part of radical activity seems to depend on the character and activities of local clans.

The religious-political awakening of Islam (and of radical Islam) coincided with the growth of a radical nationalist mood among the Russian population. This, needless to say, was bound to lead to tensions. It had to do with a major influx of Muslim workers mainly from Central Asia and the Caucasus into Russian cities.

They have not been adequately housed and do not enjoy various other essential services. They are served by a very few mosques only; resentment against them being what it is, the present mayor of Moscow has declared that there will be no more mosques in his city. However, if they pray in the streets, they are accused of disturbing public order and interfering with public transport. At the same time, safety in the streets has been affected, and in many ways it is surprising that there have not been more riots. A paradoxical situation has arisen, considered highly undesirable from the government's point of view.

While the security services have worried about the subversive separatist activities among the migrants and the local police about maintaining law and order, the Foreign Ministry has been preoccupied with the negative impression created in the Muslim world about anti-Muslim sentiment (and activities) in Russian cities. Following the initiative of the then Russian foreign minister Yevgeny Primakov (an Arabist by training), a high-level conference took place to engage in damage control. The reputation of Russia in the Muslim world had already been low following the Afghan war and the two Chechen wars. The Foreign Ministry argued that if Islamophobia were to grow in Russia, it would be a fatal blow to the Russian reputation of tolerance and integrity. Their main worry, of course, was that Russia might miss political opportunities in the Muslim world. However, Russia was saved by the American intervention in Afghanistan. Once Russia had withdrawn from Afghanistan, it ceased to be an immediate target in the Muslim world.

Following the occupation of Crimea, the treatment of the Crimea Tatars became a matter of concern to Muslims in other parts of the country. They were exiled and ill treated under Stalin during and after World War II.

The fate and activities of Russian Muslims have been of little interest to the Muslim world, mainly because of their limited presence outside Russia. Though the haj (the annual pilgrimage to Mecca) has been encouraged in various ways, only relatively few Russian Muslims have made use of what is essentially a religious commandment. Russian Muslims are claiming that many more of them would like to go to Mecca but cannot do so because the number is limited to about twenty thousand by the Saudi authorities. (There have also been complaints among those going to Mecca that there are too many members of the security services keeping an eye on militant Islamists.) The Organization of Islamic Cooperation (formerly the Organization of the Islamic Conference) abstained on various occasions from blaming or criticizing Russia, and it always refused to accord membership to Ichkeria, the political organization of the Chechen rebels. Russian goodwill was more important than solidarity with the co-religionists in Russia.

During the 1990s, something akin to a government strategy vis-à-vis Russian Islam developed. On the whole, pragmatism rather than ideology prevailed. The Russian right wing and especially the Far Right would routinely remind their countrymen that the Muslim countries and especially the Arab states were their natural allies in the struggle against the West. Dmitry Rogozin, at that time head of the far-right Rodina party, even advocated for a while the idea originally suggested by the organization of Muslims from the Lower Volga that there should be a permanent Muslim deputy president of Russia. But the policy of appeasement strategy (sometimes reinforced by "anti-Zionist" arguments) inevitably collided with the anti-Muslim resentments of the Russian street and was therefore dropped. Nor were these leaders of the Far Right willing to give up the Caucasus or make similar far-reaching concessions in exchange for political support by the Muslim countries. For these and other reasons, there has been a long-dating suspicion of Russia in the Muslim world, just as in Russia there has always been the conviction that Russia had no allies that could be trusted except its armed forces. Representatives of Hamas and other Palestinian organizations visited Moscow on various occasions without any tangible results. The only benefit derived from these activities is that Muslim countries have refrained from open support for fellow Muslims inside Russia, much to the disappointment of Muslims inside Russia. One typical example was the relative lack of political support when the Crimea Tatars came under pressure following the Russian invasion in 2014.

The specific problems of the Muslim enclaves in Northern Caucasus, which, in addition to the ones mentioned, included Ingushetia with half a million inhabitants, should be mentioned. While a major crisis had been prevented and while terrorist attacks did not have a major effect, the danger to oil and gas pipelines leading from the Caspian basin to Europe continued to exist

Russian experts and policy makers seem to be fully aware of the threats facing them in the Caucasus and possibly also in other parts of the country. That Islamic separatism is regarded as a major threat emerges from textbooks used at the university of the security forces, whose authors have no sympathy for the regions that have adopted the sharia and an Islamist orientation. But at the same time, they have not suggested how to confront this challenge, except proposing that Russia should turn to the East rather than the West for inspiration and leadership.

Another example of the confusion prevailing in the field is the Geydar Dzhemal phenomenon. Dzhemal, a Moscow public figure in his late sixties, is a poet who has published extensively on psychiatry but also serves as a chairman of the Islamic Committee of Russia. Dzhemal is of mixed Russian and Azerbaijani parentage and advocated at different stages in his life Marxist-Islamism, anti-Semitism (Pamyat), and several other ideologies. According to his teaching, world politics ("mondialization") can be understood only against the background of the conflict between the two leading superelites (the one headed by the British aristocracy and the Washington American elite). The events on September 11 were a grandiose provocation of one superelite against the United States and the Islamic world. According to Dzhemal, Osama bin Laden and the Taliban were creatures of the CIA and of Zionism together with the KGB, tools leading to a superelite domination of the planet. Connoisseurs of conspiracy theories will recognize where these theories hail from: the influence of the early Alexander Dugin.

In fact, Dzhemal cooperated closely with Dugin during their Pamyat days. Dugin subsequently moved on to the more respectable fields of geopolitics and neo-Eurasianism, whereas Dzhemal remained involved in various Islamic committees. It is impossible to know whether this farrago of nonsensical supposition is genuinely believed by anyone, how much is entertainment or deliberate confusion mongering, or how much is destined more for export than local consumption. In any case, his theories are typical of the state of mind prevailing in these circles.

Since Russia is not strong enough to counteract American and European influence (this was written several years ago), the authors of one of the intelligence textbooks suggest an alliance of Russia, China, India, and Iran (called RIKI). The authors, otherwise not distinguished by a sense of humor, mention that they are aware of Rikki-Tikki-Tavi, the heroic mongoose in Kipling's *Jungle Book*. The countries mentioned behaved very well in the past and did not exploit the state of Russian weakness (in the 1990s) after the breakdown of the Soviet Union. (Walter Laqueur, *Harvest of a Decade: Disraelia and Other Essays*, 2011)

Tatarstan

While the tension in the Caucasus continued, great comfort was drawn from the fact that Tatarstan and Bashkortostan were quiet. The media reported that the local population had benefited from the oil and gas boom and that the hold of the traditional Islamic establishment there was strong. True, some radical preachers had arrived there from Saudi Arabia as well as Kuwait and Qatar, but the great majority of the population had no wish to live "in medieval conditions" such as preached by some hothead new clerics from abroad out of touch with local conditions.

The situation seemed under control until suddenly on July 19, 2012, an attempt was made to blow up the car of Ildus Faizov, the supreme mufti of the region. He escaped with injuries, while one of his assistants was killed. This led to detailed investigations and debates, and the picture that emerged was less comforting than the earlier reports. When members of the local parliament met a few weeks later, Artem Khokhorin, head of the local Ministry of Internal Affairs, made it known that for the last thirteen years there had been a virtual state of undeclared war in the region. During that period, Tatarstan had been systematically infiltrated by preachers from certain Arab countries. Some were foreigners, others were local people who had studied in Mecca and

Medina—in other words had been indoctrinated by Salafi teachings. Furthermore, the constitution of the congregation who came to the mosque on Fridays and holidays had changed: Half or more were newcomers from Central Asia who had been brainwashed by Salafis at the places where they had come from. The same had happened in other parts of Russia, such as the Stavropol region (where Muslims now constituted more than a quarter of the population), even in southern Ural and western Siberia, which according to some reports had become one of the main targets of the Salafists. The president of Bashkortostan (formerly known as Bashkiria), which had been relatively free of problems, now reported that religious fanaticism was becoming a political threat. The issue was not that the traditional leadership had been unaware of these trends; they had cultivated the radicals. It was that if the attempt to kill Faizov had succeeded, his successor would have been one of the leading Salafi preachers in the country.

Within a short time after the assassination attempt, Ramil Yunusov, head of Kazan's biggest mosque (the biggest mosque in Eastern Europe), left posthaste for London to improve his English-language skills (according to a spokesman). He has not returned since. While no one accused him of direct involvement in the attack, he had been the leading religious/ideological opponent of the mufti. Further, he had studied for several years in Medina, was considered a charismatic preacher, but at the same time was on good terms with the religious establishment. More generally speaking, the younger Saudi-trained preachers were more popular than the establishment clerics who had the support of the secular authorities and the Russian security services.

If the Kazan events had been an exception and of purely local character, they would not have attracted wider political attention. But they were not untypical. To again quote Alexey Malashenko: "In some previously docile parts of Russia, the Muslim population is becoming radical, even extremist. Even before the attempt to kill the mufti there were attacks, some of them successful, against preachers considered moderate, including al Tirqawi, a spiritual leader of the Tariqists (a Sufi sect): Some observers regard the present situation as the beginning of the Caucasization of the Volga region."

True, there is the occasional tendency to exaggerate Salafist influence; establishment preachers are inclined to denounce all their opponents, whatever their views, as Salafists. But there is no doubt that the problem of radical Islam has been spreading and becoming more acute. And it is no longer confined to a few concentrations but has spread to most places where Muslims live in Russia.

What could Russian authorities do to limit the influence of the extremists? They could switch their support from the traditionalists to the more popular (especially among those who have an influence on the younger generation). But it is doubtful whether these preachers would cooperate at a time when there has been a nationalist radicalization among Russian communities.

Furthermore, the danger of infection has grown from neighboring countries such as Kazakhstan. Kazakhstan has been much better off economically than the neighboring Muslim republics, but this has not prevented the spread of Islamic extremism and terrorism. In December 2012, the government of Kazakhstan announced for the first time that the caliphate army posed a threat to national security. This followed several suicide attacks in the republic.

Some of the terrorists hailed from the Caucasus, others had been trained in Afghanistan. However, the Kazakh police also established that there had been local terrorist training centers for attacks within the country. Since Kazakhstan under the Shanghai Cooperation Organization can count on Chinese and Russian help in such emergencies, the size of the present danger should perhaps not be overrated. On the other hand, hundreds of thousands of Kazakh "guest workers" and even more from the neighboring republics now live inside Russia. Radical influences among them will have an immediate effect.

Alarmist reports about Russia becoming a Muslim country within a generation or two are probably exaggerated. But no great political acumen is needed to understand that serious problems are likely to arise well before the Muslim community amounts to 51 percent of the population. Putin's population strategy and "Russia for the Russians" are policies that cannot be combined, and it remains doubtful whether Russia will be able to carry out a policy leading to the integration of the many millions of newcomers. Legislation in recent years does not give the autonomous republics a great deal of autonomy; on the contrary, it is now more limited than in the past.

Moreover, it is not only the "Russia for the Russians" crowd that makes life difficult for Putin. The Russian Orthodox Church likewise opposes what it regards as the official appeasement of Islam; it wants to preserve its old/new status as the state religion. On top of all this, the majority of public opinion is opposed to the official policy.

Russian foreign policy vis-à-vis Islam and Islamism has been undecided, trying to keep all options open. With America still looming as the great threat, Islamist antiactivities should have been welcomed without reservation, and very often they were. But with the American and NATO withdrawal from Afghanistan, that country is bound once again to become a Russian problem as a base for jihadist activities in Central Asia, for Russia is near and America far away. Still, Russian government strategy is dominated by the American shadow and the conviction that what helps the United States must be bad for Russia. It may take a long time for Russia to unlearn its obsession with the Western danger. It has been Russia's destiny to see dangers and enemies in the wrong places and overlook real ones. Such inclinations have deep roots and are unlikely to disappear soon.

Opposition

The post-Soviet governments had to face domestic resistance from the beginning. In the early days, this had mainly to do with changes in the constitution, particularly with the leading role of the Communist Party in the political life of the country. Later on, this specific obstacle had been cleared and the country had been democratized, at least as far as its laws were concerned.

With Putin's rise to power, a contrary trend asserted itself: The Russian people wanted stability and order more than freedom and democracy. Gradually, freedoms that had been achieved were again curtailed or ignored in practice. It was widely maintained that the Western forms of democracy were not suitable for Russia, certainly not in present conditions—after the breakdown of the old system and the general upheavals of the 1990s. This happened partly because of the difficulties of the transition from the communism period and the mistakes that were committed during these years. Left open was the question of whether any other form of democracy would suit Russia. The very terms "democracy" and "democratic" acquired a negative connotation.

With the curtailing of political freedoms, demonstrations ensued—and this led to further restrictions. The opposition manifested itself in protests against elections that (it was alleged) had been falsified. There were also peace marches and similar activities. In the beginning, these events were headed by dissidents of the late Soviet era, but gradually a new generation of protesters came to the fore, younger people such as Alexei Navalny and Sergei Udaltsov, the former gravitating more to the right, the latter to the left. But "left" and "right" were also changing their meaning and were no longer as important as they had once been. The demands of the Left had little to do with Marxism-Leninism, and their patriotism was at least as loud as that of the others. The main issues were now corruption and the absence of political freedom. Vladimir Ryzhkov, who had once been deputy prime minister, noted that for years no new political party had been recognized by the government and that this was typical in the absence of political freedom. Whereas the state party United Russia with its youth organization Nashi (Ours) had been given every advantage, they were in fact "crooks and scoundrels," according to a famous Navalny formula.

A charismatic young lawyer, Alexei Navalny defined himself as a nationalist democrat (or vice versa). He also appeared as a speaker at meetings of far-right organizations. It was generally assumed that he had only a few thousand faithful followers, so it came as a surprise that hundreds of thousands voted for him in the Moscow mayoralty elections in September 2013 against Sergey Sobyanin, who was Putin's candidate. Navalny had no financial backer, no powerful organization, but he still had his breakthrough as a blogger. How, then, to explain that Navalny and other such protesters have not succeeded against the official candidates?

As usual, there is more than one reason. Virtually all those active in Russian politics at the present time agree that change will not come as the result of elections. If an opposition candidate were to win, it is believed he would be arrested for something—embezzlement, rape, mass murder, a traffic offense, or not paying taxes. He could also be killed.

A second reason: Within the many splits among the opposition, there are countless little parties that seem unable to join forces for common action. Sergei Udaltsov is ideologically close to the Communists and acted as chief of staff of their leader. But in a recent interview, he said that he did not want to see that leader as the next president. His misgivings may well be valid.

Furthermore, Putin has solid backing from certain sections of the population, including retired people, state employees, the church, and the working class. Backing for the opposition comes mainly from the intelligentsia and sections of the middle class. The supporters of Navalny and Udaltsov may believe in the personal honesty of their favorites. However, Navalny's strong nationalism and Udaltsov's proximity to the Communists do not inspire confidence.

The Putin government has a virtual monopoly on the media. Censorship was officially abolished under Gorbachev in 1990, but self-censorship is strong indeed. All the major television channels belong to owners who can be relied upon not to broadcast material negative or critical of the government; only a few TV and radio stations such as Echo Moskvy and Dozhd are still independent. Inconvenient journalists have been threatened, physically attacked, and in some cases even killed.

Are the Russian media at present more or less free than in czarist days? There are certain interesting similarities: The writing of Karl Marx could be ordered and bought in Russia before 1917 in English and German but not in Russian. Today, news items may be published in the *Moscow Times* that will never appear in the Russian-language media. Books in Russia, as in the West, are no longer widely read, whereas most people receive their information from the newer media.

There is, however, one big (and undesirable) hole as far as the authorities are concerned—the Internet, from which many Russians get their information about events in Russia and abroad. For this reason, the government has been trying for some time to push through legislation that would make this impossible by establishing a "national Internet" such as exists in other authoritarian regimes. It could be argued that such an action would inevitably be interpreted as a move by the regime from authoritarian to totalitarian. For this reason, some nonauthoritarian countries retreated from taking such a measure, having considered the implications. Even short of censorship legislation, the Russian authorities have been able to shut down offending Web sites, and the head of VKontakte, Russia's largest social-networking site, was compelled in 2014 to leave the country. In these conditions, in the absence of freedom of information, the government and the state party have a virtual monopoly on information.

If United Russia, Putin's state party, was not a success, Putin's personal popularity remained consistently high. Following the Sochi Winter Olympic Games and the invasion of Crimea in 2014, it approached a record 90 percent. The patriotic/nationalist policy was a winner: Even part of the democratic opposition that did not approve of Putin's policy in the Ukraine crisis agree with him that Crimea was part of Russia and should belong to it again. As long as Putin could play the patriotic/nationalist card without endangering world peace or causing a major deterioration in the economy, the prospects of the opposition being able to make significant headway were minimal.

Could Russia develop toward full-blown fascism? Some observers have argued that Russia has already reached this stage. But such assertions, while understandable from an emotional-psychological point of view, could hardly withstand rigorous analysis, nor are they helpful in understanding the dynamics of contemporary Russian politics. Boris Nemtsov, one of the leaders of the democratic Solidarnost movement and an erstwhile deputy prime minister, declared that in the spring of 2014 Russia had become a dictatorship. Although a strong case could be made in favor of this assertion, one could not feel altogether happy with such a categorical statement. For Russia had not been a free country even before, and it was not a total dictatorship even after, despite the fact that the trend toward a dictatorship was unmistakable.

It is difficult to find a common denominator for the political regimes commonly referred to as "Fascist" in twentieth-century Europe. Nazi Germany was not "Fascist," and Fascist Italy was not Nazi. It becomes even more difficult to find common denominators if one also considers the smaller European countries are also considered. This has partly to do with the time factor—the Fascist era did not last long—the second World War II broke out a mere six years after the Nazis had gained power. The very term "Fascist" is of limited use for analysis and understanding.

It is unlikely that all Fascist or para- or quasi-Fascist countries and movements would have developed in the same way. There were obvious differences between large and small Fascist countries—the big ones tended toward expansionism and military aggression, the smaller ones did not, even though they might have been militarist in inspiration. Fascist regimes all shared certain features—for instance, the presence of a leader and the cult of this leader. Regimes that did not impose the domination of a single state party, or that accepted more than one party and more than one ideology, were more likely to be military or right-wing populist dictatorships that were not Fascist in character.

There was in Russia in recent years certainly the beginning of a personality cult (see the anthology edited by Helena Goscilo, *Putin as Celebrity and Cultural Icon*) though in comparison with the Stalin cult it was quite modest. It was probably because of the intensity of the Stalin cult and its often ludicrous character, which had not left a good impression even among Communists, that a Putin cult was bound to be halfhearted. From time to time, attempts were made to present him as the "father of the nation." But he was not a father figure, and such attempts were almost certainly bound to fail. His public persona was that of a patriot and a member of the *siloviki* but lacked other attributes thought necessary for a great leader. There was the strong macho element he had in common with Mussolini. While Mussolini seldom showed the upper part of his body uncovered—his favorite sports were equestrian—Putin quite frequently while exercising or engaged in judo or other sports, displayed his well-developed torso. In Germany among the Nazi leaders this was not considered *comme il faut*, nor did Hitler, Göring, or Goebbels have the figures that people were proud to display or to have seen. Ebert, the Social Democratic president, was once photographed in a bathing suit: It did him considerable political harm in the 1920s. Ulbricht, the East German leader, was a gymnastics freak but appeared always fully clothed.

The history of political parties in Russia is very short. And while it is true that after the disintegration of the Soviet Union political parties were represented in the Duma, it is not clear whether they were bona fide organizations, who was behind them, who guided and financed them, and whose interests they represented. However, is it not possible that at a time of crisis, these pseudoparties might suddenly turn into independent bodies with a will and a policy of their own? And is it not possible that one day such a situation might arise?

The State Party

The current leaders of Russia had learned in their youth that a strong political party was needed as a transmission belt to run the country. As long as there were elections and other condiments of a democratic regime, this was needed to mobilize the masses and to conduct propaganda to get the message of the ruling stratum to the people. Gorbachev in his later years and Yeltsin had ruled without a party, but this had created a variety of problems for the leader and those around him. For they needed support—money and activists for all kinds of purposes. They did not want to be too dependent on the oligarchs and the local governors, even though the governors had originally been elected locally whereas now they are appointed by the Kremlin.

In the last days of the Yeltsin regime, various smaller pro-Kremlin groups united and the current state party came into being in preparation for the Duma elections of 1999. They declared themselves to be opposed to left- and right-wing extremism, a centrist, anti-Fascist party. Putin was at one time its leader but later bowed out, as did Dmitry Medvedev and also Sergey Shoygu, who had been its formal leader.

This party has always been the strongest in the Duma, scoring between 49 percent and 72 percent of the total vote; its support was highest in 2007–08, when prosperity was at its peak. Of course, there were frequent accusations of ballot stuffing and other types of fraud, but investigations always proved inconclusive.

In any case, the establishment of a single state party as the country's leading force has not gone over very well in recent years. Putting up a countrywide youth organization was even more difficult. It took a long time, and in the end did not amount to a dynamic force. It came into being in 2005 in competition with the "orange revolutions" in some of the republics that had split away. It attracted few members; according to rumors those who joined had been found among football fans and showed up only when they were paid for attending demonstrations. According to their official program they were against the extreme Right and Left, against fascism but also against excesses by antipatriotic oligarchs. It was apparently a creation of Surkov, Putin's chief of staff and main ideologist up to 2011. He did not show much aptitude as an organizer in this assignment, and Nashi was hardly ever much in appearance. All the essential ingredients for a dynamic, effective youth movement—above all enthusiasm—were missing. Probably not all of them were thieves and rascals, as Alexei Navalny had maintained, but they seemed to have been politically rather useless.

Lacking both a political party, which according to the old constitution should be what currently serves as the engine and transmission belt in the country, and an official ideology in the face of an authoritarian regime, Russia cannot exist simply as a society of admirers of Putin. Even for this purpose, an effective organization—along with a group of like-minded people with common interests—is needed. To a certain extent, these have been the members of the KGB (now known as the FSB). According to the famous "vertical system" of government, they are authorized to give orders to the police and judiciary. They may threaten or buy the media. They can establish working alliances with some who have key positions in government—or even place some of their own people in such positions.

Students of political movements and fascism in particular have tried to find features common to them—a "Fascist minimum"—ten, twelve, or fourteen ingredients have been pointed out. Fascism in power always had a leader; it was never ruled by a committee. There always was a single state party, and the absence of such a party immediately raises questions as to the true character of such a regime. A Fascist regime had a monopoly (or a near monopoly) inasmuch as the propagation of its ideas was concerned, and it also had a monopoly (or near monopoly) with regard to political violence. There was no independent judiciary under fascism.

At the same time, each of these regimes were different in some respects. The Russian regime was quite unique inasmuch as it was the first that mutated from communism to an order quite different—be it of the Far Right or semi-Fascist or whatever. While it is interesting to point to these differences between them, not too much mental energy should perhaps be devoted to the categorization, because more often than not these regimes (or movements) are in a state of transition.

The absence of an official ideology after a period of oversaturation with ideology is certainly fascinating, but it is not at all clear whether it will last and how long it will last. There are periods in history in which the absence of a doctrine or belief system can be tolerated, at least temporarily, whereas during others it will be unthinkable. In a similar way, there are periods even in the history of dictatorships during which a minimum of repression will be sufficient to stay in power, whereas during others a great deal will be needed (or will be thought to be needed). If the fear of chaos is great, those in power will not constantly have to prove that a strong hand is needed. The same is true if the dictatorship is of relatively recent date or has shown its efficiency in the recent past.

Is it possible to maintain such a regime under these circumstances?

And what of the opposition? What are the prospects for its success in a political system such as the one currently in power in Russia?

When a regime or a ruler has been in power for very long, a process of routinization sets in, in which the demand for change becomes intense and frequent—unless, of course, that regime has been phenomenally successful in everything it has handled. And even then the hold of the party in power may be endangered if its own power base is deeply split.

Opposition to the Putin regime currently comes to a certain extent from members of the extreme Right, who maintain that the present rulers are not sufficiently aggressive and antidemocratic. However, the increasingly repressive measures taken by the government, the popularity of the takeover of Crimea, and the strong support for the Ukrainian separatists have muted their voices for the moment. As for the democratic opposition, popular support appears unlikely given the current climate, in which a majority of Russians seem to be perfectly content with authoritarian rule.

The Putin regime is based largely on power resting at the center, with regional interests being ignored. It could well be that an opposition representing regional interests would stand a much better chance, but this has not yet been tried.

7 | THE NEW NATIONAL DOCTRINE

Back to the Roots

THE SOVIET UNION COLLAPSED IN THE 1990S, BUT THE IDEOLOGY on which it was based had suffered from utter exhaustion for a long time before. True, the classics of Marxism-Leninism were still ritually quoted when deemed necessary, but the dynamic, revolutionary spirit that had been so noticeable in the 1920s had vanished. What could replace it? Another revolutionary impulse seemed out of the question; a new Left could be detected in American and European universities, but not in the Soviet Union.

Nationalism and religion seemed the obvious answer, as had been the case before the revolution of 1917. But czarist Russia, especially in its last phase, was not an attractive model except for dyed-in-the-wool monarchists (and even they complained about the weakness of Nicholas II). Those in search of a new ideology had to go further back—perhaps to Nikolay Karamzin, who had written about love of country and national pride some two hundred years earlier. In his *History of the Russian State,* he had glorified its accomplishments. True, Russia had been in chains during long periods, but the same had been the case with other nations in Europe. Anyway, the chains had been broken gloriously. Peter the Great had united Russia with Europe: "We looked at Europe . . . and at one glance we assimilated the fruits of her long labor." Russia's army had defeated the strongest army in Europe. In brief: "What nation in Europe could boast of a better fate?"

But Karamzin as a guide seemed a little remote in 2000. He admitted that Russia's primary achievements had been in the military field—largely because it had to fight for its existence. Military leaders such as Alexander Suvorov said many profound things ("The bullet is a fool, use the bayonet"), and Mikhail Kutuzov was right in refusing to give battle to Napoleon until late in the day. But the Russian nobility were still talking French to one another. And the intelligentsia was still not happy. In his often quoted "philosophical letter" (1836), Pyotr Chaadayev wrote:

> It is one of the most deplorable facts of our peculiar civilization that we are still discovering truths that other peoples, even some much less advanced than we, have taken for granted. The reason is that we have never marched with the other peoples. We don't belong to any of the great families of the human race, we are neither of the West nor of the East and we have not the tradition of either. Placed as we are outside of time, we have not been taught by the universal education of the human race.

And later on:

> We are alone in the world, we have given nothing to the world, we have taught it nothing. We have not added a single idea to the sum total of human ideas; we have not contributed to the progress of the human spirit, and what we have borrowed of this progress we have distorted. From the outset of our existence as a society we have produced nothing for the common benefit of all mankind, not one useful thought has sprung from the arid soil of our fatherland. . . .

This "philosophical letter," needless to say, was written in French.

The Slavophiles bitterly dissented. The Russian people (Ivan Aksakov wrote) are not interested in politics. For this reason, the government was wrong to continually take measures to prevent a revolution in its fear of a political uprising, an event that would be contrary to the very essence of the Russian people. The Russian people were seeking moral freedom, the freedom of the spirit. Leaving the kingdom of the world to the state, the Russian people set their feet on the path of inner freedom, that of the spiritual life: the kingdom of Christ.

Fyodor Tyutchev was one of the greatest and most underrated Russian writers. Tolstoy put him above Pushkin; Pushkin is broader, he wrote, but Tyutchev is deeper. Having lived abroad many years, Tyutchev followed events in Europe with great interest and reached the conclusion that there were only two parties in Europe, the revolutionary party of the West and the conservative party of Russia. Although he was appointed chief censor, he was not really a conservative. He welcomed the reforms of that time, above all the abolition of serfdom. In "Russian Geography," he wrote:

But where are their limits, and where are their frontiers?
To the north, the east, the south and the rising sun.
The fates will reveal them to future generations.
From the Nile to the Neva, from the Elbe to China
From the Volga to the Euphrates.
This is the Russian empire and it will never pass away
Just as the spirit foretold and Daniel prophesied.

Tyutchev's love of Russia burned alongside a persecution mania. He wrote his sister that European countries would miss no opportunity to harm Russia. But his marriages and love affairs were mostly with German ladies, and friends reported that his French was better than his Russian.

What could the old Slavophiles offer to patriots by the year 2000? Even fellow Slavs could not be trusted; the Poles were traitors. One of the leading late Slavophiles despised European consumer mentality and praised Byzantine values. These were the views of Konstantin Leontiev, consul in Albania. Nikolay Danilevsky, who is frequently invoked with Leontiev, was a naturalist (but he rejected Darwin) and became famous because of *Russia and Europe*, his broadside against the West. Europe was not just strange (alien) to us, but hostile, its interests diametrically opposed to those of Russia.

It is doubtful whether Leontiev and Danilevsky should be considered Slavophiles. They thought the time of that movement had passed. They were antiliberal and anti-Western, and this endeared them to Alexander Dugin and others who adopted them as their mentors. The historical base on which this ideology was constructed was weak, to say the least. For when Russia was dealing with nineteenth-century Europe, the main country was usually Germany, which at that time could hardly have been considered "liberal."

Danilevsky and Leontiev were also among the discoverers (or inventors) of Russophobia. Leontiev had no time for idealizing the Russian peasant or the other Slav peoples. He was an obscurantist—so much so as to being almost modern and a prophetic realist. Toward the end of his life, he reached the conclusion that Western capitalism and liberalism had no future in Russia—since the Eastern Orthodox (Byzantine) tradition could not be revived, the only future for Russia was in some form of state socialism, which would provide the necessary measure of discipline (and repression), without which the whole fabric of society would unravel. This is an exceedingly modern way of describing the contemporary Russian situation.

Leontiev was a deeply pessimistic thinker and also very honest. He thought the systematic glorification of Russia's past a delusion, the dreams about Russia's future a mere chimera. The best one could hope for was to preserve the status quo with all its imperfections. In other words, he was ahead of the thinkers of the radical Right of our time. As a conservative, he despised Slavophilism, which he thought vulgar, democratic, and potentially dangerous. He opposed the aggressive foreign policy of the Slavophiles in the Balkans and the domestic Russification in the

Baltic countries and elsewhere. His literary views were quite different from those of his conservative contemporaries. He preferred Tolstoy to Dostoyevsky, both as a writer and as a patriot.

Leontiev had little influence in his lifetime, very much in contrast to Danilevsky, who was widely read. Danilevsky's magnum opus appeared in the major European languages. His politics were initially liberal, and in some ways he always remained a radical—he was the most eloquent spokesman of a Russian imperial mission. He is often compared with Oswald Spengler and Joseph Stalin, but such associations should not be exaggerated. Like Spengler, he believed in the rise and decline of civilizations. Like Stalin, he envisaged a totalitarian system of sorts. But his perspectives, naturally, were removed from twentieth-century barbarism. He believed in the decay of the West and anticipated a long and bloody struggle with Europe, out of which Russia would emerge victorious. As a scientist, he did not hesitate to introduce to Russia up-to-date technologies and science. He was opposed only to copying alien cultural and political models: parliamentary democracy, the class struggle, and Western plutocratic imperialism. Some of Danilevsky's beliefs were so ridiculous that they generate doubts about his sanity—for instance, when he wrote that Western statehood was based on violent oppression, serfdom, and enmity, whereas Russian governance was founded on goodwill, freedom, and peace. On other occasions, his comments appear perfectly sane, if somewhat extravagant.

His advocacy of Russian expansion was not motivated by neogeopolitics and other newfangled theories he would have thought utter nonsense; he was inspired by a belief in spiritual values and a world historical mission. Like Dostoyevsky, he believed the Russians were the only God-fearing people and would save the world: They were the body of God. Only the Orthodox had preserved the divine image of Christ in all its purity, and they could therefore act as a guide for other peoples who had lost their way. This much Leontiev and Dostoyevsky had in common.

It is difficult to believe that those who currently invoke Leontiev and Danilevsky have actually read them. If they had, they would be deeply troubled.

According to these anti-Western thinkers, the attitude of the Europeans toward Russia was one of Russophobia. This was imprecise, although not entirely far-fetched. It was not only the European Left that saw in Russia the main enemy to freedom and progress, a hotbed of reaction at home and abroad.

The tradition of seeing in Russia a barbarous (or at least semibarbarous) country despite what Peter the Great tried to do goes back to the early nineteenth century and the publication of the so-called *Testament of Peter the Great*—which was a forgery by a Polish writer in France. The classic work in this field was the Marquis de Custine's *Russia in 1839.* Custine was a staunch French monarchist and conservative; his sexual orientation would have landed him in trouble in contemporary Russia. (But this was true also of Sergey Uvarov, the Russian minister of education who coined the famous phrase "Orthodoxy, absolute rule, and *narodnost.*") However, what Custine witnessed on his trip to Russia exceeded his worst fears. He became the author of the famous phrase about Russia being an absolute monarchy, a system mitigated only by assassination. He was particularly annoyed by the constant and all-pervasive government spying. The Russian people (he wrote) had been turned into a nation of mutes and automatons (robots, in contemporary language); its mentality was one of slaves. Whereas in France this kind of despotism was a transient evil, in Russia it was deep-seated. Custine had several conversations with the czar. Had the emperor the will and the power to change the system of government? He doubted it. Custine's book (two volumes of some eighteen hundred pages) was banned in Russia, but some copies found their way into the country. It was published in full in Russia in 1996 for the first time.

Was it the superficial work of a malevolent French dandy, unfair and incorrect? It was a book with considerable weaknesses, if only because Custine had spent most of his time in the country's two biggest cities. But he had by no means arrived there prejudiced; he was a sharp observer, and he did not invent his stories. As George Kennan wrote many years later, if the Custine report was not perfect as a description of Russia in 1839, it was an excellent picture of Russia under Stalin.

What Karl Marx wrote about Russia at the time could be regarded as an excellent example of Russophobia. But Marx was no Russian expert, no insider. For this, one has to turn to the diary of a Baltic German named Victor Hehn, an educated man employed as a lowly librarian. His *De Moribus Ruthenorum* (1892) was a devastating account of all the bad features of life in Russia, above all the superficiality of even the educated Russians, the inefficiency, the lies, the pretensions, the corruption. He found nothing to like, let alone to admire, in Russia. The book is also less than fair (to give but one example: Pushkin and Lermontov do not appear in it at all, and Gogol is presented as a minor writer with major faults).

Considering that Hehn wrote in the 1860s (by which time more than half of Dostoyevsky had been published and *War and Peace* had begun to appear, not to mention Tyutchev, Turgenev, and others); that *Dead Souls* and *Revisor* were major works by any standard; and that the middle of that century was a poor time in the annals of German literature—this is a display either of profound ignorance or of colossal impertinence. In any case, Russophobia means "fear of Russia," and neither Custine nor the others mentioned were afraid of Russia. They looked down on it, and this may have caused even greater offense.

Was Otto von Bismarck a Russophobe? He served at the time as Prussian ambassador in Russia. He moved in other circles, and his main interest was not in Russian culture. He was not exactly afraid of Russia, but the warning he left to German foreign policy makers was, "Do not go to war against Russia." Not surprisingly, Bismarck became a favorite of Russia nationalists, then and now. Such feelings were reciprocated: When Alexander II was assassinated, the conservative Berlin *Kreuz-Zeitung* published the news under the headline OUR EMPEROR HAS DIED.

There were no political parties in Russia during this period; they appeared fifty years later, just before, during, and after the first Russian Revolution. It is at this time that radical nationalist organizations were born, and it is in this period that some of the present-day ultrapatriots are finding their inspiration.

This trend—of growing militancy and the feeling of a need to be organized—was by no means an isolated Russian phenomenon; it could be observed in all major European countries. It was based on the fear that the Left was making constant progress, that the countries of Europe were perhaps even facing the danger of revolution. In France, for instance, this mood led to the emergence of the Action Française and similar groups. The Dreyfus affair had split the country and created a substantial reservoir of goodwill and support for the Far Right. In Germany, the ultranationalist trend did not lead to the creation of a major political party. Rather, the reaction was cultural: The Conservatives, the leading right-wing party, managed to absorb and integrate this mood in its own ranks. It became more anti-Semitic, more antiliberal and bellicose.

In Russia, a growing terrorist movement and the revolutionary ferment led to the foundation of various groups with names such as the Union of the Russian People (SRN), which attracted people from various sectors of society. Support came from the clergy and the police, from sections of the upper class, but even more strongly from the lower middle class and Okhotny Ryad. This was the name of a street and a small quarter in the center of historical Moscow where the city's meat market was located. People living there were often recent arrivals from the countryside, rough and of little education, bewildered by town life and the rapid pace of social change. The fairly strong criminal element in these neighborhoods gave rise to the Chernaya Sotnya (Black Hundreds) movement, which played a prominent part in (or was the main instigator of) the pogroms in Russia in 1905–06.

According to the various official declarations issued by the Black Hundreds, they would never call for the murder of anyone, let alone participate in such actions. They simply wanted to mobilize the masses, something traditional conservatives were incapable of doing. Their leaders believed that but for their activities, the czarist regime would have crumbled in the wake of the lost war against Japan.

The Black Hundreds were a halfway house between the traditional conservative/reactionary forces in Russia, which had been assemblies of notables, and modern fascism, capable of mobilizing the masses. It was an inchoate movement; its character and activities varied from place to place. Most of their members believed in violence, and many pogroms took place, primarily in the south, where the majority of Jews resided.

According to the "pale of settlement" policy, few Jews were permitted to live in Moscow and the cities of Russia proper.

The Black Hundreds had no charismatic leader and no strong, efficient organization. Its declared aim was to stop the revolutionaries who wanted to ruin Russia. But its most prominent victims were not the revolutionaries, but Mikhail Herzenstein and Grigori Iolles, two parliamentarians of the centrist Kadet party. The unofficial Black Hundreds slogan was "*Bei Zhidov, spasai Rossiu*" ("Beat the Jews and save Russia"). Perhaps Russia had to be saved, but it was by no means clear that beating the Jews would do the trick. For the Jews were not the main threat.

A few government ministers supported the Black Hundreds, but the majority despised them and thought that the riffraff was doing more harm than good. Even among the clergy, support was by no means total. Of the roughly seventy members of the clergy elected to the Duma, a quarter, perhaps even a third, were liberals of sorts. Even Ioann of Kronstadt, the patron saint of the movement, had condemned the Kishinev pogrom (1903), in which forty-nine Jews were killed. He subsequently retracted this and put the blame on the Jews. He was later beatified.

The czar believed in the Black Hundreds, calling them a "shining example of justice and order to all men." But the czar was politically unimportant. The Black Hundreds lost whatever steam they had; the SRN still enjoyed the support of about 10 percent of the public, had a few sympathizers in the Duma and a few media supporters. SRN publications were financed in part by the government, which in this way exercised a measure of control over them.

In brief, the SRN and the Black Hundreds were permitted to be more populist than the mainline right wingers, but only up to a certain point. For instance, they demanded that the czar should be closer to the people, less distant—an old demand of the Slavophiles. Occasionally, they criticized local bureaucrats. But they were not permitted to go too far with their racialist slogans—this would have been unwise in a multinational empire.

After the revolutionary fever had subsided, the SRN was no longer of importance and the Black Hundreds became a topic of interest for historians and political scientists. Some of their leaders would cause minor scandals in the Duma, but this was considered entertainment and had no political impact. A few survivors returned in their old age to the Soviet Union in the post-Stalin period. And some émigrés foresaw the decline of internationalism and the rise of a new nationalism inside the Soviet Union. The main figure of this camp, Smenovekhovtsy was Nikolai Ustryalov, formerly a member of the Kadet party and a Slavophile. He returned to Russia and called on his political friends to do the same. But his timing was wrong. He should have waited another fifteen or twenty years to be on the safe side. Ustryalov was arrested and shot in 1937. This was in contrast to General Brusilov's fate, a World War I hero (who had commanded the famous Brusilov offensive), who also returned; when he died in 1926, he was given a state funeral.

It was in this period, the years just before and after the first Russian Revolution, that *The Protocols of the Elders of Zion* and the anti-Masonic literature made its appearance. The concept of a worldwide conspiracy by Freemasons went back to such opponents of the French Revolution as the Abbé Augustin Barruel. In the beginning, there was no reference to the Jews because Jews were not part of France's political life. The connection was established only later in the nineteenth century, when the conspiracy became Judeo-Masonic. But there was a lack of resonance among the public. Very little was known about the Masons in Russia; the lodges had been outlawed in 1822. There should have been a great readiness to believe in the omnipresence and nefarious activities of these hidden forces, but there was not, and it took almost a century for views of this kind to gain wider currency.

It took even longer for the present hysteria about the hidden sinister forces in Russia to materialize. There had been a renaissance of this kind of propaganda in Nazi Germany, but there was an important difference: The Nazis were not really afraid of the occult forces, which they used as a propagandistic stratagem. The Nazis felt themselves infinitely stronger than their enemies, whereas in Russia there seems to have been genuine fear vis-à-vis *Zhidomasonstvo.*

In most discussions about the emergence of the new Russian anti-Western doctrine, one important protagonist is usually underrated or ignored altogether—the Orthodox Church. Mention has been made earlier of Metropolitan Ioann St. Petersburg and Ladoga, sponsor in the post-Soviet period of *The Protocols of the Elders of Zion*. But Ioann was a central figure not at the beginning, but toward the end of this particular school of Orthodox theology, which goes back to such leading figures in the history of the Orthodox Church as Seraphim of Sarov, Ioann of Kronstadt, and several others. They have become not just church thinkers of great influence, but objects of a veritable cult. Their eschatological preaching about the coming of the Antichrist, the appearance of a false Messiah, the end of days, the final struggle between the forces of Christ and Satan in which Holy Russia, chosen by God, would play a central, decisive role: These and other elements of paranoia have figured prominently at both the center and the periphery of the Orthodox Church for a long time.

According to earlier versions, the Antichrist (born in Russia) was the son of the devil and a prostitute belonging to the Israeli tribe of Dan, but eventually a secularization and politization took place and the Antichrist came to stand for all the enemies of Holy Russia: the Freemasons, the Enlightenment, the heretic Catholic Church, the Russian agents of modernism, and many others. In this way, the metaphysical "beast" symbolizing the Antichrist became the nonmetaphysical America, concentrating all the forces of evil. To achieve its victorious mission, Holy Russia would have to establish a powerful empire, this being the meeting point of the forces of the Orthodox Church and Russian nationalism.

The idea of the katechon and parousia (the second coming of Christ), the final struggle and the end of days, has appeared and still appears in countless variations in Russia and at all levels of sophistication. It has to do with the second coming of Christ, which would be preceded by the appearance of the Antichrist. It is interesting how certain concepts of New Testament theology, some of them quite obscure, found their way into this kind of modern political mythology.

Ironically, this motif also appeared under communism in "The Internationale," as *la lutte finale*—the final decisive struggle. At present, it is put forth by writers such as Arkadi Maler and Mikhail Nazarov, virtually unknown outside Russia but widely read in that country. This school of thought deserves far wider attention than it has received so far, because it is essential for an understanding of contemporary Russian politics. It greatly helps to understand the paranoiac fears and hopes that have become so pronounced in recent years—fears of disasters ahead, hopes of redemption and final victory.

The Russian Party Under the Soviets

When glasnost became official policy with Gorbachev's ascension to power, among those benefiting from a much greater freedom of speech were the liberals, those who had been persecuted under the old regime. But it soon appeared that the nationalists and especially the "ultras" also received much greater freedom of movement and expression. This first manifested itself in the activities of Pamyat, a group active principally in Moscow and St. Petersburg that had its roots in the movement for the preservation of national monuments. Pamyat (named after a novel by Vladimir Civilichin) in 1982 asked for permission to hold meetings and demonstrations, which it duly received. Headed by Dmitri Vasiliev, a photographer, it was very noisy and received a great amount of publicity. But it was not clear what it stood for, other than anti-Semitism. It left open most questions: What, for example, were its convictions with regard to Stalinism and the ancient regime in general? This lack of clarity, it soon emerged, was not accidental, for it brought together people of very different political convictions. Vasiliev identified himself as nonparty Bolshevik, but it was not clear whether this was genuine and, if it was genuine, what it meant in practice. As one writer noted at the time, the atmosphere resembled the early days of the Nazi movement in Munich.

Flaunting anti-Semitism had certain advantages. First of all, it was almost legal; it had been preached by official Communist Party organs for a long time, as long as it was called anti-Zionism. There had been a wave of anti-Zionist literature, but it had been clear even to people who were politically illiterate that those preaching it had not Theodor Herzl or Israel in mind, but the Jews.

Pamyat soon began to split in various parts, and it ceased to exist well before the death of its leader in 2004, a perfect example of all that was wrong with Russian extreme nationalism. But it is useful to remember that the sharpest criticism came not from foreigners or Jews and Masons, but from Russians, perhaps because they knew it better than people abroad. No one described it more mercilessly than Nikolai Berdyaev, who wrote of the nationalist doctrine and practice of the Russian Far Right that it was "barbaric and stupid, pagan and immoral in inspiration, full of Eastern wildness and darkness," an orgy of the old Russian dissoluteness.

What was not known before glasnost (except perhaps to a select few in Moscow) was that the "Russian party" had much deeper roots going back in time, especially in the middle level of the Communist Party apparatus. It had been known in a general way that in the 1930s there had been under Stalin's initiative a turn from proletarian internationalism to Soviet patriotism. There had been the Pokrovsky affair in 1936: A veteran Bolshevik, a professional historian, and for a while deputy minister of education, Mikhail Pokrovsky wrote several histories of Russia in an old-style Leninist spirit that debunked all the old nationalist stereotypes. His extreme antipatriotism was probably the decisive factor in the turn in Soviet historiography; as a result of his derision, Alexander Nevsky and Dmitry Donskoy, even other traditional heroes such as Ivan the Terrible, all returned to their rightful place in Russian history.

The turn to patriotism had its limits, however, and it was only under Stalin's successors that the Russian party gained supporters even at the highest level. One of its chief supporters was Alexander Shelepin (1918–1994), who had made his career in the leadership of the Komsomol, the Communist youth organization, and had been head of the KGB between 1958 and 1961. He had been a protégé of Khrushchev's but later became involved in the successful coup against him, hoping (according to some evidence) to succeed him. This had been a miscalculation. Shelepin retained his seat in the Politburo for some time but gradually was squeezed out. Under his leadership, the Russian nationalist element in the party apparatus became stronger and received greater freedom of maneuver—but all within limits.

Transgressing the rules by not paying at least lip service to the party ideology or by contradicting it openly could be dangerous. A few nationalists who had disregarded the rules found themselves in the gulag. But their number was very small compared with those who demanded more democratic rights. Other leading protectors of the nationalists were Yuri Melentiev, also in the Komsomol leadership, and above all several highly placed officials in the top office of the Russian Federation Communist Party.

Whereas under Leonid Brezhnev the Russian party had (almost) a free run because the first secretary had no interest in ideology, its freedom of maneuver was more limited under Yuri Andropov, who disliked these ultranationalist deviationists. But Andropov's tenure was to be of short duration, and their setback only temporary. There were various indications of a rise in nationalism during the late Soviet period, with the appearance of the *pochvenniki*, a group of "village" writers from the 1960s, perhaps even earlier. One could mention Mikhail Sholokhov (1905–1984) in this context, but he kept himself very much apart from Moscow group activities and with age became a prima donna. His *Tikhiy Don* (*And Quiet Flows the Don*) was a work of outstanding quality and had little in common with the official party line of socialist realism. It was in fact a work so much superior to anything he wrote in later years that doubts (probably unjustified) arose as to whether it had really been his work or written at least in part by others. He was a true conservative who despised the city writers and demonstratively kept himself apart from urban life and anything the city stood for.

The case of Leonid Leonov (1899–1994) was in some respects similar to Sholokhov's. A major writer in the 1920s and 1930s, he permeated his last novels (such as *Piramida*, on which he worked for more than forty years) with a mystical nationalism and religiosity to the detriment of their literary merits. They were hardly read. In the age of glasnost, he joined the camp of writers of the extreme Right, protesting against the democratization of the country and other such innovations and reforms that were contrary to his beliefs. It was a sad case of the decline of a major writer, but it is of interest in showing that the Russian party was not an isolated faction but had the support of some writers who had once been thought wholly identified with the Communist system.

The *pochvenniki* proper began their work in the 1960s and included several writers of genuine talent such as Vasily Shukshin, Vasily Belov, and Valentin Rasputin. Shukshin, perhaps the most gifted of them, died young; he had been engaged in making films as much as in writing books. Belov was anything but a political dissident, but since his topic was village life he could not make a secret of his conviction that the collectivization of agriculture had been a great mistake, in fact a tragedy. It led to urbanization; Belov thought life in the city amoral (and partly blamed the West for it). The true values of Russia had been in the villages—but village life had been degrading in the Soviet period. Belov tended to idealize the prerevolutionary village; he had never known it, and this was probably the inevitable result of his negation of city life. Ironically, Belov was to spend most of his later life in Moscow, having become a political figure in the Writers Union and other organizations.

Belov's origins were in the Altai region, and he died in 2012; Shukshin came from the vicinity of Vologda in the north. Rasputin was a native of Siberia, and he is still alive as these lines are written and opted for staying in his native region of Irkutsk. Like the other village writers, he had been a fighter for many ecological causes such as opposition to the project to deroute the direction of the flow of the Siberian rivers and the protection of Lake Baikal. With perestroika he became the most politicized of all the surviving village writers, commenting in open letters to the Russian people and its leaders on current events. He became one of the staunchest fighters against liberal and democratic innovations, identifying himself with the policy of the czars and the commanders of the "White" anti-Communist armies in the civil war. Critics charged Rasputin with extreme antimodernism and idealizing pro-revolutionary village life and therefore being hopelessly unrealistic. It is true that Rasputin's politics involved him in many contradictions; thus he came eventually to praise Stalin, who after all was also responsible for the collectivization of agriculture. But the charges of embellishing village life seem at least exaggerated. His powerful novel *Pozhar* (*The Fire*) is in no way in the tradition of romanticism but describes the scene in a very small town in which a fire has broken out—in particular the actions of the townspeople engaging in orgies of drunkenness and pillage instead of trying to combat and extinguish the fire. The narrator, a local policeman having lost all hope for life in his native village, decides to leave his hometown.

Lastly, the Russian party and the movement for the preservation of national monuments. There were such groups, some of them eventually with many members, first in Moscow and later on elsewhere. Historians have been divided in their opinion of how much importance these groups were in the context of the nationalist revival. They abstained from issuing political declarations, but it is beyond doubt that from the beginning most were under the control of Russian nationalists. The main group, founded in 1965, celebrated the six hundredth jubilee of the Battle of Kulikovo. But there was also a meeting devoted to Lenin's struggle against Trotsky that had nothing to do with the preservation of monuments but gave an opportunity to discuss Trotsky's invented relationship with the Zionist movement. But since, in truth, they did not care about Zionism either, the real motive must have been anti-Semitism. On other occasions, group visits were arranged to the neighborhoods west of Moscow, where in the year 1941 fighting had taken place.

Seen in retrospect, it would appear that the Russian party did not make significant progress. The same people always attended its meetings, and its message did not reach a wider public. However, certain literary publications were firmly in their hands, notably the monthlies *Molodaya Gvardiya* and *Nash Sovremenik.* The former gravitated more toward Stalin and Stalinism; the latter expressed the views of Russian nationalism *tout court.* In this way, they could reach hundreds of thousands of readers. The ideological contrasts did not disappear, and there were serious differences of opinion, but it appeared they were not unbridgeable. Anatoli Ivanov, the editor of *Molodaya Gvardiya,* had engaged in antireligious propaganda, whereas *Nash Sovremenik,* as the organ of the village writers, stood for a rapprochement with the Orthodox Church and was basically anti-Communist. Even such seemingly inoffensive events as the Battle of Kulikovo, in which Dmitry Donskoy had defeated the Tatars, could cause conflicts. For the Eurasianists wanted collaboration rather than strife with Russia's Asiatic neighbors, of whom they thought highly: Why therefore celebrate war rather than peaceful coexistence with Russia's closest partners? To a certain extent, the differences could be swept under the carpet—for instance, by making Stalin a Russian nationalist who was not really a Marxist (which was, in fact, half-true).

This trend toward unity in the ranks of the Russian nationalist party continued and became even stronger under glasnost; the differences between (former) Communists and the Far Right tended to disappear, and often it became impossible to say whether a certain writer belonged to one camp or the other.

With the dawn of glasnost, the Russian party could come out in the open. True, the circumstances were not always auspicious. The Soviet Union was falling apart, as was the Russian Empire. What "the gatherers of Russian lands" had achieved over centuries vanished within a few months. The various coups, the attempts to overthrow the new government, failed miserably. But it was precisely because of these disasters that the Russian party received fresh impetus as the conviction grew that the country had to be saved from utter ruin. And there was only one way to save and restore the empire, to regain as much as possible. For as a small, unimportant country, Russia could not survive. Its only hope was to emerge as a great power with a great mission.

Ivan Ilyin Rediscovered

"An elite without an ideology is a threat," Alexey Podberezkin wrote in 2014, in the first issue that year of *Zavtra*, the organ of the Russian Far Right. Whether this statement is correct is open to doubt. In its history, Russia has been afflicted by many dangers and even disasters, but most have been the result of a surfeit rather than a deficit of ideology. If Podberezkin did not do too well in the presidential elections, scoring only 0.1 percent, this was probably because he offered too many ideas at the same time—a blend of radical nationalism, Orthodox Christianity, and post-Stalinist doctrine. More or less the same mixture was offered by other parties, which made it difficult to decide whom to support. Podberezkin was an adviser to the leader of the Communists, but not a member of his party, and voters perhaps could not make up their minds whether he was a conservative revolutionary or a revolutionary conservative.

But it is certainly true that until recently most Russian political parties tried to keep all options open. And the ideological fare was so rich that everyone could find something appealing. However, of late the search for something more specific and tangible has been going into overdrive. On the initiative of President Putin, all governors and senior politicians in the service of the state were sent three books for Christmas 2013 reading: Vladimir Solovyov's *The Justification of the Good*, Nikolai Berdyaev's *The Philosophy of Inequality*, and Ivan Ilyin's *Nashi Zadachi* (*Our Tasks*).

This is heavy fare, and it is doubtful that politicians in any other country have been confronted with such demands. All three writers are theologians, but the books recommended by Putin did not deal with God or Satan.

Vladimir Solovyov was a late-nineteenth-century writer dealing in many fields, who had a powerful influence on both his contemporaries (including Dostoyevsky) and subsequent generations. With his poem "Pan-Mongolism," he could be regarded as the forefather of Eurasianism. However, he was anything but enamored of what he regarded as the East of Xerxes. He was a religious thinker, but his attitude was ecumenical—he stood for reconciliation between the Eastern Church and Catholicism. This did not make him popular among official Orthodox circles, whose attitude toward other Christian churches was hostile; nor was he admired for regarding pravoslav anti-Semitism a disgrace.

Nikolai Berdyaev hailed from a family of the nobility, many of whom had served in the army. He belonged to the generation after Solovyov and died an émigré shortly after World War II in Paris. A man of great erudition, he was no doubt the best known of the Russian religious thinkers in the West. Having no academic qualifications whatsoever, he became a professor in prerevolutionary Russia, an unprecedented achievement, and had few equals in the field of Russian intellectual history. He was a passenger on the notorious ship on which one hundred sixty Russian intellectuals were exiled to Germany in 1922 on Lenin's orders.

But the Berdyaev book sent to the politicians was neither on Christian ethics nor on truth and revelation; it was a defense of economic inequality, something in the nature of a Russian predecessor of Ayn

Rand. This is surprising for a number of reasons. In his early years, Berdyaev was a man of the Left (he was even exiled for a number of years), and as a theologian he must have known Timothy 6:10 about the lust for money as the source of evil and Mark 10:25 about the rich man, the camel, and the likelihood of passing through the eye of a needle. John Rawls's *A Theory of Justice* had not yet been published in Berdyaev's day, but he must have known that while an overdose of equality was bad, too much inequality caused no end of trouble. On the other hand, Putin must have known that the general trend in the world is toward excessive inequality, partly as the result of globalization.

Putin also should have known that economic inequality in Russia is greater than in all other developed or semideveloped economies. About 110 Russian citizens are reported to control 35 percent of household wealth, largely comprising money made in the natural resources sector over the last twenty-five to thirty years. This has become not only a major political problem, but a very serious economic issue, a real obstacle to further economic growth. For if wealth is concentrated in so few hands, demand will be limited. In these circumstances, elementary political and economic common sense would seem to dictate a strategy of spreading wealth more widely. In Berdyaev's book, America's great wealth is explained with reference to inequality of property and income.

The third and most troubling ideological authority recommended by Putin is Ivan Ilyin. Putin and his colleagues believe that the long search for a new doctrine has ended and that in Ilyin they have found the prophet to present their much-needed new ideology.

Ilyin was well-known among Russian émigrés in the 1920s and 1930s, subsequently forgotten, and rediscovered only recently. Widely republished in recent years, he has been frequently quoted by Putin in speeches and articles and also by other leading Russian figures close to him. As the Russian minister of regional development put it: "The demand for his ideas in today's Russia is so strong that sometimes there is a feeling that Ivan Ilyin is our contemporary."

Born in Moscow in 1883 a stone's throw from the Kremlin, Ilyin came from an upper-class family, many of whom served in Russia's army. He studied law in Russia and Germany (his mother was Russian of German origin) and wrote on Hegel, Fichte, and the philosophy of law. In later years, he became engaged with religious questions, and he too was a passenger on the philosophers' ship of 160 undesirables expelled from Russia in 1922. Ilyin settled in Berlin, where he worked in the Russian Scientific Institute, primarily as a political lecturer and writer. He was devoted entirely to the struggle against bolshevism, which he saw as the greatest danger to mankind. He edited *Mankind on the Brink of the Abyss,* a collection of essays devoted to the misdeeds of the Bolsheviks; the book was widely translated and disseminated. However, Ilyin still had difficulties with the Gestapo, was dismissed from his job in July 1934, and found it next to impossible to be employed as either a writer or a lecturer. It is true that the Nazis dismissed him from his job; it is less frequently mentioned that his place of work was part of Joseph Goebbels's Ministry of Propaganda. With the help of composer Sergei Rachmaninov, he moved to Switzerland, where he lived up to his death in 1954. Putin personally initiated the transfer of his remains to the Russian capital in 2005, and he was reburied in a Moscow monastery. In the last two decades, almost thirty of his books have been republished in Russia.

What attracts Putin and other leading Russian figures to Ilyin's writing? What were his ideas for the rebuilding of a post-Communist Russia? Among his generation of Russian émigrés, Ilyin was one of the two theologian/philosophers giving more than routine thought to Russia's future. While Georgy Fedotov, a major theologian and philosopher, was a humanist and democrat, Ilyin never made a secret of the fact that he stood for a monarchy and autocratic (but not totalitarian) dictatorship. After World War II, Fedotov published an article that argued that czarist Russia could in no way be the model for a post-Communist Russia. What would Russia believe in when bolshevism has died, when the revolution and the counterrevolution were over? Fedotov asked. It would be Russian nationalism, he answered, but what form would it take? As of today, the answer would appear to be Ivan Ilyin, but the counterrevolution may not be over yet. Ilyin was the only thinker whom Putin quoted in his speeches as a president: in his presidential addresses of 2005 and 2006 and in his speech to the State Council the year after. In 2009, Putin went to the Sretensky Monastery to lay flowers on Ilyin's grave.

Ilyin advocated a strong central power for post-Communist Russia, with few rights for non-Russian regions such as Ukraine or the Caucasus, which may help to explain his popularity among the present-day Russian leadership.

Ilyin's particular form of solidarism reached Russia through his influence on an organization of the exiled younger generation, the Natsionalny Trudovoi Soyuz (NTS), which adopted him as its master ideologist after World War II; when some of its members returned to Russia after the fall of communism, they carried his ideas to Moscow. It is likely that the messenger was Aleksandr Solzhenitsyn or the film producer Nikita Mikhalkov (*Burned by the Sun* and the *Barber of Siberia*), a man of very right-wing views and the son of the poet who had provided the Soviet anthem that replaced "The Internationale."

"The Lord allocated to Ilyin the gift of the seer," according to one Russian minister of regional development, giving voice to the conviction that just as Ilyin's prophecies concerning the disintegration of the Soviet Union were correct, so are his predictions of hostile attempts to undermine Russia's sovereignty after the fall.

But not all of Ilyin's ideas were as seductively influential. Indeed, some were embarrassingly wrong. "What did he do?" he wrote of Adolf Hitler. "He stopped the process of Bolshevization of Germany and with this provided an enormous service to Europe."

Ilyin, in other words, did not foresee that far from closing the door to bolshevism, Hitler opened it by unleashing World War II.

"Europe does not understand the Nazi movement. It does not understand it and is afraid," Ilyin wrote. "And the more it is afraid, the less it understands. The less it understands, the more it tends to believe all the negative rumors, all the horror stories of 'eyewitnesses,' all the frightening predictions. Radical left wingers in virtually all European nations create an atmosphere of ill will and hatred. Unfortunately our Russian [émigré] press is gradually also drawn into this, the [Jewish-liberal] emotions gradually become categories of good and evil."

Ilyin wrote that while he understood the emotions of German Jews, he categorically refused to judge national socialism and recent events in

Germany from their point of view. Hypnotized by liberal democratic views, Europe was blinded as far as the Bolshevist danger was concerned.

"To this day European public opinion has failed to understand that National Socialism is by no means radical racialism which does not respect the law," Ilyin asserted. "The spirit of National Socialism does not lead to racialism." It does not lead to negation, but generates a positive and creative spirit to tackle the tasks that confront all nations. The same calumnies were brought against the Russian émigrés and against Mussolini.

To summarize: Ilyin was not a Nazi, but a strong sympathizer who wholly misjudged its essence. His political judgment was utterly foolish. He was not at all aware of Hitler's racialism or did not mind his hostility toward Russia or the fact that Hitler regarded Russians as subhuman. Nor did he realize that Nazism was leading to war against Russia and that its motives were by no means mainly ideological. Ilyin was willing to embrace all anti-Communists. But for Hitler, communism was not that much of a threat; his propaganda in this respect was deliberately misleading. Up to a point, he admired Stalin. He wanted to occupy and dominate Eastern Europe and Russia.

Ilyin bitterly attacked the "Jewish bourgeois press" of Weimar Germany, which he accused of being pro-Soviet and never telling the truth about Russia. It is true that the newspapers of the period in Germany were on occasion uncritical, but their sins of commission and omission were small in comparison with Ilyin's utter misjudgments—indeed, fanaticism.

What could be said in defense of Ilyin? Not much, except perhaps for the fact that these lines (and others in a similar vein) were written early on, in 1933. But it still remains true that while being a monarchist, he considered Nazism a positive phenomenon that with some modifications and adjustments could serve as a model for the future Russia.

Did he change his views after the war? Yes, but not by very much. He preferred to comment on fascism in general, not on Nazism specifically. In an article published in 1948, he maintained that fascism had been inevitable, given Europe's left-wing chaos and totalitarianism. The healthy forces had to reassert themselves, just like a dictatorship in ancient Rome in states of emergency. This happened in Europe after World

War I and would happen in the future, too. Fascism was right inasmuch as it looked for justified social and political reforms and inasmuch as it was based on patriotic feelings, without which no people can survive. However, fascism committed several deep, serious, fatal mistakes that brought about its downfall. Ilyin listed six of them, but the first was the decisive one.

Fascism was not religious—indeed, it was hostile to Christianity. It generated right-wing totalitarianism, while the monopoly of a political party created demoralization and corruption. It also became chauvinist and idolized Caesarism.

Since Ilyin was deeply religious, fascism's lack of religion was for him decisive. But not all fascisms were antireligious: only in Nazi Germany was there intervention in church affairs and occasional persecution. Nothing of the sort occurred in Italy or other Fascist countries and movements. In some cases, there was a fairly close collaboration between the (Fascist) state and the church.

Did the establishment of a single party create demoralization? Similar questions arose with regard to the other points listed. Ilyin believed that all the deviations, exaggerations, and mistakes were unnecessary. Benito Mussolini understood that he needed the church, but Hitler with his vulgar atheism did not understand that he was proceeding in the footsteps of the Antichrist. Nor was it necessary to establish a party monopoly.

Idolizing Caesarism (Ilyin probably meant the *Führerprinzip*, the adulation of the Duce) was the greatest mistake of fascism. It was totally opposed to monarchism and inevitably led to despotism, the negation of freedom, and terrorism. Caesarism is immoral, cruel, and demagogic, despises the people, and shows disregard of law and individual rights. Francisco Franco and António de Oliveira Salazar understood this and did not call themselves Fascists, Ilyin suggested. Fascism must not lead to *folie de grandeur* and an excess of pride and superiority, which would cause its isolation and eventually its downfall.

Ilyin expressed the hope that Russian Fascists would learn from and not repeat the mistakes of their predecessors, which would fatally compromise the patriotic cause. Even after World War II, Ilyin found it difficult to see the difference between a mistake and a crime, a distinction he should have known.

On some points, Ilyin's views had changed by 1948. The monarchism he preached before World War II was not the constitutional monarchy of, say, the United Kingdom, Sweden, or the Netherlands, but tantamount to an authoritarian dictatorship. Ilyin had never been a Fascist, but in the interwar period he had moved in that direction. His views on monarchy after 1945 became vaguer. The term "authoritarian" was still used, but dictatorship had acquired a bad reputation and was dropped. However, since he was still opposed to a democratic order, what could be the political system of a future Russia?

Ilyin's views on social and economic policy were never made clear: It was not really his field. He was a solidarist of sorts, but what was solidarism? It meant different things in different countries at different times. It appeared first in France, found its most prominent spokesman in the Austrian academic Othmar Spann, and also had support in many other countries, perhaps most significantly among left-wing Catholics.

Solidarism was against anomie and the breakdown of social cohesion and bonds. It disagreed with socialism but also with free market theorists; some supreme power was needed to control the market and those who benefited most from it. The market could not be trusted to solve all problems, certainly not the most crucial.

Fascism played with solidarism but never quite adopted it. Spann had hoped that his ideas would be accepted by the new rulers in Germany, but the Nazis had no such intention. They instead arrested Spann and removed him from his chair at the University of Vienna. Solidarists were against traditional socialism, but also against laissez-faire capitalism. The present (capitalist) system should be allowed to work as long as it delivered the goods, but only under control and supervision. Solidarists preferred (and continue to prefer) to remain vague: The state is to be in charge, not the market.

Vagueness in this important field did not, however, impede the rise of Ilyin's reputation in Russia. He became the great authority to be invoked more often than anyone else, whatever the issue. Needless to say, there was occasional criticism and contradiction. Theologians disliked the fact that Ilyin had always talked and written about God—but very seldom about the church. Berdyaev and others had criticized him back in the 1920s and 1930s; as they saw it, his worldview was not really Christian, let alone Orthodox. He used Christianity to back up his political arguments, convinced that his views were right and no other views were credible.

The most extreme attacks on Ilyin, however, came from the most radical voices in the Russian émigré community. Thus Viktor Ostretsov, a Russian émigré specialist on *Zhidomasonstvo* (the cabal of Jews and Freemasons that was the leading force behind world politics and all the evil in the universe). According to Ostretsov, Ilyin was not really a monarchist or a Christian, but an agent of the Jews and the Masons. The proof was easy to find: Had he been a real enemy of the Bolsheviks, his place would not have been on the philosophers' ship of those expelled, he would have been sent to Siberia or have been shot. When he came to Berlin, he belonged to the Russian philosophers' society together with Berdyaev, a type even more suspect than Ilyin among the followers of the Russian Far Right, and Semyon Frank—a converted Jew. Need one say more? The headquarters of this society was in the building that belonged to the Jewish B'nai B'rith Masonic lodge, which had put it at the disposal of refugee intellectuals in the beginning of their stay. We do not know whether Ilyin ever visited this building in Berlin. But it stands to reason that such a concatenation of circumstances could not possibly have been accidental.

The attack by Ostretsov and like-minded crackpots did not affect Ilyin's authority in contemporary Russia. Why mention it in the first place? Because it shows that the madness and persecution mania mentioned earlier among contemporary writers in Russia did not come like a bolt out of the blue. It had its predecessors. It is impossible to say how far this affliction will spread or has spread already.

8 | FOREIGN POLICY AND THE PETROSTATE

For a long time, the main preoccupation of Russian policy makers, as well as the rest of the country, was with domestic issues. Unless there was a minimum of stability at home, unless it was clear who was running the country, unless the economy functioned to at least some extent, Russia was an object of politics, not a normal power pursuing its own interest. Gorbachev and Yeltsin had also been negotiating with outside powers, but their main assignment, as they saw it, was to limit the damage that had been caused; the Russian economy had collapsed, and the country urgently needed foreign help. A change came only gradually, a few years into Putin's reign as president. Putin provided the minimum of stability that was needed, but this alone would not have been sufficient. It came not as the result of a spiritual awakening or because Russia suddenly regained its self-confidence and sense of purpose. It came for more prosaic reasons—the growing demand from world markets for oil and gas and the steeply increasing prices paid for these raw materials. Within a few years, Russia found itself strikingly better off. If instead of Gorbachev and Yeltsin (or another member of the reform party), Yegor Ligachev, once Gorbachev's main rival, had come to power, he would have benefited from this turn for the better. The Communist Party and its leaders would have been praised in 2005 for achieving this turn in the fortunes of the country. The Soviet Union would still have collapsed, because the system was essentially rotten, and the fall of the regime could have come with even more devastating consequences. But it might have happened only two or three decades later in a world situation quite different from the one in 1991.

Striking misjudgments prevailed in both West and East concerning the events taking place in the Soviet Union, partly because everything happened so unexpectedly.

In Washington and the European capitals, there was enormous relief that the Cold War had ended. If it was not interpreted as the end of history, it was certainly seen as the dawn of a new peaceful era. With Russia on the road to democracy, the danger of war had been exorcised, military budgets could be drastically reduced, and Western countries could at long last devote their efforts and resources to tackling long-neglected domestic issues. Most observers followed events in the former Soviet Union with a mixture of goodwill and a steady decline in interest. Some Western observers thought that Russia's road to freedom and democracy would be long and arduous, but this was by no means the majority view. Even with the benefit of hindsight, it is difficult to explain this unwarranted optimism; given Russia's past and present condition, it was rooted in wishful thinking. Very few considered the likelihood that the loss of empire might not have been the end of the story and that, as quite often happens in history, an attempt would be made to regain what had been lost.

The German precedent should have been remembered: Totally defeated in 1918 and powerless, Germany was able to return as a great power within a mere fifteen years. It should have been realized that when new tensions arose, they were not being provoked by Putin and the KGB. Like the German people in the early 1930s, a majority of Russians wanted not only a good life, but to be part of a great power, if possible a superpower. It would have been wrong to accuse the Russian leaders of keeping their true intentions secret. There had been complaints even by Gorbachev and Yeltsin that too much had been expected from the West and that Soviet concessions had not been reciprocated in the 1990s. Steps had been taken by the West (such as expanding NATO) that were consid a provocation in the Kremlin.

Some of these complaints were difficult to understand—for instance, those concerning purely defensive measures by the United States (such as installing radar and some other components of missile defense in Eastern Europe to deal with the Iranian threat). But the West failed to take into account traditional Russian fears and suspicions. Be that as it may, it was not true that the Russian leaders failed to make their position clear. This was done perhaps most clearly in some of Putin's speeches. Nevertheless, up to about 2003 the key words as far as American-Russian relations were concerned were friendship, cooperation, engagement, freedom agenda, equilibrium, bilateral, pragmatic, and so on.

People in Moscow expected help from the West, but it was not clear in what way the West could have helped except by World Bank support. But there was also the suspicion, small in the beginning but steadily growing, that the West would take advantage of Russia's weakness. Some went further and expressed the conviction that the fall of the Soviet Union had been engineered by Western imperialism. Zapadophobia (fear of the West) grew in Russia by leaps and bounds. There was a deep-seated conviction that any initiative that was good for the West was bound to be harmful for Russia and should therefore be rejected. The radical Right, which had emerged as a force to reckon with in Moscow, was praying for a revival of the Cold War. Russia faced bankrupcy more than once in the 1990s and the economy would have collapsed but for Western bailouts. But this fact was mentioned seldom if ever by Russian leaders.

During this period, the United States was still mentioned occasionally as a "strategic partner." Russian leaders more often invoked the BRIC countries (Brazil, Russia, India, China) as their new favorite partner. This was not taken too seriously in the West because the BRIC had little in common either politically or economically, nor was there much interest in a close collaboration with Russia. Moreover, some of them faced serious domestic and/or economic problems.

This Russian attitude found its concise formulation in a polemical speech by Putin at the Munich Security Conference in February 2007. It was a strong attack against unipolarity—meaning the United States, which had emerged as the sole remaining superpower. Under the cover of spreading democracy, the United States was using military force all over the globe, thus endangering world peace.

Some Western leaders were shocked by the fierce tone; they should have been grateful to Putin for clearing the air. They should have been aware that, as Angela Merkel put it in a talk with President Barack Obama at the time of the Ukraine crisis, Putin lived in a different universe. This was true. However, they had been mistaken in assuming that their universe was the norm and Putin's the outdated exception. They had also been mistaken in their belief that given its demographic and other weaknesses, Russia was no longer important; this was probably true from a long-term perspective, but it was wrong with regard to the next decade or two, given Europe's weakness and America's apparent desire to reduce its activities in world affairs following Afghanistan and Iraq. As far as Washington was concerned, Russia was still in a position to cause a great deal of mischief.

Putin had given due warning. Why did the Europeans not invest more in the Russian economy? He could have blamed the Chinese even more when they took a hard look at the Russian economy and decided not to invest, but this he could not do. He upbraided the West for its "colonialist attitude." He expressed his anger on various other occasions. And it was not only the mood of one person: He had the support of public opinion, the majority of the people. It found its expression in a variety of political documents, such as "The New Russian Foreign Policy Concept" (2013) and the Plan Oborony (the new military doctrine of 2010). These documents were hardly noticed in the West, on the assumption that if important changes were taking place in Russian thinking, they would hardly be discussed in detail in official documents of this kind.

But on this occasion the Kremlin was quite outspoken. It emphasized the international power shift from West to East, from Europe to the Asian-Pacific region. Whereas previous such documents (2005–06) discussed the need to liquidate the remnants of Cold War attitudes, this was now ignored. In earlier documents, the possibility of interaction with NATO had been considered, but this too was no longer part of the agenda. Instead, the need to establish closer relations with China and India received high priority. In contrast with isolationist trends in America and European foreign policy, Russian foreign policy grew more expansive, something many in the West failed to see. New problems and new opportunities turned up, including interest in the Arctic and Antarctic regions. Since Russia had become stronger, it could take the initiative in various directions.

Russian foreign policy makers, needless to say, would not discuss all their foreign policy problems in the limelight; there was a limit to glasnost. At least some of them must have known that the whole Eurasian concept was a dubious and windy one (as a prominent British diplomat put it). Russia was part of Asia, but not a very important and welcome one, and the countries of Asia were not waiting with bated breath for its appearance. Russia was not welcomed with great enthusiasm in Asia; it was considered essentially a European country.

Furthermore, the shift from West to East in world politics was a mixed blessing from the Russian point of view. If Russia did not move with great caution, it would end up as a junior partner, playing second fiddle to China. In its anger about the West, Russia was strongly tempted to ignore this, given the traditional suspicions concerning Western policies. Russian emotions could easily prevail over sober, critical judgment. It was the old story of Russian policy makers detecting threats where none existed or were not of great importance. Perhaps it was inevitable, perhaps Russia needed the lesson of being a junior partner in order to free itself from concepts and prejudices of a past age?

If the Eurasian concept had at least a weak base in geopolitical terms, what can be said about the orientation toward the BRIC countries? In a Russian concept paper about the participation of the Russian Federation in the BRICs, there were many pages about the great benefit of the strategic objectives of such an alliance, about strong support for generally recognized principles and norms of international law, of the Russian Federation standing in favor of positioning the BRICs in the world system as a new model of international relations overarching the old dividing lines between West and East and North and South. Declarations of this kind were showing that Russian diplomats had mastered the United Nations political gobbledygook. But what had it to do with the realities of world politics? What strategic benefits were likely to accrue to Russia from a close collaboration with Brazil and South Africa?

The realities of world politics were the deterioration of relations with the United States. Ukraine was a constant bone of contention well before the Crimea crisis of 2014, Georgia, Syria, the assassination of Alexander Litvinenko in the United Kingdom, the fate of some adopted Russian children in the United States, the Iranian nuclear bomb, and the defector status given in Moscow to Edward Snowden (the American revealer of secrets who had been told by Putin in person that in Russia such practices did not occur). These and other irritations bedeviled relations between the two countries.

President Obama was still moderately optimistic, talking about a reset in relations and promising President Dmitry Medvedev that if and when reelected, he would be able to devote much more energy to a reset to improve relations. But it all came to nothing. The Russians tried to explain to the Americans that their concept of (sovereign) democracy—with the emphasis on sovereign rather than democracy—was different from the Western and especially the American concepts. "Sovereign democracy" was an invention of Vladislav Surkov, the leading idea man in the Kremlin and also Russia's best *piarchik* (public relations expert); not for nothing had he been president of the all-Russian advertising agency.

As far as many Russians were concerned, democracy meant disorder, if not chaos. The Russian system had to be authoritarian at least to some extent, and to harp on democratic values and human rights in these circumstances was pointless and counterproductive. But this did not register for a long time in Washington and other Western capitals. Perhaps it could not be accepted, if only because it was needed as a counterweight against the permanent anti-American propaganda of the Russian media.

Russia and the European Radical Right

Why did Russian relations with the West go wrong? A Russian version by Maxim Bratersky published in *Global Affairs* (2014) is interesting and superficially, at least, partly plausible. It certainly gives an indication of the ideas underlying the conduct of Russian foreign policy at the present time and in the years to come.

The reasoning in brief goes as follows: Russia's 2012 presidential elections were a watershed in relations between Russia and the rest of the world. Integration into Western structures as an ideology was replaced with preserving Russia's independence and turning toward partners in the east and south. The goal of dissolving the national economy into the world market was changed for ensuring the country's reindustrialization, laying the foundation for its economic independence, and establishing an economic association of its own.

The strategy of looking for compromises with Western leaders gave way to restructuring the world system in cooperation with non-Western countries, where Russia would be one of the leaders. In Russia's foreign policy philosophy, the values of the naïve liberalism of the 1990s were replaced with ideas of realism and statism. The vacuum in Russia's foreign policy ideology was filled with an idea of gathering the Russian world and giving priority to the protection of traditional Christian values. This development was more or less inevitable, because the West believed that Russia had lost the Cold War and from the beginning followed an anti-Russian policy. It wanted to turn Russia into a semicolony technologically and financially dependent on the West.

The West was strongly opposed to the preservation in Russia of a political regime that could concentrate resources on politically prioritized areas. In the 2000s, such a form of integration stopped suiting Russia, and it raised the issue of a "big bargain," including (among other things) a visa-free regime between Russia and the EU. In the mid-2000s, the EU began to limit opportunities for productive investment in Europe by Russian capital.

Contradictions between the West, above all the United States, and Russia came to a head in 2008 after the Georgian-Russian conflict provoked by Atlantic initiatives and by a deadlock in negotiations for a strategic cooperation agreement between Russia and the EU. In 2009, after the G20 summit in London, Russia came to the conclusion that the existing financial and monetary system controlled by the West was at variance with its interests. The idea of integration with the West was finally sidelined because of an information war launched by the West against the Sochi Olympics, the Syrian crisis, and an acute conflict that broke out in Ukraine.

This briefest outline of the Russian version of events. It raises many questions: For instance, unprejudiced readers might be interested to know in what way the two wars in which Russia became involved during the last decade against Georgia and Ukraine/Crimea protected Christian values, as claimed by the Kremlin. They might want to know more about "the information war" in connection with the Winter Olympic Games and whether "gathering" could be a synonym for imperialism. Such quibbling, however, will not take one very far toward an understanding of the doctrine underlying Russian foreign policy.

The truly interesting aspect is the chronology, or rather chronological sequence, of events. While the Bratersky article argues that a basic change in Russian policy occurred in 2009 or at the latest in 2014, an article by Yuri Afanasiev, published in *Perspective* in February 1994, entitled "A New Russian Imperialism," provides a different timetable and explanation, based on the official "Russian military doctrine" of 1993. Among the basic principles, it mentions a strong Russia as the most effective guarantee for the entire territory of the former Soviet Union; assumption of the role of peacemaker in all territories; the obligation to protect Russians in the near abroad; opposition to the extension of NATO; and defense of the interests of Russians at home and abroad. This the author says could be well-founded, but it created concern because the article states that Russian interests extend not only to the entire territory of the former Soviet Union but also to the countries of the former "socialist camp," even if they believe they had freed themselves from Moscow's control and have no desire to return to it.

In the 1990s, Russia was more than once close to bankruptcy and not in a position forcefully to pursue its aims. It depended on bailouts by the West by way of the World Bank. However, in the years after, following increased demand for oil and gas, the change in situation enabled the Kremlin to conduct a more aggressive policy. The author also mentions the assumption that this course of action was determined at least to some extent by a feeling on the part of the authorities of the "loss of past greatness" and the suffering from an inferiority complex. It is the voice of a country that "feels humiliated and insulted now that it is no longer listened to as in former times." In brief, there was no dramatic change in 2008 or 2010, only a change in circumstances that enabled Russia to pursue its foreign political aims.

These comments are of interest, partly because they were prescient and also because they are relevant with regard to the question of whether another policy by the West might have prevented present and future tensions with Russia. It is possible that the West could have helped Russia regain its former position as a superpower, even if it meant acting against the wishes of the regions and republics that did not want to be part of the Soviet Union; but it is not clear why it should have done so. Furthermore, given Russia's deep suspicion of the West, the Russian "ultras" would likely have believed that such Western help was in some hidden, unfathomable way aimed at hurting Russia. Any favors extended by the West were a priori suspect.

If relations between Russia and the United States deteriorated after 2006 to reach a nadir in 2014 with the Crimea/Ukrainian crisis, there was a similar process in relations with the European Union. Europe, in contrast to America, was heavily dependent on Russian energy supplies and Russian imports from Europe, especially of luxury goods. The Russians could threaten Europe with all kinds of countermeasures, but not too bluntly. An interruption of gas and oil supplies would immediately have reduced Russian earnings and induced the West in the long run to reduce its dependence on Russian oil and gas.

European investments in Russia also remained well below Russian expectations, partly because of doubts about the health of the Russian economy, but also because of political uncertainties. There were frequent irritations. The Russians were unhappy about the Kosovo situation, the British complained that Moscow refused to extradite a person thought to be involved in the murder of Alexander Litvinenko, the KGB defector. Russia had high hopes with regard to relations with Germany, its historical partner in many ventures. What had happened between 1941 and 1945 had been forgiven; Putin had good memories from his years in

Saxony. Gerhard Schröder, a former German chancellor, became an employee of Gazprom, the leading Russian oil company. Schröder declared that Putin was a 100 percent democrat, a statement that probably embarrassed Putin a little because he had tried hard to make it clear that he was a sovereign democrat, not a democrat in the Western sense. There is no reason to doubt Schröder's statement that he and Putin were close friends. But could the fact that he was employed by the Russians have also been a factor of some relevance?

EUROPEAN interests as far as relations with Russia were concerned were not identical with American. Europe's dependence on Russian energy supplies quite apart (about a third of total requirements), there were traditionally Europe's closer trade relations. Hence it came as no surprise that European countries dissociated themselves from certain American initiatives with respect to Russia that were considered too harsh and aggressive. The imposition of sanctions following the Crimea/Ukraine crisis was one example, but there were others. On the other hand, there was no unanimity inside Europe; the countries closer to Russia, such as Poland and the Baltic republics, felt themselves more directly exposed to Russian pressure and therefore in greater need of protection. At the same time, no European country wanted to divorce itself entirely from American foreign policy. Russia tried to make the most of the differences between the European Union and the United States, but with limited success. For if there were deep-seated suspicions of the outside world in Russia, there was no great trust in Russian intentions in Europe, either. Suspicions increased whenever Russia acted provocatively even on relatively minor issues such as a Russian cyberattack against Estonia. Russia regarded Europe as a continent in decline, but not to be written off entirely in view of its economic importance. Russia had obvious misgivings with regard to European plans to achieve greater integration, whether it was through establishing a European army or enacting a European foreign policy or approving a common energy policy. A united Europe would have meant a stronger Europe, and this was the last thing Russia wanted. A divided Europe meant a weaker Europe and many opportunities for Russia to play out one country against another.

There were several EU attempts to draw Russia closer to Europe before the crisis of 2014. Most ambitious was media mogul Silvio Berlusconi's project to make Russia a full member of the European Union. Berlusconi, who served three times as Italy's prime minister, had established a close personal relationship (he believed) with Putin, but his constant problems with the law in Italy made it impossible for him to pursue his project. More modest were the projects aimed at ENP (European Neighborhood Policy) and common economic and other spaces. But Russia did not favor projects of this kind; it preferred to have Europe join its own pet scheme—the Eurasian Union. In this, Europe had very little interest.

In addition, Russia has been cultivating several potential Trojan horses in the ranks of the European Union. This refers above all to Hungary, where an antidemocratic policy has become the new official state doctrine; and to Greece, which ideologically is not particularly close to the new Russia but is in an almost desperate search of friends and sympathizers in view of its weak economy and great domestic difficulties. It applies in particular to Bulgaria, where the pro-Russian Plamen Oresharski government—consisting of a coalition of formerly left-wing and far-right parties, exceedingly corrupt by any standards—managed to hang on to power for more than a year in 2013–14. The Russian search for allies is understandable, and as is the fact that it cannot afford to be choosy in its pursuit. But it is still remarkable that it ended up with an array of the least savory forces in all of Europe.

It seems a long way from the class struggle to solidarism, from historical materialism to a philosophy of idealism, from militant atheism to the Orthodox Church, from proletarian internationalism to staunch nationalism and chauvinism. But as Russia has shown, the transition is by no means impossible, even within a short time.

Once upon a time, there had been a Communist International, and Moscow could count on the sympathy and support of the radical Left in Europe. But those days are gone, probably forever, and if Russia wants allies in Europe, it must look in a different direction. As Sergey Baburin, Vice Speaker of the Russian Duma and one of the leaders of the Far Right, put it, succinctly if somewhat bluntly, in an interview with Sergey

Ryazanov in *Svobodnaya Pressa* entitled "Our Fifth Column in Europe," Russia has strong potential allies in Europe—namely, the forces of the extreme Right. The old slogan "Workers of the world, unite" has been replaced by "Nationalists of all countries, unite." They are anti-American, anti–European unity, and anti-NATO and can be counted upon to support Russia in various ways.

This idea had occurred to Russian leaders for a number of years as Russian policy at home and abroad had become more and more right-wing and nationalist, both ideologically and in political practice. The European Left, especially the Communists and former Communists, had been very slow in realizing this. Some of them were still thinking of Moscow as the bulwark of progressive mankind, socialist in orientation. Why this happened is not easy to explain. In part, it was probably genuine ignorance of the changes in Russia; in part, such reluctance to accept these developments may have been psychological, mere wishful thinking.

Leaders of the European extreme Right had been invited to the Russian capital well before the Baburin interview. The French *Naitonal Front* was even given a Russian loan to finance its campaign. As support for these politicians and ideologists (some of them quite close to neo-fascism) became stronger, largely as the result of a growing aversion against Brussels, the European ultranationalists gained political importance. The European fans of Putin were attracted by his religious inclination and his image as a critic of such decadent Western ways as homosexuality and of course as a leading anti-Americanist.

Russia and the European right-wing extremists certainly have common enemies, but to what extent do they have common values and beliefs? It would be too facile to dismiss this new budding alliance as a pure marriage of convenience. Russia has moved to the right and to a significant extent very far to the right. How far it will eventually move, only the future will tell. But since old-style conservatism is no longer very attractive (or effective) in the modern world, it needs a good measure of populism, and this is bound to bring it fairly close to fascism. Could it manage in the long run without a single state party, without a leader and a leadership cult, without a heavy propaganda machinery and repression? Only if it proves to be very successful and popular. In the long run, this is not at all certain.

An alliance between Russia and the European Right is in no way unprecedented. It had been part of European politics for a century—from the Congress of Vienna (1814–15) to the Russian Revolution. The Soviet connection with the European Far Left has been of shorter duration.

Russia had always been on the lookout for friends and agents of influence in Europe, mainly to embellish its image in Europe, which had not been as good as it wanted. At the beginning of the nineteenth century, the outlook seen from Moscow had been promising: Russia had defeated Napoleon, the anti-Napoleonic forces, the nationalists and patriots—especially those from Germany such as Baron vom Stein; Karl August von Hardenberg; Johann Yorck; August, Count Neidhardt von Gneisenau; and Ernst Moritz Arndt who had congregated in Russia or cooperated with the Russians. But soon after, a countermovement developed. Russia stood for oppression. In a number of conferences (Olmütz, Karlsbad), it coordinated the ban on freedom of expression. Agents of influence such as August von Kotzebue and Leopold von Gerlach were operating, but Kotzebue was assassinated, and for public opinion, especially democratic opinion, Russia was the enemy par excellence. Alexander Gorchakov, the Russian foreign minister, followed, broadly speaking, a pro-German line, just as Bismarck was pro-Russian.

But public opinion was bitterly opposed to Czarism; Russia's only friends were on the Right. Admiral von Hintze, a confidant of the German emperor, wrote in a report to Wilhelm II a few years before the outbreak of the war that there was a common interest in holding down the Poles and the Jews. This trend became particularly pronounced toward the end of the century with the anti-German Triple Entente. The main task of Russian diplomats and the agents of the Okhrana (the Russian secret police operating inside the country and abroad) was to try to create a climate at least somewhat more sympathetic toward Russia.

Russia found a number of talented agents, such as Olga Novikoff in London and several ladies in Paris—some operated out of conviction, others because they were paid well. French newspapers and periodicals from the leading dailies to the *Revue diplomatique* and the *Revue des deux mondes* received substantial subsidies. Alexander Benckendorff, a

Russian diplomat in London, sent a list of the newspapers with whom he had established contact to his ministry. It was a very impressive list, and the newspapers for whatever reason played down the importance of the 1905 revolution and the pogroms as well as other unpleasant occurences. The situation today is similar. Russians not only buy *The Independent* and the *Evening Standard* in London but also newspapers in Paris. In Germany, the conservatives were divided as far as the attitude toward Russia was concerned. The arch-conservative *Kreuzzeitung* was in favor of Russia, but after Bismarck's resignation, the voices calling for a preventive war became louder. It is reported that the situation at the present time is not dissimilar except that financial support is now provided not by embassies or secret agents but by corporations and business offices.

Russia and China

Russian-Chinese relations are now among the most important aspects of Russian foreign affairs, in both the short and the long run. They have improved considerably over the last twenty years. Most of the sources of immediate conflict, such as the border disputes, have been removed. Nevertheless, there is a yawning gulf between the extravagant rhetoric on partnership and the limited realities of cooperation. There are common interests, especially in the field of energy supply with Russia as a supplier of oil and gas, but these interests are seldom coordinated. This would be in neither the Russian nor the Chinese tradition of conducting foreign policy, which is dictated more by suspicion than by goodwill. In a wider perspective, China needs Russia less than the other way around. The balance of power between the two countries has changed profoundly and will continue to change. Fifty years ago, there could be no doubt as to which was the stronger of the two countries. Today, the population of China is about ten times larger than Russia's, and this trend is bound to continue as the one-child policy in China has been virtually abandoned. The disparity in GNP is becoming more striking, and changes take place far more quickly than is realized by most. In 1993, the economy of the two countries was about equal. Today, the Chinese economy is four times larger.

Ten years ago, Russia was of importance to China in providing advanced conventional weapons systems and some limited missile defense cooperation. Today, most of what China needs is produced at home. Russian fears of China getting too strong militarily might be one reason its arms exports to India have grown substantially, but in view of Sino-Indian tensions, this may cause political problems.

After ten years of negotiations, an agreement was reached in May 2014 about Russian oil and gas supplies to China. This was an important step for both countries, for Russia because of the need to reduce its dependence on the European market, for China because of its enormous and permanently growing energy needs. But in view of recent and coming breakthroughs in the field, such as shale gas production (China having perhaps the greatest reserves in the world), the importance of an agreement of this kind should not be overrated. Paradoxically, with the widening of cooperation and the emergence of new common projects (such as the three concerning Sakhalin oil fields), the more formidable the Chinese presence in the Russian Far East and Siberia, the greater the political implications. This at a time when the question of whether Russia will be able to hold on to its territories in Asia is becoming more topical. With U.S. withdrawal from Central Asia and Europe's standing in world affairs becoming weaker, potential conflicts between Russia and China will loom more strongly than in the past, when cooperation between Russia and China was rooted to a considerable extent in the perception of a common Western (American) danger. As this danger is beginning to recede, the base for cooperation is shrinking.

The main emphasis of Russian policy in Asia (and particularly regarding China) is on economic relations—Russian exports to China, Japan, and South Korea amount to $150 billion, and a further expansion has been predicted. But for this to happen, Russia needs substantial investments to strengthen its infrastructure, mainly in the field of transport. China will help in this respect, but it is driving a hard bargain, as with its negotiations over the price of oil and gas in the 2014 agreement, and this will not change in future.

In 2014, Chinese commentators uttered surprise about the lack of Russian interest in Chinese investments in economic initiatives in the border regions. Whereas the Chinese had been showing little interest in investing in major central enterprises in Russia, they were willing to invest in the Asian border regions but had always encountered difficulties and resistance on the part of the Russian bureaucracy—this despite the fact that such Chinese investment was needed. For the Chinese, this was not a matter of overwhelming importance, but they seemed to have been peeved by Russia's resistance.

Since the 1990s, the Shanghai Cooperation Organization (SCO) has been in force, encompassing Russia, China, and several other countries and providing a framework for cooperation in various fields. Annual meetings and various confidence-building measures followed. Eventually, in 2001, a more permanent mechanism was established, which was meant to deal primarily with security problems (including antiterrorism maneuvers). They provided protection to the Central Asian republics against "color revolutions" such as happened in Ukraine or protests against local governments such as that in Tiananmen Square. In other respects, the SCO has not been put to a test. There has been much talk about a comprehensive strategic partnership, but little action. Russia and China have common interests in Central Asia—for instance, if a serious terrorist threat were to emerge. But while moving cautiously, they remain rivals in this region both economically and politically.

The Chinese likely have no wish to become directly involved in the administration of the territories in Asia at present under Russian control. But the situation in future is a little more complicated. If Russians truly believe that the relationship between the two powers will not be affected by the fact that the population of one of them is about ten times larger than the other, and the disproportion with regard to the GNP and industrial output almost as striking, they may be in for a surprise. One of the main Russian complaints about Europe and the United States during the years after the breakdown of the Soviet Union was that they were not treated as equals. It will be fascinating to observe how much equality there is likely to be in future between two countries as unequal in most respects as Russia and China.

The relationship between China and Russia has become more that of an elder to a younger brother. During a recent international conference, an Asian scholar referred to Russia as the most recent but also the weakest power on the continent. Russia, needless to say, wants to be a partner rather than a brother, especially not a younger brother. The question arises as to whether it can escape this kind of relationship. Probably not, as long as the United States is considered the main threat by the Kremlin. It is the price Moscow will have to pay short of a fundamental political and psychological reorientation.

The Near Abroad

Russia's relations with the republics that seceded when the Soviet Union collapsed is an issue that has featured prominently in the media and need not be discussed in great detail. The belief among Russian nationalist ideologues that their country cannot exist except as a great empire is deeply rooted and goes back a long time. To many Russians, a number of the regions that were lost (such as Ukraine) are still considered to be parts of Russia proper. Moreover, millions of ethnic Russians now find themselves outside Russia.

True, the Russian Empire had not existed for millennia, contrary to what numerous Russians believed. Many acquisitions were of relatively recent date. Crimea joined Russia under Catherine the Great in 1783, Georgia in 1813, Azerbaijan in 1813. The conquest of the Northern Caucasus took longer; the natives found in Shamil a talented guerrilla warlord and the fighting took about two decades.

Moldova had changed hands and was divided countless times and became part of Russia only in the nineteenth century. The majority of those living in the Baltic countries had been German-speaking for centuries. Lithuania, Latvia, and Estonia had been independent for a short time only between the two world wars. Today, hundreds of thousands of ethnic Russians live there, but they (or their parents or grandparents) had arrived there only under Soviet rule after World War II. Siberia had been explored beginning in the sixteenth century, but it was sparsely settled only in the nineteenth century. Vladivostok was founded by a lieutenant and twenty-eight sailors in the 1860s. Even in those days, half of its residents had not been Russians. Novosibirsk, the largest city east of the Urals, is just over a hundred years old; Irkutsk, which comes next, was founded earlier, in the eighteenth century.

Central Asia became part of Russia in the eighteenth and nineteenth centuries. Russian settlers began to arrive around this time, but primarily just to northern Kazakhstan and the big cities. The Russian protagonists of conquest were named von Kaufman, Georg Steller, Przewalski, Martens, Mannerheim—which indicates that they were not descendants of Rurik. Their message to the Russian public was that the locals of Turkestan (as it was then called) were dying to become part of Russia, but not everyone agreed. Alexander Blok, in a famous poem about the Scythians wrote:

> You are millions, we are hosts, hosts, hosts.

Nevertheless, even if of recent date, by the nineteenth century Russia had become an empire, and its loss in the late twentieth century was a painful blow. It should have been clear that attempts would be made to recover as much as possible of the past glory if the opportunity arose. Many wondered, however: If the United Kingdom and France had accepted the loss of empire, why couldn't Russia? Perhaps because of Russia's conviction that it could not survive except as a great power.

As the Russian economy recovered following the oil and gas boom, the invasion of Georgia took place (2008), Crimea and eastern Ukraine were regained, and attempts were made to recover the initiative in other directions.

For their part, the Central Asian republics indicated a willingness to establish normal, even close, relations with Russia—provided Moscow did not intervene in their domestic affairs unless asked to do so. And such an arrangement may suit Moscow: These are poor countries and with the exception of Kazakhstan have few prospects for substantial improvement in the foreseeable future. Direct rule by Moscow would generate a conflict with China, provoke domestic resistance, and above all commit Russia to invest heavily in these parts without any hope of a quick return.

The United Kingdom and France had realized in the twentieth century that from an economic point of view, the ownership of an empire involves few rewards and a heavy price. The Soviet Union had a similar experience in the 1970s and 1980s. There were constant complaints even under Brezhnev that the Central Asian republics were not pulling their own weight but constantly needed financial help. The new Russia has to pay a heavy price for Chechnya and Dagestan, and the moment Crimea was recovered there were urgent demands for immediate financial support. In brief, empires were no longer a bargain.

Why should the Kremlin engage in a policy of expansion at a time when it faces serious problems at home? The impression was gained among outside observers that the Russian leadership was not aware (or at least not fully aware) of the danger of losing Siberia and the Russian Far East in view of the demographic issues and the disparity of economic power between China and Russia in these parts. But such an impression was wrong: The Russians were quite aware.

Back in 2001, Alexei Kudrin, the outspoken Russian finance minister, had spoken about the need of urgent and massive Russian efforts to improve the situation in these areas. Otherwise, China and other Asian countries would steamroll Siberia and the Russian Far East. When Dmitry Medvedev was president, he declared in a speech in Kamchatka that unless Russia made substantial progress developing the economy in the Far East, it would turn into a raw materials base for more-developed Asian countries, and if efforts were not speeded up, Russia could lose everything. Similar declarations were made by other Russian leaders, and Putin also promised much-needed assistance. But very little happened: Immigration of Chinese, legal and illegal, continued; for political reasons, the Russian authorities may have found it impossible to take drastic action against it. Siberia and the Russian Far East became progressively more dependent on Chinese services, imports, goods, and labor.

Something akin to a Siberian separatist movement developed, and two concessions were made by the Kremlin. The first was that residents of Siberia were permitted to give "Siberian" rather than "Russian" as their nationality in their internal passports. Second, in May 2014 Putin appointed General Nikolai Rogozhkin as his envoy plenipotentiary in Siberia. Unfortunately, Rogozhkin, however loyal and talented, specializes in the field of internal security not economic development, having neither the experience nor the financial resources to deal with economic development. And since Putin was preoccupied with the fallout of the Ukraine/Crimea crisis, this new appointment was unlikely to solve the problems of Russia in Asia. Three months later, meetings by citizens considered Siberian separatists were banned, even though their demands were quite moderate.

Anatoly Antonov, a nationalist demographer at Moscow State University, published a number of projections the same month Putin appointed his new representative for Siberian affairs. According to Antonov, Russia's population will halve within the next fifty years. Applied to Siberia and the Russian Far East, this would mean a decline from about forty million to twenty million. Given such a prediction, could Russia hold on to the vast territories between the Urals and Sakhalin? Migrants from Central Asia arrived in Russia in great numbers after 1990. But they were not warmly welcomed by the local population and after 2010 many of them returned to where they had come from.

A paradoxical and from the Russian point of view unexpected situation may develop. With the American exodus from Afghanistan and to a large extent from the Middle Eastern countries, Russia will face competition from China. The Kremlin would like to evade a situation of this kind, but it is difficult to see how this can be achieved. Suspicion of America and enmity against the West have been an integral part not only of the Russian security forces, but of the population at large. Following a lull in anti-Western propaganda in the 1990s, it became fairly strong in the decade after. A return of America and other Western countries to Central Asia or the Far East is most unlikely. This means that wherever in Asia Russia will try to strengthen its position, it is bound to confront China, not the West. In these circumstances, any attempt to pursue a strong anti-Western line would be recognized as an act of desperation. To avoid relinquishing its Eurasian fantasies, Russia may be forced to accept its reduced status as a "younger brother," playing second fiddle to Beijing.

If Russia is willing to behave as expected by Beijing, being a reliable supplier of oil, gas, and other raw materials at reasonable prices, China may well abstain from more direct intervention in what is now Russia in Asia. The demographic balance is very much in China's favor, but no one really wants to settle in Siberia.

What could a Russian government do to reverse a trend of this kind?

If ethnic Russians at present living outside Russia were to return to what many consider their homeland, this would certainly slow the process, but it would not affect the situation in Asia. Putin's policy of absorbing non-Russians, mainly from the Central Asian republics, and integrating them could be another step in this direction. But this is based on the assumption that there will be a readiness on their part to be integrated. Antonov believes that in another ten to fifteen years, the government in power, realizing that the fate of the state depends on demography, will promote the image of larger families. This would involve raising the salaries of men to a level that will allow them to support such families in comfortable homes. It would also imply about a tenfold increase in health care funding and also family incentives to European levels. It is by no means certain that funding for a policy of this kind will be available. Finally, historical experience has not shown that rising living standards lead to an increase in the birthrate.

Discussions on demographic problems may seem not to belong to an analysis of foreign policy. But it appears likely that considerations of this kind will have a direct and decisive impact on Russian policy with respect to the near abroad.

Russian Oil

The energy sector is the key to Russian domestic and foreign policy. It is also the best-known, most thoroughly analyzed and documented aspect of Russian affairs, for which reason there is no need to discuss it in great detail. The contribution of oil and gas exports has risen during the last hundred years from about 7 percent to about 50 percent. The term "petrostate" has been applied to contemporary Russia not without reason, for the attempts to variegate the Russian economy have not been successful so far, and it is unlikely that they will be successful in the near future. It is Russia's only major weapon in foreign policy. The popular support for the government, the stability of the country, the well-being of the population, the allocation for defense, and many other issues depend on the export (and the price) of oil and gas.

If so, then how to explain that oil and gas exports did not prevent the breakdown of the Soviet Union? Largely because global demand was less at the time and the price of oil much lower. If the Russian economy doubled in size between 2000 and 2008, it was owing to oil exports and the price of oil and gas. If there was a plunge in 2008, the cause was the decline in demand for oil and gas. At the same time, the export of oil and gas was an important political weapon. If Belarus had to pay only a fraction of the price Ukraine did, the reason was not economic. In the 1970s, Russia's satellites in Eastern Europe had to pay much less than countries that did not belong to the Council for Mutual Economic Assistance. The Soviet Union was in the fortunate position of being able to produce relatively cheap oil, but as time passed, production became more expensive, and prices for foreign consumers, even political allies, went up, which caused resentment abroad. The central political problem was Europe's dependence on Russian oil and gas: Russia supplied about one-third of Europe's needs.

Our concern in the present context is not with the history of Gazprom, one of the most powerful international companies, or the tug-of-war concerning the various pipelines, or the many other fascinating developments in this field that took place in recent decades. Our concern is limited to the likely political repercussions of oil and gas exports from Russia. Unfortunately, developments in the energy sector are largely unpredictable, although they will be of great importance for a long time to come for producers and consumers alike.

The European Union has been unable to agree on a common energy policy. With the centrifugal forces inside the EU having gathered strength, it is unlikely that this will change soon. There is, of course, a limit to the pressure Russia can threaten or apply—if the price of supplies is increased beyond a certain limit, consumers will look for alternatives in various directions. Furthermore, Russia will have a vested interest in European prosperity, for a downturn of the European economy will mean a decline in Europe's demand for gas and oil.

How does Russia see its prospects? Russian authorities have always been stressing that they are willing to do business with all countries, that their main interest is to maintain stability, and that political considerations should not interfere with these fundamental economic interests. This is a perfectly sensible attitude, but in fact political considerations have taken precedence over economic issues. Is this going to change in future?

According to a report of the 2014 International Energy Forum, Russian experts envisage a growing demand from the Asian Pacific region. They also expect a volatile situation as a result of politics interfering with oil and gas supplies. The considerable impact of shale gas and shale oil supply has turned the United States from an importer to an exporter of energy. According to Russian experts, the unconventional fuels will also have a significant impact outside America within the next ten years, although no one can predict how great this impact will be, how this will affect prices, how it will influence European dependence on Russian supplies, or whether it will lead to greater use of renewable energy sources or other approaches.

Specific Russian problems include a reluctance on the part of international companies—for both political and economic reasons—to provide the massive investment Russia's oil industry desperately needs. Furthermore, there is widespread belief that the prospects of the export of natural gas from Russia are more promising than the prospects of oil.

The dramatic decline of the price of oil in 2014 (and concurrently the fall of the value of the ruble) may well be temporary, but it points to a great weakness in the structure of the Russian economy and its political consequences. The price of a barrel of oil reached almost $150 at one stage (2008). As these lines are written it is at $52.

Putin had the good luck to come to power at a time of rising demand and rising prices for oil and gas, especially after 2004. Realizing the paramount importance of the export of oil and gas for the survival of the regime led him to renationalize the industry. This too is most unlikely to change. Even the most daring experts are unlikely to venture beyond these seemingly obvious predictions.

9 | SOURCES OF FUTURE CONFLICTS

QUO VADIS, RUSSIA?

The question has been asked many times. Today, as before, a discussion of this kind is bound to take Nikolai Gogol's famous scene in his great novel *Dead Souls* about the speeding troika as its starting point:

> And you, Russia of mine—are you not also speeding like a troika which no one can overtake? Is not the road smoking beneath your wheels and the bridges thundering as you cross them and everything being left in the rear, and the spectators, struck with the portent, halting to wonder whether you are not a thunderbolt launched from heaven? What does that awe-inspiring progress of yours foretell? What is the unknown force which lies within your mysterious steeds?

It is a wonderful opening of a great novel, the troika swift as a bird and the awe-inspiring progress. But as a description of contemporary Russia, it is a bit over the top. Are the oligarchs and the *siloviki* truly overtaking the whole world? Is our troika forcing all nations, all empires, to stand aside? Above all, whither are you speeding, Russia of mine? But there is no answer as yet.

Nor should one exaggerate the speed of our troika. Past attempts to predict future trends in Russia point to the difficulties and limits of such endeavors. Consider one study published in 1990, carried out when Gorbachev was in power and the Soviet Union still existed. *Soviet Union 2000: Reform or Revolution?* (edited by Walter Laqueur, New York, 1990) assessed the prospects of political change as follows:

> The style of Russian politics for centuries has been authoritarian and so has been to a large degree the mentality of rulers and ruled alike. This may change, but only as the result of a cultural revolution affecting wide sections of the population. Such revolutions have occurred, but they have always taken a long time to unfold. It is easy to replace one set of rulers with another. It is infinitely more difficult to eradicate the mentality of unfreedom, to inculcate a spirit of civic responsibility, initiative, tolerance, and willingness to compromise. These features were never ranking high on the tsarist or Bolshevik political agenda. The transition from a totalitarian regime to a democratic system, even a guided democracy, is a period of enormous tensions and *difficulties*.

The study further assessed correctly the likelihood of authoritarian rule and the improbability of the introduction and maintenance of a democratic system in Russia:

> A desire for change will not result in the adoption of Western liberal ideas and values. Liberalism was never deeply rooted in Russian history, its influence was limited, by and large, to sections of the intelligentsia, and even among them it was adopted by only a minority. Today, the general belief is that Western-style liberalism may be well suited for Western-style liberal society, especially for smaller countries in which social and national conflicts are not rampant. But in a society such as the Soviet Union which lacks this, any such institutional change would be a disaster. The country has

> never yet reached such a degree of maturity needed, nor is it likely to do so in the foreseeable future.
>
> Some leading intellectuals are preaching the virtues of greater tolerance, more freedom of speech, and common sense rather than doctrinaire fanaticism in politics, and they look with envy to the higher political culture of some European countries. Even the greatest optimists among them feel the need for a strong hand to control the reform for a long time to come. They point to the fact that every reform in Russian history from the importation of potatoes onwards has been introduced by order from above, usually against much resistance.

This at a distance of twenty-five years seems a fairly accurate description of Putinism, with its "vertical" style of command politics. What could not be foreseen at the time was the disintegration of the Soviet Union and the subsequent attempts to restore it, the chaotic conditions of the Yeltsin era, and how far the reaction against it would go—the emergence of the oligarchs and the *siloviki*. Nor was the growing influence of the Orthodox Church fully appreciated. The experience of the *Russia 2000* study shows that it was far easier to predict long-term trends than short-term events.

A second study, published by the Center for Strategic and International Studies (CSIS), had the great advantage of proceeding after seven years of Putin's rule, as the country had calmed down and an internal balance of power had emerged. Whereas the 1990 study did not attempt to achieve a consensus among its contributors but merely presented individual opinions, the CSIS study more ambitiously attempted just that, only to realize that there were wide divergences of opinion and a consensus could not be reached.

It presented various scenarios for a ten-year period (2007–17) and got much of it right. But it underrated the extent of the hardening of domestic and foreign policy and the influence of various ideologues of the Far Right on the policy of the regime. It overrated the impact of some trends, including the high level of education of the population; this had been true in the past but has declined in view of the reduction of allocations for education by the government. The diversification of the economy was overrated. All leading spokesmen agreed on the necessity to work toward this aim, but little has been achieved.

Skolkovo, which was to be the center of innovation, ran into serious trouble early on mainly as the result of squabbles among various bureaucracies, and there were charges of corruption. It was one of the reasons for the downfall of Vladislav Surkov, Putin's long-term chief of staff.

The CSIS study stated, "It is not only entirely possible, but likely, that Russia will be the largest economy in Europe by 2017." Judging from a 2014 perspective, this seems unlikely; at present, the Russian GDP is trailing not only the German GDP, but those of France, the United Kingdom, and even Italy. This could change, but not in the near future.

Russia's Identity

Any discussion of Russia's future has to start with its demographic prospects. The history of such forecasts is replete with mistakes. For the three decades after the Franco-Prussian War of 1870–71, which France lost against Germany, it was commonly assumed that the French would die out. Similar predictions were the fashion in the 1920s, even though France had been among the victors in World War I, but the bloodletting that had occurred had been so horrible that this seemed the obvious perspective. In 1974 the Club of Rome, a greatly respected semiofficial think tank predicted that the world would come to an end very soon as the result of overpopulation because "we were breeding too much and too because fast."

Since then there has been greater caution; forecasters have often submitted an optimistic as well as a pessimistic scenario, and sometimes even a third somewhere in the middle. Inasmuch as Russia is concerned, the forecasts have ranged from "the bear is dying out" to "the Russian situation is not worse than that of other countries."

Nevertheless, there are certain figures that are not in dispute; the trends are similar to those of other developed countries. The Russian fertility rate was 6–7 percent a hundred years ago. It went down to about 1.9 percent in the 1960s and is at present 1.6 percent. This is slightly more than in other East European countries but less than the reproduction rate of 2.1 percent. It means that in the decades to come Russia's population will decline, not immediately but quite substantially in a span of 20–30 years. Russia's population is 143 million at present; according to U.S. statistics, it will be down to 109 million by 2050. According to Russian statistics, it will decline only to about 130 million. There are many estimates in between. The more optimist projections are based on a number of assumptions such as substantial immigration at the rate of 400, 000 or more a year and improved health services (which will ensure people live longer). Tax relief and direct grants may be given to families with two children or more. To these and other unpredictable factors could be added the possibility that Russia may occupy and incorporate further territories with Russian speakers such as Eastern Ukraine and Transnistria, in which case the outlook will improve from a Russian point of view—certainly in the short run.

On the other hand, a price will have to be paid for most of the measures that may (or may not) be taken to boost the birthrate or the size of the population. Massive immigration of non-ethnic Russians will provoke xenophobia. During the first decade after the fall of the Soviet Union, the majority of immigrants were ethnic Russians from states like Kazakhstan. But most of those who wanted to immigrate have by now done so.

Those who can now be expected to immigrate to Russia are mainly non-Russians. The number of illegal immigrants is unknown; estimates vary between 10 and 20 million. Most illegal immigrants in Russia now, as well as those who are likely to come, are Muslims, which may create social and political problems. According, to the Moscow Institute of National Strategy, if current demographic trends continue, a very high percentage of the population of Russia (including migrants and minorities) will be non-ethnic Russians by the middle of the present century.

Official Russian policy concerning immigration rests on the assumption that non-Russians will be integrated within a relatively short period. But such willingness to be integrated cannot be taken for granted. Historical experience all over the world shows that such integration has seldom if ever taken place quickly, and quite frequently there has been considerable resistance to it. Quite often, it has taken place only superficially—such as acquiring a knowledge of the language of the host country. Russia, unlike Australia, Canada, and the United States, has not been a country with a tradition of accepting and integrating immigrants; xenophobia has been known for a long time. Such a perspective, if true or even if only approximately true, would provide an additional motive for the Russian leaders to incorporate regions of the former Soviet Union inhabited by ethnic Russians.

Why attribute great importance to this issue? Virtually all developed countries face a decline in population, and there are various reasons why this should not necessarily be considered a disaster at all. But Russia is not Belgium or Bulgaria; it is a big country with strong aspirations to great power status, a country that feels it has a mission to fulfill. What is the Russian manifest destiny, and why can it be fulfilled if it counts 150 million citizens but not half or even less?

This has been discussed for a long time, and it will continue to be debated. But before entering these deep waters, mention should be made, even if only briefly, of another consideration: Russia's great weakness as a *Raum ohne Volk* (a space without people), or rather with very few people. In 1926 a German writer named Hans Grimm had published a book entitled *Volk ohne Raum*, which almost instantly became a bestseller and remained one for the next nineteen years. The action took place in Africa, where the author had lived for a long time. He was not a member of the Nazi Party but was deeply convinced that his country was doomed because of a lack of living space. For this reason, there was a vital need for colonies that Germany had lost in World War I. Hitler, like most others of the Far Right, shared Grimm's conviction but not his concentration on Africa. He did not think that colonies in Africa would solve Germany's problems. Hence the German expansion eastward and the invasion of the Soviet Union.

The Idea of a New Empire

Any discussion of Russia's future must undertake to examine the psychically resonant concept of an eternal Russia with a great messianic mission to fulfill. This dominating mind-set is of considerable relevance in the present context, underlying present and future Russian policy. It has appeared in various forms and under various names and goes back a long time. It serves as a justification for Russian imperial policy and statism, but it is also used as a purely theological concept. For a while, it was thought even by some non-Communists that bolshevism was the Russian idea, the major contribution of the country to mankind. With the fall of the Soviet Union, the need for a new ideology arose. Under Boris Yeltsin, there was a competition for formulating a new national idea. But this was a more complicated endeavor than agreeing on a new national anthem, and it was given up—only to be renewed under Putin. Even daily newspapers participated in the search for national identity.

Since then, a great many suggestions in this direction have been made, mainly by ideologues on the right wing of the political spectrum. Philosopher Igor Chubais, for instance, has proposed Christianity, the gathering of the lands, and communitarianism. On the more sophisticated religious-philosophical level, the search went back to Byzantium, which regarded itself as the only legitimate representative of true Christianity. (After the fall of Byzantium, Russia regarded itself as the only legitimate heir to this tradition.)

The next major impetus in this search for a new ideology came in the nineteenth century. With respect to the formulation of a national idea, there was the famous definition, the so-called triad, by Sergey Uvarov, minister of education ("Orthodoxy, absolute rule, and *narodnost*"), which first appeared in an office memorandum sent in 1833 to a number of educators. The czar liked the formula, and some leading intellectuals backed it. It became the official formula up to the revolutions of 1917, even though "nationality" (*narodnost*) was a vague concept and its English translation wholly unsatisfactory.

Later on, the expression "Russian idea" was coined by Vladimir Solovyov in 1888. But the Solovyov concept of a Russian idea concerned itself with spiritual issues rather than empire building. The same was true with regard to Nikolai Berdyaev, the best-known Russian philosopher-theologian of the century after. In his famous book *The Russian Idea*, he dealt with the eschatological and prophetic character of Russian thought, the Russian people being a "people of the end and Russian philosophy being of a religious character."

Solovyov and Berdyaev were patriots, but no one has been more devastating in his comments on the paranoia of the Russian extreme Right than Solovyov. And as for Berdyaev's comments in 1908, the following observation on the chauvinism of the Far Right should suffice: "It was barbaric and stupid, pagan and immoral in inspiration, full of Eastern wildness and darkness, an orgy of the old Russian dissoluteness" ("O russkom natsionalism" in *Slovo* December 7, 1908). One could hardly think of a harsher judgment. Solovyov and Berdyaev were two of the three authors recommended by Putin to Russia's senior officials for Christmas reading in 2013. However, while Putin recommended the right authors, he chose the wrong books. He did not include what they had to say about the deformities of Russian nationalism, for they had become part of the emerging state ideology. This became clear from a document published in May 2014 presenting guidelines for official support for a Russian culture (in line with the spirit of the Putin age), based in considerable part on excerpts from speeches made by Putin on various occasions and declaring that "Russia is not Europe."

It is an interesting statement, even though no one had recently claimed that Russia was Europe. The document argues that while tolerance has always marked Russian history and culture, there must be limits to tolerance; otherwise, it might be interpreted as an ill-placed and dangerous concession to foreign (hostile) influences and as approval of traditions and values alien to the Russian spirit. In other words, it is an all-out attack against modernist trends in Russian and world culture. It mentions, for instance, Kazimir Malevich as an example of worthless artists. Such attacks are not new in history (the "Decadent Art" exhibition in Munich, July 1937). Not all modern art is of the highest value, will last forever, or fetch prices at auctions like at present. Malevich's *Suprematic Composition* (1916), sold by Sotheby's in 2008 for $60 million, the highest price ever achieved for a Russian picture. Whether this is the true worth of this "composition" or whether it is wildly exaggerated is an open question. Some of the paintings highly valued today might be considered preposterous by future generations. For the time being, auction prices will not be greatly influenced by the approval or disapproval of Malevich's antimodernist compatriots.

One of the authors of the document is the historian Vladimir Medinsky, Russia's minister of culture (and tourism), a controversial figure, as many of his colleagues claim. However, conservative cultural criticism is not only legitimate but necessary. The authors quote a number of Western and Russian cultural figures to make their case more powerful, including Arnold Toynbee, Sam Huntington, and the early Zionist leader Max Nordau, who wrote a witty, undeservedly forgotten attack against modern art in the 1890s. His name and work are now known to a few specialists only. The Russian authors also adduce as anti-modernist experts for the prosecution several authorities such as I. Rossolimo and I. A. Gundarov, who, if indeed they exist, are unknown even among the specialists. The case made in the document is legitimate inasmuch as a defense of Russian culture is concerned, assuming that such a defense is at all necessary.

If the minister of culture and tourism is guilty of massive plagiarism, as claimed by his critics, his defenders might argue that the same accusations have been made with regard to several contemporary German government ministers (the difference being that in Germany, such charges if found correct had consequences—in Russia they did not).

The fact that Medinsky's dissertation was passed generated bitter exchanges in the Russian academic world. Writing about early Western visitors to Russia, Medinsky dismissed all those who had something critical to say as liars and Russophobes—for example, Sigismund von Herberstein (1486–1566) an Austrian diplomat who knew some Russian and had therefore more access than other foreigners. His book is one of the earliest detailed reports; it was also translated in English and is generally considered a reliable, detailed source. There is some occasional snobbism in his approach, the cultivated European looking down on the primitive Russian. But since there is little doubt that Europe was at the time on a more advanced cultural level, this is not surprising, nor does it appear in an extreme form. However, for Medinsky, this is Russophobia *tout court*, and his attitude to other early visitors, including some from England, is the same, such as for instance the report of the poet, diplomat, and traveler Giles Fletcher the Elder (1548–1611), a member of Parliament who wrote *Of The Russe Commonwealth*. Medinsky says about him: "His writings are evil slander about the Russian state, its rulers and people." But he failed to show mastery of the sources of his criticism, and many of his opponents compared the level of his writing to that of a first-year student. His defenders, on the other hand, said that though his writing was perhaps somewhat unorthodox, it was permeated with love for Russia, and this in the last resort was what mattered most.

Is it the business of a government to intervene in cultural debates? Assuming that Putin and Medinsky are right in claiming that Russia and Russian culture have nothing good to expect from foreigners, that Russian culture is superior to European culture, that Russia is also morally superior, praising its openheartedness and hospitality—is such boasting helpful and in good taste? The answer could be that contemporary Russia is not a democracy (at least not as understood in the West), that it is a "guided democracy," a term invented by Sukarno of Indonesia, and that therefore Western yardsticks do not apply.

Why deal with Medinsky and the cultural guidelines of his Ministry of Education and Tourism? Because they point to a certain basic approach that will be taken by Russia's rulers in the years to come. While education in a patriotic spirit and the inculcation of the population with traditional values, putting the emphasis on achievements rather than shortcomings and failures, is natural and has been practiced everywhere, the wholesale suppression of negative events and trends and the systematic denigration of other cultures are dangerous actions even in wartime, let alone in a period of peace. It creates, perpetuates, and exacerbates conflicts and makes normal relations difficult. Would it not be more appropriate for a government to increase its support for education and cultural purposes in order to halt the decline in standards that has been going on in Russia for some considerable time? The climate of suspicion with respect to foreigners has been traditionally strong in Russia: Unless giving fulsome praise to things Russian without exception—the Russian people's deep spirituality, the Russian soul, the Russian idea, and the untranslatable *shirokaya natura*—the foreigner must be considered an enemy out to harm the country and be treated as such.

The whole approach is disconcerting. Official spokesmen of the regime will deny any hostility toward the West, which (they say) would be incompatible with the traditional friendliness and trust shown by

Russians toward foreigners. Unfortunately, the evidence points to a different direction, boding ill for Russia's relations with the outside world in the years to come.

Russophobia and Zapadophobia (fear of the West)

The search for identity continues in Russia, not on the high level of abstraction it did two hundred years ago, but still with a great deal of passion. Underlying it is the conviction that Russia is not Europe and that there is a giant conspiracy to destroy Russia. Accompanying it is another set of beliefs that whatever went wrong in Russia is the fault of foreigners; the idea that Russians too may be responsible is alien and inappropriate. Thanks to this mind-set, Russia has no need even to consider a little self-criticism.

The intellectual roots of this thinking go back to the impact of German romanticism, which coincided with the war against Napoleon and the rise of nationalism in Europe. The German Romantic school had an enormous influence in Russia, and no philosopher was more popular than Friedrich Schelling, who was almost thought to be a Russian philosopher, just as Friedrich Schiller was believed to be a Russian poet. Among Schelling's correspondents were Fyodor Tyutchev and Sergey Uvarov, the future minister of education and author of the famous "triad" ("Orthodoxy, absolute rule, and *narodnost*"). Schelling was a philosopher of wide interests, largely responsible for the ideas of a "national soul" and a world soul (*anima mundi*). These concepts in turn go back much further and had to do with what Schelling called "the spirit of nature"; but they could also be applied to politics. In the case of Russia, they led to messianism and the belief in a manifest destiny. This gave the Slavophiles a new impulse. Konstantin Aksakov wrote that the West (the Western soul) was exhausted and in decline. Conscience was replaced by law, inner motives by regulations. It was Russia's historical task to continue its search for a national idea from where the West had gone wrong.

Such disillusionment was not, however, limited to the right wing and the Slavophiles. Alexander Herzen had come to the West full of admiration and willing to follow the Western lead, but after a few years disappointment set in. The same with Mikhail Bakunin, who arrived in Berlin a confirmed Westerner. But the first thing he saw on the wall of a building was a giant Prussian eagle, under it an inscription announcing that this was the workplace of a tailor. The inscription read:

Unter deinen Fluegeln
Kann ich ruhig buegeln.

Meaning, "Under your wings can I safely iron."

But Bakunin and his friends had not come to the West to iron in safety. They hated pragmatism.

From this kind of disillusionment, it was only a step or two away from distancing oneself from the West and the search for a national idea. Much of the time, the Russian intelligentsia could not make up their minds whether their country was moving toward a brilliant future or a disaster.

They were not willing to give up hope entirely: Slavophiles such as Ivan Kireyevsky declared that they still loved Europe. But many believed that only Russia was still in full bloom of its forces in the age of maturity, although even early on in the age of Mikhail Lermontov there were dire forebodings:

> The day will come for Russia, that dark day, when the czar's diadem will fall.

Similar forebodings appeared in European countries, but how seriously should they be taken? It was an age of great confusion, not only among Russians, but also among those who were trying to understand Russia from afar. The Russian intelligentsia was asking: Should we stick with Europe or leave it for good?

Such negativity toward Europe was rooted not so much in disillusionment as in a feeling of inferiority. And since Russia never believed in the virtues of moderation, this led to the dangerous extremes of hostility and suspicion. It would have mattered less if such animosity had been limited to a small minority, such as can be found in every country. But there is reason to believe that it became a majority view from the days of the Slavophiles.

German Romantics were forever in search of the famous blue flower, just as Russian nationalists were looking for the Russian idea. Neither search was successful, for there was no blue flower and no Russian idea except on the level of mythology. But since myths were needed, attempts were made to produce them synthetically. Artifical flowers, if well done, may look like the real thing, but they are not real flowers—and the same goes for the Russian idea. When Berdyaev was looking for the Russian idea, he meant God's view of Russia. The searches in our time aimed at articulating (or perhaps transforming) a religious and metaphysical search into a pragmatic quest for a state ideology, which the authorities thought was needed to establish unity and a sense of common purpose, away from cosmopolitanism. Those who failed to accept the new consensus were traitors and had to be eliminated.

There is general agreement that Russian attitudes toward the West and democracy have deteriorated over the last decade or two. When asked in 2008 whether Western society was a good model for Russia, around 80 percent said "no," about the highest negative response rate in Europe and one of the highest in the world. Russia's Levada Center—an independent sociological research organization based in Moscow—carried out an investigation that reached more positive results: About 60 percent were in favor of democracy rather than a strong hand. But of this 60 percent, about half wanted a democracy in consonance with Russia's needs, which could be interpreted as Putinism rather than democracy.

These negative attitudes are no doubt closely connected with the negative concomitants of the reforms of the 1990s, the emergence of a class of oligarchs. They were also influenced by massive doses of indoctrination by the official media. It was assumed by some that attitudes toward democracy would change for the better with growing prosperity, but this has not been the case. Standards of living have improved, but this has not generated more democracy.

Even when all allowances have been made, there is no doubt that support for the strong hand in Russia is as powerful as ever and belief in democracy rather weak. If anything, the situation in this respect has deteriorated, and the question arises as to whether and in what conditions it may be possible to witness a lessening of the hostility toward the West and support for freedom and democracy.

However, at the same time, the pressure for regional autonomy has been growing all over this immense country, probably an inevitable process precisely because of its very size. It is by no means identical with separatism, but it still faces bitter hostility on the part of the Kremlin and its insistence on the preeminence of state power and an unwillingness to make concessions. It is easy to foresee tensions in the context of these conflicts. The opposition lost the battle against the government because it showed insufficient patriotism at the time of the reconquest of Crimea. But it could well be that these new tensions, the demand for more regional autonomy, could be the new main battlefield between the central power and a rising opposition—namely, the strong local interests.

A few years ago, the Valdai Discussion Club, a semiofficial Russian institution established in 2004 to promote dialogue between the Russian and international intellectual elite, commissioned a report on the Russian national identity. It consulted men and women from all sides of the political spectrum, and there was general agreement that a Russian identity did exist. But what was it? Historically, the Russian character is freedom-loving and long-suffering: "We are open to other cultures and religions," it said. "We are brave and cordial. We are showy and talented. We have strong willpower and know how to win. However, we have forgotten most of the qualities on this list in the course of the past twenty years. On the other hand, we allowed ourselves to promote the worst qualities of our national character: sloth, pessimism, predatory individualism, irresponsibility, and total mistrust of others." The report also mentioned a "finely tuned sense of fairness, which is a wider notion than justice in the Western world." It noted that over the past twenty years, the values of Russia's citizens have changed, and not for the better. Among values of today's Russians, material well-being and consumption take first place: 55 percent in 2006, compared with 31 percent in 1986. Given Russia's highly unequal income distribution, this leads to an even greater fragmentation of society and growth of social tensions.

The quest for a definition of Russian national character and for the Russian idea of tomorrow is bound to remain elusive. What are the prospects for moderation, for a lessening of anti-Westernism and mistrust, for a restoration at least in part of the values of freedom and humanism, for a turning away from autocracy to greater freedom? If the reactionaries have been strong in Russia, the party of freedom, even if very weak at present, has a deep tradition in the history of the country. What are its prospects in the foreseeable future? Such sea changes in the mood have occurred in many countries throughout history, and they can by no means be ruled out in Russia, even if the chance may appear dim at the moment. In what circumstances are they likely to occur in Russia?

History shows that such changes have taken place, for instance, in the case of a lost war or a major economic crisis. But they have also occurred when the party in power outstayed its welcome and failed to deliver its promise. It has happened out of boredom or with the appearance of a new generation—the result of generational conflict. It has happened for no apparent reason at all or because the party in power and its ideology lost whatever dynamism and attractive power it initially had. There is no full accounting for all these conditions, just as there are no full explanations for the fact that some nations in history rise and others fall, that some recover from setbacks that appear devastating, irreversible, and final, whereas others never recover.

Some of the factors accounting for final decline or sudden recovery can, however, be singled out.

The Economic Future

There are many varying economic predictions for Russia, and they come from all quarters. The aforementioned Valdai Discussion Club envisages four scenarios. According to a highly optimistic one, the revenues from oil and gas exports will be high, in the range of $146 per barrel. Therefore the government will be able and willing to carry out long-overdue economic reforms. In this case, Russian growth will be higher than in most other countries, and the per capita income in 2030 will be equal to that of Switzerland at present.

According to a more pessimistic forecast, the price of oil will be low, there will be no reforms, and the Russian economy will stagnate. In this case, Russian growth will be lower than elsewhere, about 2 percent, and per capita income will be about that of the Czech Republic at the present time.

More likely, according to Russian economists, are two "centrist" scenarios. One rests on the assumption that the price of oil will be $94 a barrel, but sweeping reforms will be carried out. The other prognosis rests on the assumption of a relatively high price for oil ($140 per barrel), but there will be few reforms and on a local level only. In this case, a per capita income similar to that of France at the present time is expected. As these lines are written (January 2015), Russian forecasts predict recession—a change in the fortunes expected only in 2017.

In the course of these debates, which took place in November 2012, some interesting facts emerged. Sociologists reported that there is a substantial desire for reforms among those whose income is above average. However, some 68 percent of them want their children to study and work outside Russia at least for a number of years, and 37 percent want them to leave Russia for good. Why? Partly, no doubt, because of the general uncertainty about the future of the country, but mainly perhaps because the prospects of finding a suitable job for talented young people are bad.

Members of the Valdai group believe that the existence of a Eurasian economic sphere, including Kazakhstan, will have a positive effect on economic growth.

Another optimistic report published by Pricewaterhouse Coopers in 2013 sees reasonable chances for Russia to become Europe's leading economy by 2030 and stay that way, surpassing Germany. However, this projection rests on the utopian premise that strict economic policies, not politics, will be the decisive factor driving the Russian economy.

Less sanguine is the prognosis made by Evsey Gurvich, a well-known Russian economist. He believes that the great majority of Russians want to live well but also wish their country to be a superpower. He doubts that both aims can be combined at the present time. Russia currently spends twice as much (4.5 percent) on military expenditure as the NATO countries, and the money needed for the armed forces will be available only if the health and education budgets are cut. Unless taxes are substantially increased (the current maximum rate is 13 percent), a higher military expenditure will mean lower life expectancy and lower literacy. Even at the present time, according to UN statistics, Russia places 134th out of 207 countries in life expectancy—lower than that in Bangladesh, Guatemala, Honduras, and other countries. Gurvich believes that the 2014 Crimea sanctions will have little immediate effect; however, they could significantly reduce the amount of foreign investment. In this case, the Russian growth rate will not be higher than 2 percent in the years to come and could even decrease to 1 percent.

The desire to have guns and butter at the same time may be psychologically understandable but is very risky. The attempt to accomplish this in the postwar period resulted in the "greatest geopolitical disaster of the century" (Putin), the collapse of the Soviet Union. In order to achieve substantial growth, Russia has to regain the trust of foreign investors; otherwise it will have neither guns nor butter and remain on the level of Turkey or Indonesia. Even at the present time, investments in Russia are relatively low, about 20 percent of the GNP, which is lower than the average for emerging markets. Furthermore, most of the investment at present goes to the energy sector, which is precisely the model from which, everyone agrees, Russia should try to get away, the dependence on the export of natural resources.

The Russian policy to regain some or all of the territories lost with the breakdown of the Soviet Union is acting as a booster of morale and has added to the popularity of its government. But it comes at a price.

Even before the incorporation of Crimea (the cost of which was $7 billion in 2014), Russia had to allocate substantial funds to South Ossetia and Abkhazia and to prop up the regimes in Belarus and Transnistria. The self-proclaimed eastern Ukraine republic owes Moscow at present $4 billion in unpaid gas bills. Russia has given substantial funds to Armenia, Kyrgyzstan, and Tajikistan to maintain its influence in these parts, for keeping military bases in these countries and other purposes. It is unlikely that these allocations will decrease in the years to come.

Exact figures for these outlays do not exist. When Crimea was part of Ukraine, about two-thirds of its budget had to be covered by Kiev; Russia also contributes two-thirds of the Tajik budget. Altogether, the cost of empire at the present time could be in the range of $25 billion to $35 billion a year, which is about 6 percent of the Russian budget, not counting the cost of military and police forces. These are not enormous figures, but they are likely to increase; and if Moscow cannot fulfill its obligations or reduce its allocations, this will cause disappointment and resentment among the recipients, who had great and growing expectations as far as their relations with Russia were concerned. At the same time, there is bound to be grumbling in Russia if Russian health and education budgets are affected along with the funds originally scheduled to pay for the modernization of the Russian economy.

Russia will be able to pay the price for empire—if its economy flourishes. All depends on the price of oil and gas. And the level of oil prices depends on a number of circumstances that cannot be predicted, such as the world economic situation and the demand for oil and gas. It depends on the political situation in the Middle East, whether this region will be able to maintain or even increase its supplies. It depends on the political will of the EU, whether it will be able to agree on a common energy policy in order to lessen its dependence on Russian and Middle Eastern supplies. It depends on technological progress, which may make the use of alternative sources of energy considerably cheaper. It depends inter alia on the state of the infrastructure of the Russian oil and gas industry, whether Russia will be able to extract and deliver the amounts needed at costs to the producers that are not exorbitant.

There is a close connection between the cost of empire and economic factors.

The record of the Russian economy in the Putin years has been impressive. Putin's main aim as far as the economy is concerned was stability. This was a sensible policy, but the very good years that generated even higher expectations for the future might be over. It seems unlikely that the modernization of the Russian economy will make significant progress in the years to come. It is expensive, and there is much resistance against it, which brings us back to the price of oil and gas. If Europe's political weakness persists or even deepens in the years to come (which appears quite likely). The Russian economy does not have to fear a collapse. The reconquest of some of the last of their territories may also compensate for painful economic problems. But a weak Europe also means a weak economy and less demand. Given these uncertainties, all attempts to provide a helpful prognosis are bound to lead to a series of major question marks.

The Face of the Younger Generation

Basic political change has sometimes come as the result of an economic crisis, at other times following a war, won or lost. But it has also happened as the result of a new generation coming to the fore. Sometimes this has led to violent change by radical movements of a younger generation, such as fascism and communism. Sometimes such change has happened gradually, without a major upheaval.

One such example is the movement of a younger generation that emerged in France around 1900. Up to that time, the mood of that country had been largely pessimistic (indeed, defeatist) following the lost war against Germany; it was widely believed that France was finished. But then a new generation emerged—bored with the prevailing pessimism, preoccupied with sports, optimistic on the whole in outlook. Patriotic and even militarist rather than pacifist or defeatist, it built the Eiffel Tower, was the first to fly over the English Channel, and believed in the future of France.

The character of the younger generation in Russia, needless to say, is of paramount importance when thinking about the future of the country. Yet traditionally, little attention has been paid to it. In the late 1920s, a German student named Klaus Mehnert went to the Soviet Union and wrote a book that became something of a classic. He had been born in Moscow and in later years was to become a leading German Sovietologist. Mehnert observed that in the early years after the revolution, young people figured prominently in Soviet fiction, embraced as symbols of the country's future. In later years or under glasnost, however, they were replaced by public opinion polls and sociological investigations.

The younger generation of the 1930s and, to a certain extent, those of the 1950s and 1960s were on the whole optimistic. As the favorite song of the time was putting it, "*Molodim vezde u nas doroga*" ("*For the young all roads are open in our country*").

It was easy to be optimistic at the time when young—little did they know who went to summer camps about the harsh realities of life, about the cruelties of politics. It was the generation in the century before them that had been at the forefront of the struggle against despotism (and among the vanguard of the terrorists)—these young people had been among the most ardent supporters of the Communist regime, at least in the first decades.

As for the present, the investigations report that the key word concerning the young generation is "anomie," a term coined by the sociologist Émile Durkheim in 1893. It means social disorder, alienation, purposelessness, and even lack of hope. It means a breakdown of social bonds between the individual and society. Mention has been made earlier of the increasing number of young Russians wishing to live abroad—this despite the fact that they have reason to believe they will be better off remaining in Russia (as opposed to immigrating to the West) than were their parents before them.

During the early days after the fall of communism in the Soviet Union, there was much optimism in Russia. Unfortunately, not much has remained of this optimism. How to account for it? According to recent studies, Russian young people feel alienated, misunderstood by their parents, and above all discriminated against. Some blame the high divorce rate and domestic violence. But the fact remains that while the young were until recently optimistic about the economic future of their country, they are now rather pessimistic concerning their own future, their chances to enjoy their careers, and the likelihood of making a decent living. They feel exploited. They believe that outside Moscow it is difficult to get a satisfactory job; in Moscow the chances are better, but the competition is much fiercer.

Their attitudes toward politics are highly contradictory. Support for Putin and his style of governing is greater among the young than among the older generation. But only some 24 percent reveal any interest in politics. Some 80 percent distrust the government, political parties, the parliament, and politics in general. It seems to be a matter of both distrust and boredom. Their knowledge of politics is very limited. They believe that Russia should be a great power not only respected but feared by others. It should be ruled by a strong hand. The main task for the president is to keep order in the country. The most popular politician after Putin is Vladimir Zhirinovsky, which is a sad reflection of their political maturity and moral values, their failure to understand the difference between a vision of the future of their country and a circus performance. The political outlook of this generation is largely shaped by government television. This indoctrination has been defined as "Western-style entertainment minus democracy" and it has been quite effective.

Opinion polls that took place in 2008 and more recent ones from 2014 carried out by the Levada Center* did not show any major deviation from these trends. On the contrary, Putin's approval rating following the events in Crimea and eastern Ukraine among respondents eighteen to twenty-four years old rose to 92 percent, higher than in the older age groups. There was overwhelming support for the manifestation of strength, near total identification with government power, and hatred against the enemy—the West and Ukrainian nationalists. More than 70 percent expressed satisfaction that Russia had again become a great power. When asked whether they preferred Russia as a great power respected and feared by other countries or as a country with a high living standard that was not one of the world's strongest powers, 56 percent expressed their preference for the former variant. Again, such enthusiasm was somewhat lower among the older age groups.

On the other hand, the polls of 2014 showed almost total ignorance about the character of Russian society and its institutions; the knowledge of the younger generation was limited to their immediate surroundings. According to the great majority, there was a national leader deciding all important political issues concerning the present and the future of their country; the rest of the people had no influence on this, and there was no reason to change this state of affairs. Active participation in politics was not an issue, nor were any reforms of the system needed.

*The figures given in this section are based on the most detailed study on the subject at present available: Denis Daflon, *Youth in Russia: Portrait of a Generation in Transition*. 2009. Swiss Academy of Development, in cooperation with the Levada Center.

These opinion polls do not clarify to what extent these views reflect a permanent state of mind regarded as normal. Nor did they indicate whether this patriotic and profoundly antidemocratic upswing was a temporary phenomenon, likely to be affected by setbacks of the government on the foreign or domestic front. They seemed to show that Putin and other spokesmen of the regime were correct when they pointed out in discussions with the West that there were basic differences between Western democracy and the specific Russian type of "sovereign democracy."

According to the evidence gathered, money and the adulation of power define the ideology of the younger generation. This is no longer *Homo sovieticus*. In its place, it seems, we are experiencing *Homo putinus*.

What has become of the great idealism and the revolutionary spirit of sacrifice of young nineteenth-century Russians? Once upon a time, there was the conviction that money was nothing, all that mattered was the boundless fervor to live in freedom and to build a new society and create a selfless new human being, a model for all mankind. The vision was naïve and utopian, but even those politically remote from these views could not fail to be impressed. The present lack of vision is striking.

For a while in the 1990s, it seemed certain Western fashions would find followers in Russia—punks, rappers, drivers and ravers, BMX, hashish consumers, heavy metal freaks, and young people spraying their slogans on the walls. But this was limited to a few big cities, and it did not last long. Elsewhere there was nothing but the traditional boredom and right-wing patriotism—although no one knew how deep it really went, except that foreigners (and oligarchs) were disliked. However, all across the country having money was thought to be of great importance.

Oppositionists in the younger generation exercised their rebellion through membership in various sects, including Oborona (Defense), Pora (The Time Is Ripe), and Da (Yes); but all of them turned out to be aimless, free-floating, and usually short-lived, thanks to a lack of inspiration on the part of their leaders.

Then someone in the leadership of the ruling United Russia party came to believe that the country needed a youth section (mainly as a counterforce against the possibility of a "color revolution" such as happened in Georgia and Ukraine). So in 2005, Vladislav Surkov, Putin's chief of staff, created Nashi.

Under Surkov and Vasily Yakemenko, Nashi's leader, the movement tried to attract conformist young people by using avant-garde techniques. In essence, Nashi was created to appeal to nonpolitical young people who still needed a dream, a certain image of the future. Unfortunately, the highbrow Surkov proved to be too much of a creative ideologist at a time when Russia needed less-politicized "effective functionaries" who could engage in more-concrete actions.

This new policy was outlined by President Putin, who went to one of the main annual camps of Nashi at Lake Seliger (near Tver), and other government speakers. Whether this new policy would succeed still remained an open question.

The political leadership was apparently not aware that a movement of this kind had to emerge from among the youth rather than the ruling elite of an older generation. There was nothing spontaneous about Nashi; there was no genuine need or desire. It was an artificial creation, and those responsible for it seem not to have been aware that such ventures seldom succeed. Nashi had at one time more than one hundred thousand members, but once the "color revolution" danger to the regime has passed, the movement ceased to be a political factor of any importance and lost government support. In 2010, Yakemenko announced that Nashi would cease to exist.

Various youth organizations continue to exist in Russia, including some with an ecological agenda, but the politically active ones are found mainly on the extremist wings, following the lead of the Communists and the neo-Fascists. The ideological differences between these two, once again, are not great. The Communists have little in common with the traditional Left and nothing at all with Marxism and internationalism; they have embraced not only patriotism but big-power chauvinism and have been looking for approval by the church. Those of the extreme Right share much of the program of the Communists. The two extremes have a common enemy—the liberals and the democrats, whom they call "liberasts." They pretend to believe that all gays are liberals and democrats and vice versa. These two camps have frequently appeared together in demonstrations.

The influence of the extremists has often been overrated because they are the only ones able to mobilize thousands in their demonstrations. It is easily forgotten that such numbers do not mean much in a city of twelve million to fourteen million inhabitants such as Moscow. Given Putin's strongly nationalist line and his turn against some oligarchs and big business, much wind has been taken out of their sails. But what if the economic situation deteriorated and the expectations of wide sections of the population were not fulfilled? What if overall political support for the present regime were to shrink?

By 2014 Putin and the government had reached the conclusion that Nashi had been a failure; both Surkov and Yakemenko were out of favor. Nashi had been too brash (harassing foreign ambassadors and opposition figures) but not hip enough. Their activities had been belligerent but did not have much response. But when the government faced demonstrations by all kinds of opposition groups at the end of 2011, Nashi failed to mobilize young people and to offer any alternative. Since then, it has almost disappeared from the scene and the headlines.

According to polls by the Levada Center, about 50 percent of Russians believe that their country needs an opposition; only 23 percent think it can manage without one. There is no opposition in the present Duma. The young generation of 2015 will be tomorrow's voters. It is difficult to see the future opposition in this generation, but unforeseen circumstances may push them in this direction.

This *molodaya gvardia* (young guard) of 2014–15 is a strange generation, with often contradictory views and attitudes. It admires Putin but has no sympathy for politicians. Political apathy is dangerous, because it could mean that radical minorities may impose their views on the majority at a time of crisis. It is nationalist, but many of its members would prefer to leave Russia. It is also a sad generation: The suicide rate among young Russians is three times higher than in any other European country. According to many reports, the actual figures for youth suicide may be even higher than the official figures suggest because outside big cities "accident" is often given as the cause of death rather than suicide.

It is a conformist generation, in no way revolutionary, but there is nevertheless growing tension. As in other developed countries and societies, there was an unwritten social contract in the past; parents took care of their children, and when the parental generation grew old, the young took care of them. But now there are fewer young people and the old live longer. There will be a heavier burden on those who are young today. It is not an ideal generation for the kind of empire building Putin envisages or indeed for achieving any major purpose unless it can be done quickly and without much effort and sacrifice. The main interest of this generation is in business and financial security rather than the political character of the regime, whether there will be more or less freedom in Russia. The opposition cannot therefore expect much support from this age cohort.

Political and social attitudes may change, but it is too early to say in what direction.

Central Asian Conflicts

The first years of the Putin era were devoted to economic and political stabilization and consolidation. Once this aim had been achieved, the main task became to strengthen Russia's foreign political standing. Russia was no longer a superpower, and much territory had been lost. But given an auspicious international constellation, a weakened America, and a disunited Europe, the prospects improved for recovering at least some of what had been lost with the fall of the Soviet Union. Putin's strategy rested mainly on the idea of a Eurasian project, but one that did not rule out recovering positions lost in Europe. This was based on the assumption that Russia was not only a European power, but also had a major presence in Asia and that Asia was going to play a role of increasing importance in world affairs.

It was a risky strategy. Russia's presence in Asia is weak as far as its population is concerned—the number of Russians in the Far East has fallen by about 20 percent in as many years. Above all, increased Russian activity in Central Asia could lead to a conflict with China, which has also shown growing interest in these regions.

There had been substantial tensions between these two countries earlier on, culminating in fighting in 1969; but border disputes were settled in the Gorbachev years, and in 1998 a hot line was established between Beijing and the Kremlin to deal speedily with local crises if such should occur. During the last two decades, the border areas have been demilitarized and there have been a series of agreements between the two countries, mainly of an economic character—the energy trade, the building of pipelines to facilitate the export of oil and gas. However, Chinese and Russian interests in this respect are not identical. Both countries want to increase oil and gas output, but Russia wants to keep control over output and wishes to keep prices high, whereas China as a consumer wants low prices. As a safeguard, China has recently purchased several Kazakh oil companies. The Central Asian republics, in particular Kazakhstan and Turkmenistan, fear Russia more than China because of its physical proximity—Russia has military bases in the Central Asian republics, whereas China has not—and would like to play out one against the other. The Russian minority in Kazakhstan has been well treated—so much so that they nominated Nursultan Nazarbayev, the Kazakh president, for a Nobel Prize in 2013. Under a different leadership the situation could deteriorate, but given the country's delicate situation even a future leadership will probably act cautiously.

The two governments have referred to their relationship as a "strategic partnership." Russia supported China whenever the Tibet and Taiwan issues came up in an international forum, whereas China always defended Russia's activities in the Caucasus. Military maneuvers have taken place under the auspices of the six-member Shanghai Cooperation Organization, which is largely preoccupied with the security of the area to face threats of terrorism and separatism. However, the treaty's cooperation does not extend to an exchange of state-of-the-art military technology; Russia refrained from supplying to China most modern atomic technology.

An energy deal in 2014 envisaging a thirty-year gas supply from Russia to China estimated at $400 billion has been hailed by Moscow as a political achievement of great importance inasmuch as it will lessen Russian energy trade dependence on its European customers. Also in 2014, Russia established the Eurasian Economic Union with Kazakhstan and Belarus. Opinions differ as to the significance of this common market in the political and economic arenas. According to Putin, the long-term intention is to enlarge the customs union to all post-Soviet states (excluding only the Baltic countries). Armenia and Kyrgyzstan have indicated their interest to join the union, although some in Armenia oppose such a move, claiming it would limit its national sovereignty. China and other Asian countries have shown no interest thus far in joining this body, but neither have they opposed its existence.

Broadly speaking, both Russia and China have moved carefully in Central Asia in order not to infringe on each other's interests. At present, China's interest is limited to energy supply and certain minerals. Neither Russia nor China has so far shown any interest in the physical occupation of Central Asia. Russia has tried to maintain its traditional dominant political position in the area, but this has not generated any opposition on China's part as long as its economic interests remain secure.

However, from a long-term perspective it seems doubtful whether Russia will be able to hold on to its present position because the demographic imbalance will probably be overwhelming. The ethnic Russian population in Asian Russia might decrease to below thirty million, whereas the population of the five Central Asian Muslim republics will likely reach eighty million and the Chinese will maintain a population in excess of one hundred million in the border provinces. Such a disproportion is bound to have political repercussions. Russia may still be able to hold on to its presence, but only in a weakened position to which it has not been accustomed in the past and to which it may find difficult to adjust in future.

Which other regions are likely to be bones of contention in the years to come? The Arctic has become an area of dispute between Russia and the West, with conflicting territorial claims by five countries: Canada, Denmark, Norway, the United States, and Russia. These claims also concern the opening of sea routes that have become accessible in the wake of global warming and more pressing now given the deterioration in relations between Russia and the West.

There have been various international agreements based on a United Nations convention, but the law of the seas is not precise, leaving open many questions concerning control of the Arctic maritime region. According to maritime law, there is a territorial water zone of twelve nautical miles that allows coastal states to set laws, regulate use, and exploit resources. In addition, there is a contiguous zone of a further twelve nautical miles that allows the introduction of laws concerning pollution, taxation, and customs. Last, there is an exclusive "economic zone" of two hundred nautical miles to control all living and nonliving resources.

The two-hundred-mile economic zone has given rise to these conflicting claims. Russia, Canada, and Denmark (Greenland) all claim the Lomonosov Ridge, which is as big as half of Europe. The control of the Northwest Passage is yet another bone of contention. These and various other such claims could be peacefully resolved; unfortunately, there is no certainty that this will be the case.

It is further believed that substantial oil and gas fields exist in the region, such that Russian eagerness to own as many Arctic oil and gas fields as possible—despite the technical difficulties and overwhelming expense involved in extracting oil and gas in the area—would be understandable in light of the fact that some fields on the Russian mainland are approaching exhaustion. Hence the call for a strong Russian military presence and demonstration of force in the Arctic voiced, for instance, by Dmitry Rogozin, a leading nationalist spokesman and deputy prime minister: "It is crucially important for our national interests in this region. If we do not do that we shall lose the battle for resources which will mean we'll also lose a big battle for the right to have sovereignty and independence."

Russia at one time maintained military bases in the Arctic, but following an understanding about the demilitarization of the Arctic, they were not further developed. However, in May 2014 Putin announced a reopening of the bases to protect Russia's strategic interests in the Arctic. This in turn led to an announcement by the NATO secretary general to the effect that the members of NATO would have to address the issue in light of Russian actions. The United States has been reluctant to get involved in the Arctic disputes, but other NATO members closer to the scene (such as Norway and Canada) have expressed concern following the Russian military buildup. Some Russian commentators have even predicted a war over the ownership of Arctic oil and gas within the next ten years.

Very little is known outside Russia (and not much more inside the country) about some of the territories that were at one time part of the Soviet Union and whose future status is in dispute. Transnistria is one such region, as are Abkhazia and South Ossetia—the latter two located in the Caucasus. They ought to be mentioned here because according to historical experience, even very small territories can trigger major political conflicts. About the Gagauz, a minority in Transnistria, little is known. Even their origins are in dispute among the experts (Bulgarian or a steppe tribe). Nevertheless, they figure prominently in the conflict and discussions between the Kremlin and the Republic of Moldova.

The Republic of Moldova, with Kishinev (Chisinau) as its capital, came into being with the breakdown of the Soviet Union. Romanian is the official language. However, it is also home to a considerable number of Russians, Ukrainians, and Gagauz. Most of the Russians and Ukrainians had moved during the Soviet period to the area east of the river Dniester and now represent a little more than half of the population, and the Communist Party has remained the strongest political group. The Russian-Ukrainian-Gagauz area felt discriminated against, which led to a split; a law giving this region almost full autonomy had been introduced but was not confirmed by the Moldovan parliament. Armed clashes took place, and in two votes (1991 and 2006) a majority expressed the wish to secede and unite with Russia, whereas Moldova was moving toward the European Union. Russian economic and military influence was strong in the Transnistrian area; Russian troops were stationed in the breakaway region. The area has a national anthem, Russian textbooks are used in local schools, and the Transnistrian currency is the ruble; however, Moscow did not press for unification at an early date. This issue came up only at the time of the Crimean crisis in 2014. Moldova's economic situation is extremely bad; that of Transnistria is even worse, with a very low per capita income.

The Republic of Abkhazia considers itself an independent state and wishes to remain independent. It is recognized by four member states of the United Nations (Russia, Venezuela, Nicaragua, and the South Pacific island of Nauru). Abkhazia has been fighting Georgia, of which it was a part, several times since the breakup of the Soviet Union. South

Ossetia too was part of Georgia but declared its independence in 1990. As the result of almost permanent unrest, many Ossetians fled to Russia's North Ossetia, whereas many Georgians moved to Georgia. The South Ossetian issue led to the war between Georgia and Russia in 2008. The region is of no strategic importance, exceedingly poor, and economically wholly dependent on Russia.

The real issues at stake regarding the recovery of the Russia Empire are not the splinter regions, but Ukraine and the Caucasus on the one hand and the extent of Russia's influence on the Eastern European countries on the other. Russia will oppose any close military involvement of these countries with the West; whether it will be able to prevent closer political and economic relations of these countries with Western Europe will depend on the balance of power and Europe's reliance on Russian oil and gas supplies.

Russian political and economic weaknesses have been discussed in some detail, and a spectacular change for the better seems unlikely in the near future. However, the movement toward European integration, agreeing on a common political, economic, and energy policy, has shown equal signs of weakness. Europe's weakness could induce a Russian foreign policy aimed at extending its influence, even if the power base on which such a policy rests will be brittle. Russian imperial ambitions might be limited, but Western weakness could lead them into temptation.

There is an abundance of Eurasian political and economic projects, but will they provide stability and prosperity in this part of Asia adjacent to Russia? Of the five Central Asian republics, two are doing relatively well, whereas the present condition and future projects of the others remain dismal. Turkmenistan has substantial oil and gas fields, mainly on the eastern shore of the Aral Sea. Kazakhstan has also become a major supplier of oil, gas, and certain rare minerals. The country attracted considerable investments from the West and the East. It also became the site of an important oil pipeline to China. Under the SCO, the security of the area seems to be safeguarded. But the question remains open whether in an emergency these agreements will provide internal stability. Domestic tensions cannot be ignored.

Tajikistan's civil war among various clans and ethnic groups

(1992–98), barely noticed outside the area, left more than one hundred thousand dead and created more than a million refugees. Full control by the government has still not been established. While regular warfare seems highly unlikely between the republics, other forms of conflict may occur as a result of general misgovernment as well as specific issues such as control of the drug trade, which constitutes an important unofficial part of the gray economy of the area. Local governments are frequently closing their borders, causing considerable hardship to the population even if smuggling continues. Tensions among ethnic and religious groups go back far in the past. While governments such as those in Kazakhstan and Uzbekistan tend to pursue a nationalist secular policy, conservative Islamic trends prevail in many regions, and unrest generated against this background will continue to add to a climate of instability.

It is difficult to assess the prospects of the militant Islamic movement, because most of their activities take place underground. It seems probable that at least some of the militants of the Afghan war will invade the Central Asian republics.

The militant movement most active in Central Asia has been Hizb ut-Tahrir, a pan-Islamic political organization founded in Jordanian Jerusalem in the 1950s and intent on establishing an all-encompassing Muslim state (caliphate). At present, it is banned in almost all countries, including those of the Arab world. Its prospects in some Central Asian countries such as Kyrgyzstan should not be underrated.

On the whole, the Central Asian republics have successfully suppressed terrorist groups. Chinese Uighurs who are Muslim have been arrested and returned to China. However, there is a great deal of dissatisfaction among the population of some regions, and the influx of militants from Afghanistan could change the situation. Given the corruption at the local level, "goodwill" on the part of the authorities could be bought in certain regions; such a state of affairs might appear favorable for the production of weapons of mass destruction. However, similar conditions prevail in other global regions such as Somalia or Yemen that might be considered preferable from a logistic point of view.

So far, mention has been made of a likely recurrence of terrorism in Kazakhstan, but the situation in Uzbekistan is not dissimilar. The roof organization IMU (Islamic Movement of Uzbekistan) has failed so far in its aim to overthrow the government at home, but it may have a second chance with the return of Uzbek jihadists from the battlefields of Afghanistan, Syria, Iraq, and other countries. At present, Uzbek jihadism is based mainly in the Uzbek "diaspora" of neighboring Tajikistan, some Arab countries, and Turkey, where young Uzbeks have been studying and become radicalized. Some of them are only too eager to resume the struggle at home, and the local government may not be able to confront this challenge.

It remains to be seen whether the SCO can deal with these threats. Russia has shown little enthusiasm to include Kyrgyzstan and Tajikistan in its Eurasian projects, aware that they would be a burden rather than an asset. From Moscow's point of view, it would be preferable to install pro-Russian quasi-independent governments. However, such a scheme may encounter domestic nationalist resistance, and the risk of failed countries at Russia's border would not disappear. Hence the likelihood that parts of Central Asia will remain danger zones.

I have not been dealing with Ukraine and Moldova, with the Baltic republics, or with Georgia and Azerbaijan, all countries that were once part of the Soviet Union or the Soviet bloc. Moscow regards them as part of their zone of influence and does not want any change in this respect. This could be achieved by maintaining a Russian physical presence directly, but it is certain that the countries (or regions) concerned will want to keep a maximum of independence. Whether they will be able to count on support for their endeavor from other powers, including Europe and the United States, no one can say. It depends on the international balance of power and above all the demand and supply of oil and gas. An uneasy arrangement may emerge, but temporary and local conflicts against this background are almost certain.

EPILOGUE: *KAMO GRYADESHI, ROSSIYA?*—*QUO VADIS,* RUSSIA?

How do Russians envisage their country's place in the world fifteen or twenty years from now? A year or two ago there was a great deal of pessimism, but there has been a significant change in the mood of the Kremlin and the country at large, tempered of course, to some extent, by the economic crisis. According to public opinion polls, most Russians think of their country as a superpower; among experts, this view is less widely to be found. As they now see it, the West is in retreat, isolated. The rules of the game dictated by the EU and Washington for a long time are no longer the same. The expansion of NATO and the EU to the Russian periphery has been halted. These views are shared by mainline, moderate Russian commentators such as Sergey Karaganov, Aleksander Lukin, and others, to wit: Until recently, Russian dignity and interests were trampled underfoot. Of particular annoyance to the Russian political class were systematic deceits and hypocrisy and broken promises. Unable and reluctant to toe the line, Russia has now given up attempts to become part of the West.

Now the West is losing its leadership over the world economy, its military advantage is dwindling, and the main reason was the West's refusal to put an end de facto and de jure to the Cold War. The West systematically pressed ahead with expanding its zone of influence and control militarily, economically, and politically. Russia was treated as a defeated nation, its interests and objections ignored. Yet Russians do not consider themselves losers. Of particular annoyance to Russia's political class were systematically and hypocritically broken promises and declarations. Russians were told that the "spheres of influence" policy was outdated. But in the rest of the world it was known that this was simply not true, and it was a mockery and caused distrust. The motivation of the EU expansion was to make Russia believe that the geopolitical and sociopolitical retreat of the West was over. It was to camouflage the irreparable crisis of the European integration project. This was very painful to the political class of the Western countries since it questioned its moral and political legitimacy. The West also wanted to sabotage Russia's Eurasian project to re-create the Asian European Economic Union. The language was not always clear, but the intention was. Russia did not like Europe. It was not part of Europe, and anyway, Europe was finished, or almost finished.

As for the "hypocritically broken promises," Putin and the other Russian spokesmen have declared many times in later years that the West promised Russia that NATO would not move eastward, but that this promise was not kept. The documents (by President George H. W. Bush, James Baker, and Helmut Kohl) show that Gorbachev did indeed want an undertaking of this kind, but it was never attempted. Instead, Western (above all, German) economic help was promised to avert the then threatening Soviet state bankruptcy. It could be argued that Western leaders should perhaps have accepted such an undertaking in view of NATO's weakness and its inability and unwillingness to take a strong stand in the case of a threat. But this is not what happened, and the official Russian version of later years about a "betrayal" is therefore based on a misunderstanding or, more likely, invention. Russian statements were very often contradictory, expressing fear and boasts at the same time. On one hand, the Russian leaders maintained that the West was encircling a weakened Russia, on the other, there were almost weekly assertions by Putin and others that there was no country militarily stronger than Russia and that it was able to destroy the United States. If NATO expanded eastwards it was not because America or other NATO members exerted heavy pressure on Russia's neighbors to join but because these small countries felt threatened by a country so frequently invoking its imperial mission.

Perhaps NATO should not have admitted any further members. But it is by no means certain whether such a concession would have calmed Russian nerves or whether, on the contrary, it would have been interpreted as a sign of weakness and an invitation to Russia to expand.

It was not true that the West tried to keep out Russia all along. It invited Russia to join the G7, the Council of Europe, the World Trade Organization, and other such bodies. But for the emergency help extended in July 1998 by the World Bank and the International Monetary Fond amounting to more than $22 billion, Russia would have been bankrupt—but this fact was seldom mentioned. The impression was created that Russia wanted more. It wanted Europe to join its Eurasian ventures in a way that Russia would emerge as the leading power with the exclusion of the United States. And for such ambitions not much support could be found in the West.

This in broad outline is what leading Russian experts have been saying and writing. But the more sophisticated among them seem to feel that this is not the whole story. Sergey Karaganov, one of the leading contemporary observers of the Russian scene, still feels uneasy, and he is not alone. The decline of the West is welcome news, but there may be a price to pay. Karaganov sees dark clouds on the horizon—economic, demographic, and political. Russia is now at the zenith of its power; fifteen or twenty years from now it will be weaker. If so, Russia should be looking for allies. Perhaps the predictions about China's future power are exaggerated? Perhaps that country too will face major problems in the years ahead? In any case, Russia might be well advised to keep all its options open, not to end up as a satellite of some future superpower. Putin seems to be dimly aware of such a need, but perhaps it is not yet advisable to say so openly.

The more cautious, less triumphant Russian commentators point out that until the second half of the 2000s, Russia's strategic goal was integration with Europe on acceptable terms. Moscow emphasized the European nature of the Russian state and Russian civilization and proposed a concept of synergy of European capital and technologies and Russian natural and human resources. This would have made Europe competitive in the global economy. It would have formed a third superpower in the world alongside the United States and China. Russia sought equal integration, and some European countries were interested; but the EU as a whole was not, especially the new (Eastern European) members supported by the United States. Thus another historic opportunity was missed.

Much of this assessment was new and startling to Westerners—the reference to the European nature of the Russian state and civilization, which was strongly denied much of the time; the assertion that a powerful Western propaganda machine was relentlessly engaged much of the time in anti-Russian propaganda, in particular in connection with the Sochi Olympic Games. Westerners must have been surprised to learn that they wanted to continue the Cold War at any price. But above all, they will be baffled by the idea—which allegedly existed and was rejected—of the great lost opportunity of Russia looking for integration in the West.

This remains the position of the moderates, also called "the peace party." They consider the conquest of Crimea a welcome fait accompli and believe that the pressure on Ukraine should continue. Russia should defend its interests with an iron fist, as Karaganov puts it. But the pressure should be political and economic rather than military, which is too risky and may have undesirable, even dangerous, consequences.

Valery Gerasimov, chief of staff of the Russian armed forces, gave a speech in early 2013 in which he ruminated on the changing character of contemporary war, which is carried out by small special units, political and economic measures, and cyberwarfare. Mass armies, he maintained, are obsolete. Western military thinkers have reached similar conclusions in recent years. There is a war party in Russia arguing that now is the time to hit back at the West in revanche for the collapse of the Soviet Union and to regain much of the power and influence Russia once possessed. The risks are small, NATO is disunited, the mood in America gravitates toward isolationism and even defeatism. If, as President Obama said in 2014, America has no strategy vis-à-vis Syria, it stands to reason that it will not react forcefully in the case of some limited Russian aggressive attack in Eastern Europe. Mutual assured destruction may still be in force in the case of an all-out nuclear attack against the United States. But a limited nuclear strike against a target in Eastern Europe would probably not cause American retaliation. The mood in the West is to a considerable extent *mourir pour Narva*? Narva is the eastern part of Estonia in which many ethnic Russians live. (*Mourir pour Danzig* was the phrase coined in 1938 by Marcel Déat, the French socialist leader who became a leading Nazi collaborator). The failure of the West to react would probably lead to the demise of NATO and diminish American prestige in the world even further. Seen in this light, the Russian failure to act would be a missed opportunity, tantamount to losing the initiative in an undeclared war that has been under way for some time.

The point of view of the war party has supporters well beyond the camp of the lunatic fringe and ultranationalists. They admit they want to eliminate the liberals and democrats at home and worldwide; they fervently hope for a confrontation with the West; they believe that Brussels is "the center of world fascism." These claims are sometimes bewildering because the West has been told time and again that fascism was not really the main enemy (if it was an enemy at all) but "atlanticism" and liberalism and Western-style democracy—those were the great dangers and the great evil. Even a former moderate of sorts like Sergey Kurginyan close to the Kremlin had been explaining to the West that there was much to admire in Hitler at least up to 1939. If so, why the sudden denunciations of Hitler? Because he overstepped a certain border (also called a red line in our time), a point that had also been made many years before by Ivan Ilyin, who has become the principal moral and political guide.

Is it true that a great chance was missed in the 1990s when Russia wanted to join the West and was rejected? This version of recent history is not universally accepted. Consider the view of a leading Russian historian, Yuri Afanasiev ("A New Russian Imperialism?" *Perspective* [February–March 1994]). His analysis was based on what he called "the Yeltsin doctrine" as well as the official Russian military doctrine of 1993: A strong Russia was needed, assuming the role of peacemaker and defending its legitimate state interests. This was the duty of the Russian, and it had the right to act firmly and toughly. Russia was obliged to defend the interests of Russians living in the near abroad if their rights were violated. In practical political terms, it meant that Russian state interests extended to the entire territory of the former USSR and justified the attempt to impose a particular foreign policy on all countries of the former European socialist camp. It meant the return of the great power ideology (*derzhavnost*). Such a view should not have been a great surprise even in 1994, and various reasons could be adduced in its defense. But it was difficult to maintain that this was tantamount to the ardent wish to join Europe and become part of it.

From the vantage point of 2015, this is more or less what has happened. The liberals (who were never very strong) became much weaker and eventually lost all influence. What did change was not the Russian aim (to join Europe), but the circumstances in which Russia's real national interests—regaining its erstwhile position of strength—could be pursued. In 1994, Russia was weak; it needed Western help to prevent bankruptcy. Twenty years later, both the United States and Europe had become weaker, whereas Russia's position was much stronger. Owing to the oil and gas boom, Russia had again become a great power.

Was it the fault of the West? Was there ever a real chance of Russia's integration with the West in 1989–91 if the West had only shown greater foresight, magnanimity in victory, a greater willingness to compromise? How intense, how genuine, was Russia's desire to move toward integration with Europe and the West? Given Russia's deep economic and political crisis at the time, what exactly was the meaning of "acceptable terms" and "equal partnership"?

A document entitled "Russia's Military Doctrine," published by the armed forces general staff every few years, lists the main dangers facing the country. Until a few years ago, NATO and the United States were referred to as a "strategic partner." No longer: In the 2014 version, Putin and other Russian spokesmen referred to the United States and NATO as the main enemy and were making barely veiled threats referring to Russia's nuclear arsenal and renouncing the 1987 treaty with the United States, one of several promising to limit the nuclear arms race. Undue importance should perhaps not be attributed to "Russia's Military Doctrine," the full text of which has never been published. In any case, there is reason to assume that Russia has disregarded the 1987 nuclear treaty for years. Facts on the ground are more important than official declarations of this kind. And the facts say that Russian military spending between 2007 and 2014 has doubled, whereas NATO spending has halved.

What was the decisive factor in Russian thinking, and what were the main motives? Was it the wish to protect Russian speakers living outside the Russian republic, or was it the wish to restore the borders of the Soviet Union, to re-create the old empire?

These issues will be discussed for a long time to come, when more will be known about Russia's desire for integration with the West and Western attitudes toward it. According to the evidence available at present, Russian claims about the "missed opportunity" are untrue.

It was no doubt in the interest of Russian patriots to regain great-power status. But since the West had been regarded as Russia's sworn enemy for such a long time, was it not inevitable that the Russian strategy of integration, even if wholly genuine, should have been regarded with a measure of suspicion or at least hesitation? At the time, Russia was in need of help to prevent a total collapse: should Western help have included restoration of the old borders of the Soviet Union? Would such help have earned Russia's eternal gratitude?

Some Russian analysts feel a certain unease even at a time of Russia's triumph. As Sergey Karaganov puts it:

> Today Russia is at the peak of its strength. The near future promises no chance that it can get stronger. It looks like Russia has deliberately shifted the focus of competition with the West from soft power and the economic sector to hard power, political will, and intellect. In other words, to where Russia considers its strength lies.
>
> So far the attempt has yielded positive results. But to consolidate its position at least in the midterm, Russia needs to reform its economic and domestic policies, rapidly change its elites, and formulate the goals and national idea shared by the majority of its citizens. Russia has been getting ready. A televised anti-Western campaign unprecedented since the Cold War era helped to shape public opinion. The armed forces underwent a fundamental upgrade. There were other omens of an imminent clash. The interim results are favorable.

> Russia has seized and retained the initiative. Russia's arsenal contains a wide range of economic and political tools until it has achieved its goal, which is a very risky strategy that will complicate relations with the West for a long time. The strategy will weaken Russia's position in relations with China (its maneuvering room will narrow), although moral authority in the eyes of the non-Western world will grow. This will be the case if Moscow will not lose, of course.

These are interesting ruminations, more prescient than most emanating at this time from Moscow. It is relatively easy to launch a massive propaganda campaign, but how to produce a new elite in a short period? Has Russia given up competition with the West in the economic field—and does it hope to gain its advantages by means of "hard power" and "political will"? Does it mean war? If so, what kind of war?

It should be taken for granted that even though Moscow has moved toward an aggressive nationalist, even chauvinist, policy, no one outside the lunatic fringe actually wants a major nuclear war. There are apparently some in Moscow who believe there will be no competition between Russia and China, because all China wants is to regain Taiwan. Great are the powers of self-deception. There was a time when Mao considered it desirable for Russia to go to war with the United States so that the two superpowers could annihilate or at least incapacitate each other.

Assuming that Russia is now at the peak of its strength, a statement less often heard following the economic crisis of 2014–15 should it not make the most of it? What if such a unique opportunity does not recur? But this would be dangerous, because if Russia again overstretches itself, would not the result be the same as in the past? Would it be able to hold on to what it gained at a time of a favorable constellation? Any territorial advance Russia made now or in the near future would mean a gain in domestic support for the present government. But how long would this gain last?

Russians want their country to be a great power, a superpower if possible. But they also want to live well. Two understandable aims—but can they be combined? Economic experts such as Vladislav Inozemtsev have argued in strong terms that Russia is not a superpower and cannot be one as long as it depends on the outside world, as long as it imports much of what it needs and its exports are limited mainly to raw materials. Even more critical is Russia's financial dependence on the West.

Russia faces great domestic difficulties and problems, but problems can be solved and difficulties overcome. Again, historical examples have been given, such as France's recovery after 1870–71 and the German recovery after World War I. In the late Middle Ages and early modern period, the Swedes and the Swiss were known as the best and fiercest soldiers, but this is no longer so. Britain was known as the pioneering industrial country par excellence whereas China was known as the country in which nothing ever changes. Times have changed.

The United States and Europe are passing through a period of great psychological weakness. The European project, the movement toward unity, has been running out of steam. It could be the beginning of the end, but it could also lead to a recovery.

Among the Russian weaknesses is the fatal belief in all kinds of conspiracy theories and strange ideas, such as neo-Eurasianism, neogeopolitics, confabulation, and zapadophobia, accompanied by an enduring persecution mania and the exaggerated belief in a historical mission. Such afflictions are by no means exclusively Russian, but in no Western countries have these and similar ideas gained the legitimacy bestowed upon them by Alexander Dugin and sections of the intelligentsia or been used to influence political policy as determined by Russia's leaders. Nationalist feelings have been running high in many countries at various times, but it is difficult to think of an accumulation of hatred similar to what has taken place in Russia in recent years. It could be argued that such afflictions may not last forever, they may weaken or even disappear. But at the present time, in the age of weapons of mass destruction, they are a major danger.

Quite recently with the end of the Cold War, the belief prevailed in the West that democracy was the normal state of affairs and all other forms of governance a regrettable deviation from the norm that would not last a long time. This assumption proved to be overoptimistic. The authoritarian mentality of many Russian rulers and ruled alike will change only as the result of a cultural revolution, which has not taken place so far.

This is a matter of some grief to Russian democrats, but the reality must be faced. Events during the last two decades have shown that chaos is much more feared in Russia than authoritarian rule and dictatorship. As long as half of the people believe in the greatness and goodness of Stalin, nothing else can be expected. This may change one day, but in the meantime one can only hope there will be no deterioration in the situation toward an even more severe form of rule. The Russian extreme Right and the lunatic fringe have grown in influence over the years, but full-fledged fascism seems unlikely. To a certain extent, the Stalin experience is still acting as a deterrent for many, and even those who find excuses for it do not want a repeat performance.

But a retreat from authoritarian rule toward a more democratic system seems equally unlikely. The Soviet Union under communism could count on the support of Communists all over the world. A right-wing nationalist Russia may find (or buy) a few sympathizers abroad, but not much more. The Soviet doctrine was based on the assumption that world revolution would eventually prevail everywhere. There can be no such perspective today, which poses natural limits to Russian expansion. But on the other hand, it is difficult to envisage an abdication of the present rulers, unless they are assured (as Yeltsin was) that they will not be prosecuted after their resignation—for instance, with regard to the fortunes amassed while in power.

How to achieve this? Hardly as a result of free and unfettered elections. If it were only for this reason, the transition to a more democratic regime would be difficult indeed. However, there are additional problems, such as the traditional Russian fear of freedom among wide sections of the population. Once persecution mania has become deeply engrained, it may easily turn in the wrong direction—internally, against one's own people and government. If enemies are hiding everywhere, they might be among one's neighbors; no one can be trusted anymore. A rising tide of Russian nationalism replacing the old internationalist doctrine is a double-edged sword. Once the chauvinist genie is out of the bottle, not only may it be directed against the West, it could find domestic targets such as national minorities and the millions of guest workers at present in Russia. As the ambassador of one of the Central Asian republics asked his Russian friends in Moscow: "What are you doing to our people working for you? They return home militant Islamists."

Western freedom of action to promote friendlier relations is limited. Even if Western attitudes toward Russia were guided by unparalleled friendship and respect, responding positively to all Russian demands, there is no certainty that this would have the desired effect. Self-criticism has not been in fashion in Russia for a long time; if something goes wrong in Russia, it is virtually always the fault of foreigners. According to past experience, the feeling of Russia as a besieged fortress is running deep and dates far back. For if Russia were not such a fortress, how to justify authoritarian rule, the many restrictions imposed on the population, the sacrifices demanded, and the shortcomings of the regime? For this reason, the prospects for a lasting reconciliation and better relations with the West seem not to be brilliant at the present time.

There is bound to be change. But when and how and in what direction no one can say with any certainty. Will it be for the better or the worse? Gogol's troika mentioned earlier, with its bells ringing, makes many appearances in Russian culture; it used to be an essential part of the winter scene. It appears in popular songs as well as in highbrow literature. In a popular song, the *yamshik* (coachman) gets a kiss from a pretty girl, but there are also disaster stories caused by the drunken *yamshik*. In old Russia, the coachman had to undergo special training almost as thorough as a London taxi driver. But not all of them did. And who is the passenger in Gogol's great novel? Chichikov, not one of the most positive heroes in Russian literature, but a con man, the embodiment of *poshlost*. So Gogol's troika is galloping on as before, the coach driver is not sparing the horses, and one only hopes he has a general idea where he is going and the way to reach his destination without too much risk to his passengers and the rest of mankind.

BIBLIOGRAPHY

The Pillars of the New Russian Idea

Nikolai Berdyaev's *The Russian Idea* (New York: Macmillan, 1948) is the best-known work on the subject; it deals with its religious rather than nationalist aspects. General works on the search for identity, Russia's manifest destiny, and related subjects include Wendy Helleman, *The Russian Idea: In Search of a New Identity* (Bloomington, IN: Slavica Publishers, 2003); James Billington, *Russia in Search of Itself* (Baltimore: Johns Hopkins University Press, 2004); Michael Lane Bruner, *Strategies of Remembrance: The Rhetorical Dimensions of National Identity Construction* (Columbus: University of South Carolina Press, 2002); and Marlène Laruelle, *Russian Nationalism and the National Reassertion of Russia* (London: Routledge, 2009). Another useful collection of texts is Geoffrey Hosking and Robert Service, eds., *Russian Nationalism, Past and Present* (New York: St. Martin's Press, 1998).

On political-ideological developments during the last two decades, see Victor and Victoria Trimondi, *Krieg der Religionen: Politik, Glaube und Terror im Zeichen der Apokalypse* (München: W. Fink, 2006). On the Black Hundreds, see Walter Laqueur, *Black Hundred: The Rise of the Extreme Right in Russia* (New York: HarperCollins, 1993). Vadim Kozhinov, *Pravda "Chernoi Sotni"* (Moscow: Eksmo/Algoritm, 2006), offers a defense of the Black Hundreds. Kozhinov was a literary critic and historian but also a leading right-wing ideologist. While not a Communist, he defended Stalin against his critics—arguing, for instance, that the Stalin cult was created not in the Soviet Union, but by foreigners.

For a general overview on Russian intellectual history pertinent to the subject of this book, see Andrzej Walicki, *The Slavophile Controversy: History of a Conservative Utopia in Nineteenth-Century Russian Thought* (Oxford: Clarendon Press, 1975). Also see the comprehensive anthology edited by Marc Raeff titled *Russian Intellectual History* (New York: Harcourt, Brace, 1966).

On issues of confabulation, the most comprehensive recent work is William Hirstein, ed., *Confabulation: Views from Neuroscience, Psychiatry, Psychology and Philosophy* (Oxford: Oxford University Press, 2009).

Confabulation

Vladimir Solovyov's collected works were published in St. Petersburg between 1911 and 1914. Several anthologies have appeared in English translation, in particular Vladimir Solovyov, *Politics, Law and Morality: Essays*, trans. and ed. Vladimir Wozniuk (New Haven: Yale University Press, 2000).

Most of Nikolai Berdyaev's books have appeared in English, French, and other languages, including *The Meaning of History* (New York: Scribner, 1936). There is also a long autobiographical essay, *Dream and Reality: An Essay in Autobiography* (New York: Macmillan, 1951). On Berdyaev and inequality, the subject that fascinated Putin, see Marko Marković, *La philosophie de l'inégalité et les idées politiques de Nicolas Berdiaev* (Paris: Nouvelles Éditions Latines, 1978).

Georgy Petrovich Fedotov's collected works in twelve volumes began to appear in Russian in 1996. Selected essays have been published in Russian in a number of volumes in France and the United States, including *Litso Rossii* (Paris: YMCA Press, 1976). In view of his political leanings, he is not persona grata at present in Russia.

Ilyin and Fascism

Ivan Ilyin has been frequently quoted by Putin and other current leading Russian political figures. Most of his writings were republished in Russian in recent years, including *On Monarchy and Republic* [*O Monarkhii i Respublike*] (New York: Sodruzhestvo, 1979).

The nineteenth-century Slavophile and nationalist writers most in demand in Russia at the present time are Nikolay Danilevsky and Konstantin Leontiev. Danilevsky's classic *Russia and Europe* was republished in Russia in 1995 (*Rossiya i Evropa*, 6th ed. [St. Petersburg: Glagol and St. Petersburg University Press, 1995]), and there is a biography by Robert E. MacMaster entitled *Dani-*

levsky: A Russian Totalitarian Philosopher (Cambridge, MA: Harvard University Press, 1967). On Konstantin Leontiev, see knleontiev.narod.ru and the Leontiev page in pravoslavie.ru.

Russian Messianism

Russian messianism remains a hitherto neglected subject. An important early study is Emanuel Sarkisyanz, *Russland und der Messianismus des Orients* (Tübingen: J. C. B. Mohr, 1955). Also see Leonid Kacis, *Russkaja Éschatologija i Russkaja Literatura* (Moscow: OGI, 2000).

On the Antichrist, the leading expert is Michael Hagemeister (http://www.phil-fak.uni-duesseldorf.de/v-geschichte-und-kulturen-osteuropas/ehemalige/dr-michael-hagemeister). Some of the relevant texts can be found in German translation in Bodo Zelinsky, *Das Böse in der Russischen Kultur* (Köln: Böhlau, 2008).

On the history of the "Third Rome" concept, see Peter Duncan, *Russian Messianism: Third Rome, Holy Revolution, Communism, and After* (London: Routledge, 2000).

Eurasianism

On classic Eurasianism, see Otto Böss, *Die Lehre der Eurasier: Ein Beitrag zur Russischen Ideengeschichte des 20. Jahrhunderts* (Wiesbaden: O. Harrassowitz, 1961). The basic manifesto of the movement is explained in Peter Savitsky, ed., *Exodus to the East* [*Iskhod k Vostoku*] (Idyllwild, CA: Charles Schlacks Jr., 1996). On the takeover of original Eurasianism by Alexander Dugin and company, see Marlène Laruelle, *Eurasianism: An Ideology of Empire* (Baltimore: Johns Hopkins University Press, 2008), and Dmitry Shlapentokh, *Russia Between East and West: Scholarly Debates on Eurasianism* (Leiden: Brill, 2006). Also see Herman Pirchner, *Reviving Greater Russia? The Future of Russia's Borders with Belarus, Georgia, Kazakhstan, Moldova, and Ukraine* (Washington, D.C.: American Foreign Policy Council, 2005). Wayne Vucinich, *Russia and Asia: Essays on the Influence of Russia on the Asian Peoples* (Stanford, CA: Hoover Institution Press, Stanford University, 1972), deals with the broader issues, not specifically Eurasianism.

Russian Nationalism

For more on nationalism during the Soviet period: Nikolai Mitrokhin, *Russkaya Partiya* (Moscow: Novoe Literaturnoe Obozrenie, 2003). Also see John B. Dunlop, *The Faces of Contemporary Russian Nationalism* (Princeton, NJ: Princeton University Press, 1983) and *The New Russian Nationalism* (New York: Praeger, 1985); Alexander Yanov, *The Russian Challenge and the Year*

2000 (New York: Basil Blackwell, 1987); and Marlène Laruelle, *In the Name of the Nation: Nationalism and Politics in Contemporary Russia* (New York: Palgrave Macmillan, 2009).

The Opposition

Marc Bennetts, *Kicking the Kremlin: Russia's New Dissidents and the Battle to Topple Putin* (London: Oneworld, 2014)

Oliver Bullough, *The Last Man in Russia: The Struggle to Save a Dying Nation* (London: Penguin Books, 2013)

Masha Gessen, *Words Will Break Cement: The Passion of Pussy Riot* (New York: Riverhead Books, 2014)

Ben Judah, *Fragile Empire: How Russia Fell In and Out of Love with Vladimir Putin* (New Haven: Yale University Press, 2013)

Konstantin Voronkov, *Aleksei Naval'nyi: Groza Zhulikov i Vorov* (Moscow: Eksmo, 2012)

Dugin and Gumilev

Many of Alexander Dugin's books are available in Russian and English. Among them: *Konspirologiya* [*Conspirology*] (Moscow: Arktogeya, 1992); *The Fourth Political Theory* (London: Arktos, 2012); and *Putin vs. Putin: Vladimir Putin Viewed from the Right* (London: Aktos, 2014). Many Dugin lectures are on YouTube as well as on his Web site, dugin.ru, along with a long interview with Vladimir Pozner.

Lev Gumilev has several sites on the Internet; see his portal (http://gumilevica.kulichki.net/English/) for a complete bibliography, including (among others) *Drevnyaya Rus i Velikaya Step* (Moscow: Mysl, 1989); *Etnogenez i Biosfera Zemli* (Leningrad: Azbooka-Atticus, 2013); and *Geografia Etnosa* (Leningrad: Nauka, 1993). Many of his books on the history of the Huns, the Khazars, ethnogenesis, and so on have been translated.

The Orthodox Church

S. L. Frank, ed., *A Solovyov Anthology* (New York: Scribner, 1950)

John Gordon Garrard and Carol Garrard, *Russian Orthodoxy Resurgent: Faith and Power in the New Russia* (Princeton, NJ: Princeton University Press, 2008)

Konstantin Leontiev, *Against the Current: Selections from the Novels, Essays, Notes, and Letters of Konstantin Leontiev* (New York: Weybright and Talley, 1969)

Christopher Marsh, *Burden or Blessing?: Russian Orthodoxy and the Construction of Civil Society and Democracy* (Boston: Boston University, Institute on Culture, Religion, and World Affairs, 2004)

Birgit Menzel and Michael Hagemeister, *The New Age of Russia: Occult and Esoteric Dimensions* (München: Otto Sagner, 2012). Hagemeister is the leading expert in this field; for a full list of his publications on *The Protocols of the Elders of Zion* and related topics, see his Web site, http://www.phil-fak.uni-duesseldorf.de/v-geschichte-und-kulturen-osteuropas/ehemalige/drmichael-hagemeister/.

Jonathan Sutton, ed., *Orthodox Christianity and Contemporary Europe* (Dudley, MA: Peeters, 2003)

Mikhail Vostryshev, *Patriarch Tikhon* (Moscow: Molodaya Gvardiya, 1995)

The Radical Right

A great amount of right-wing extremist literature has been produced during the last fifteen years. Among the successful practitioners is Nikolai Starikov (http://nstarikov.ru/en/), a St. Petersburg TV producer widely acclaimed as a master of conspirology second only to Alexander Dugin. Since about 80 percent of the Russian public receive information on domestic and foreign affairs from television, the contribution of producers and writers such as Starikov and Mikhail Leontiev should not be underrated. Maxim Kalashnikov has written bestsellers entitled *Voina s Golemom* (Moscow: AST, 2006) and *Putin Inkorporeyted* (Moscow: Eksmo/Algoritm, 2013). The weekly *Zavtra* (formerly *Den*) is the mouthpiece of this camp.

Foreign Policy and the Petrostate

Anders Aslund and Michael McFaul, *Revolution in Orange: The Origins of Ukraine's Democratic Breakthrough* (Washington, D.C.: Carnegie Endowment for International Peace, 2006)

Marshall Goldman, *Petrostate: Putin, Power, and the New Russia* (New York: Oxford University Press, 2008)

Thane Gustafson, *Crisis Amid Plenty: The Politics of Soviet Energy under Brezhnev and Gorbachev* (Princeton, NJ: Princeton University Press, 1991)

———. *Capitalism Russian-Style* (Cambridge: Cambridge University Press, 1999)

———. *Wheel of Fortune: The Battle for Oil and Power in Russia* (Cambridge, MA: Belknap Press of Harvard University Press, 2012)

Per Högselius, *Red Gas: Russia and the Origins of European Energy Dependence* (New York: Palgrave Macmillan, 2012)

Edward Lucas, *The New Cold War: The Future of Putin's Russia and the Threat to the West* (New York: Palgrave Macmillan, 2008)

Jürgen Roth, *Gazprom—Das Unheimliche Imperium: Wie Wir Verbraucher Betrogen und Staaten Erpresst Werden* (Frankfurt: Westend, 2012)

David Satter, *Darkness at Dawn: The Rise of the Russian Criminal State* (New Haven: Yale University Press, 2003)

Angela Stent, *The Limits of Partnership: U.S.-Russian Relations in the Twenty-first Century* (Princeton, NJ: Princeton University Press, 2014)

Jonathan P. Stern, *The Future of Russian Gas and Gazprom* (Oxford: Oxford University Press, 2005)

Strobe Talbott, *The Russia Hand: A Memoir of Presidential Diplomacy* (New York: Random House, 2002)

Dmitri Trenin, *Post-Imperium: A Eurasian Story* (Washington, D.C.: Carnegie Endowment for International Peace, 2011)

——. *Getting Russia Right* (Washington, D.C.: Carnegie Endowment for International Peace, 2007)

The Oligarchs

David E. Hoffman, *The Oligarchs: Wealth and Power in the New Russia* (New York: Public Affairs, 2001)

Richard Sakwa, *Putin and the Oligarchs: The Khodorkovsky-Yukos Affair* (New York: I. B. Tauris, 2014)

Stalinism and Re-Stalinization

Veniamin Kolkovsky, *1953: Likvidatsiya Stalina* (Moscow: Eksmo, 2013)

Maria Lipman, Lev Gudkov, and Lasha Bakradze, *The Stalin Puzzle: Deciphering Post-Soviet Public Opinion* (Washington, D.C.: Carnegie Endowment for International Peace, 2013)

Sergei Minakov, *1937: Zagovor Byl!* (Moscow: Eksmo, 2010)

Konstantin Romanenko, *Pochemu Nenavidiat Stalina?: Vragi Rossii Protiv Vozhdia* (Moscow: IAuza-press, 2013)

Nodari Aleksandrovič Simoniâ, *Istoriografiâ Stalinizma* (Moscow: Rosspén, 2007)

Putin and Putinism

Many biographies of Putin have been published during the last decade. The English-language ones are on the whole superior to the Russian, most of which either belong to the genre of hagiography or are strictly polemical. Among the books by American and British writers, the following ought to be mentioned:

Anna Arutunyan, *The Putin Mystique: Inside Russia's Power Cult* (Newbold on Stour, UK: Skyscraper Publications, 2014)

Peter Baker and Susan Glasser, *Kremlin Rising: Vladimir Putin's Russia and the End of Revolution* (New York: Scribner, 2005)

Karen Dawisha, *Putin's Kleptocracy* (New York: Simon and Schuster, 2014)

Masha Gessen, *The Man Without a Face: The Unlikely Rise of Vladimir Putin* (New York: Riverhead Books, 2012)

Luke Harding, *Expelled: A Journalist's Descent into the Russian Mafia State* (New York: Palgrave Macmillan, 2012)

Fiona Hill and Clifford Gaddy, *Mr. Putin: Operative in the Kremlin* (Washington, D.C.: Brookings Institution Press, 2012)

Richard Sakwa, *Putin: Russia's Choice* (London: Routledge, 2004)

Andrei Soldatov and Irina Borogan, *The New Nobility: The Restoration of Russia's Security State and the Enduring Legacy of the KGB* (New York: Public Affairs, 2010)

Dimitri Trenin, *Integratcia* (Washington, D.C.: Carnegie Foundation, 2006). See also his other books and articles published by the Carnegie Foundation.

The best of the books on Putin's early rule by Russian authors are those by Lilia Shevtsova, especially *Putin's Russia* (Washington, D.C.: Carnegie Endowment for International Peace, 2003); Vladimir Putin, *First Person* (New York: Public Affairs, 2000) is a series of interviews with Russian journalists on his early life.

See also:

Stanislav Belkovsky, *Sushnost Rezhima Putina* (Moscow: Eksmo, 2012)

Edward Lucas, *Deception: The Untold Story of East-West Espionage Today* (New York: Walker, 2012)

Aleksei Mukhin, *Pokolenie 2008* (Moscow: Algoritm, 2006)

Anna Politkovskaya, *Putin's Russia* (London: Harvill Press, 2004). Politkovskaya, a leading investigative journalist, was murdered. As so often happens in such circumstances, the motives and leading perpetrators were never fully and clearly identified.

Vladimir Soloviev, *Empire of Corruption* (London: Glagoslav Publications, 2014)

Russia and Islam

Gordon Hahn, *Russia's Islamic Threat* (New Haven: Yale University Press, 2007)

Aleksei Malashenko, *Islam dlia Rossii* (Moscow: Rosspen, 2007)

INDEX